HAUNTED

the Death Mother Archetype

Violet Sherwood, PhD

 CHIRON PUBLICATIONS • ASHEVILLE, NORTH CAROLINA

www.ChironPublications.com

Interior and cover design by Danijela Mijailovic
Printed primarily in the United States of America.

ISBN 978-1-63051-988-9 paperback
ISBN 978-1-63051-989-6 hardcover
ISBN 978-1-63051-990-2 electronic
ISBN 978-1-63051-991-9 limited edition paperback

Library of Congress Cataloging-in-Publication Data Pending

Table of Contents

List of Figures

Foreword

Haunted: the Death Mother Archetype is a wonder of a book. Dr. Sherwood's impeccable scholarship undergirds a transformative dance between the imaginative capacity of soul, and the harsh realities embedded in her subject matter. The heuristic research method she chose brings dual perspectives of one who is both the investigator and the investigated. With a poetic sensibility, she takes us to the neither/nor realm of soul, that liminal place where past and future dissolve into the present moment, where imagination illuminates what would otherwise remain lost in the shadows of the human condition. We find ourselves, with Dr. Sherwood, in the terrible presence of the Death Mother archetype, she who dwells in the dynamic between the unwilling (unsupported) mother and the unwelcome child. Still, in the containment of the observing mind embedded in the research, we know we are safe as witnesses and readers.

It's my intention in this foreword to invite others in the world of depth psychology, including psychotherapists, analysts, mythologists, and imaginal psychologists to read this treasure of a book. More importantly, any and all readers are invited to host, in our own imaginal world, children who before birth know in the soma, in each becoming cell the harsh reality that they cannot be contained in the embrace of the mother, she whose beating heart is a child's first reality. For these children, first moments of life find them in the bodies of women who have no capacity to care for them. Such a state of enwombed calamity may well lead to an archetypal breach, following the child through years of deep mother-loss, a situation which constellates the wounded archetypal couple, the Sacred Feminine and her Divine Child.

Dr. Sherwood's investigation leaves no room for raw blame. Hers is neither a one-sided argument, nor a judgement, but rather a more difficult journey, an uncovering of that which is hidden, resulting in a redemptive process. As I read through each page, I was reminded that just as Dr. Sherwood is called to bring to the world what she discovers in the depths, so, too, are each of us called to our unique work. A fearless guide, she moves with grace and courage among the ghosts that haunt, and the forces that threaten inner annihilation. Yet very early on, we find a first intimation of archetypal healing in the author's tender dedication, "to the unsung, and also, to Williamina McCulloch (Minnie Dean), with deepest gratitude and compassion," a reference to the profound imaginal relationship between Dr. Sherwood and 19th-century baby farmer Minnie Dean. As in many of our lives, the most unlikely participant in our healing process is the very one with whom we must engage.

Through biography, myth, story, classic literature, works of art, gripping dreams, and letters in the imaginal to and from Minnie Dean, Dr. Sherwood enters a world of soul-making foreign to modern experience. Those symbolic forms allow a gathering of inner figures whose aim is luminosity, but whose liminal nature would have them float away, into the dark unconscious, but for Dr. Sherwood's expressive capacity, in the same symbolic forms that call the figures forth.

The result of such creative play is to fix in awareness each moment of engagement, each reluctant encounter, each whisper of love. Keats' words capture the way in which such glimpses of depth, might, without research with soul in mind, slip beyond our grasp:

> *... like the passage of an angel's tear*
> *That falls through the clear ether silently.*

In Dr. Sherwood's writing, I discern particular bravery in finding and speaking truths that society finds too harsh to hear. Hers is a telling that would open cultural wounds so often left to fester beneath awareness, wounds that once opened, can begin to heal. Hers is a story too, of compassion and connection in the face of personal and cultural psychological infanticide and one of its modern iterations, closed stranger adoption. Her work is an invitation for her readers to witness the poetic imagination burrowing deep into conscious discovery. She makes the difficult choice to explore the darkness, in what she describes as a return to the scene of a crime.

Each compelling page reminds the reader of the vast in-between-domain within our grasp, if only we would choose to open our eyes to its wonder. Over and over, in Dr. Sherwood's eloquent writing, I encountered evidence of the existence of tears in the veil between worlds, openings that welcome a haunting of our days and nights, each in profoundly different ways, so that we might discover the gifts embedded within our unique wounds.

Here, I wish to speak broadly of particular sections of Dr. Sherwood's book in terms of how each resonates with my researcher's sensibility as well as my personal thirst for secrets hidden like lush landscapes in the shadow of lived experience.

In each of her three sections Dr. Sherwood delivers all that is promised: introducing and situating the narrative in her personal life, the historical context, and the theoretical lenses through which her study developed. Her careful framing of the inquiry methods and topics within, provide definitions of terms such as psychological infanticide, the Death Mother, infanticidal attachment, and heuristic imaginal self-inquiry. These early explanations act as initial guideposts, supporting understanding, and allowing us to fully embrace the subsequent discoveries that emerge from Dr. Sherwood's finely tuned intuitive intellect. The initial writing suggests that the reader will enter a sacred space with Dr. Sherwood. The narrative that follows never disappoints.

Because Dr. Sherwood navigates this multi-dimensional realm with grace and clarity, we, her readers, also find the capacity to negotiate the fine line between fact and fiction, conscious and unconscious reality, and matters between the sensible world and the ideas of the reasonable mind. In her good care, we manage to dwell in the presence of both the sublime and the devastating until we, along with Dr. Sherwood come to terms with the unconscious. Because we have entered the experience with her, beginning with her riveting prologue, we realize the transformative gift that unfolds in the work. Without her generosity in sharing her vulnerable accounts, we cannot know the profound psychological ache of many for whom being welcomed after conception was not possible. We understand, when the scene is set that the terrain we will enter is one of psychological, and sometimes, concrete child murder, and still, we choose to go. Additionally, through each division within Dr. Sherwood's book, we see a continual building of historical insight. As readers we feel a certain cohesion as we approach the theme of closed stranger adoption, a deeply complicated area within the current culture, and also, within the personal experience of the researcher.

I was reminded, in chapter after chapter, especially in the imaginal narrative between Minnie Dean and Dr. Sherwood, of Jung's understanding that the unconscious cannot be studied objectively but only through subjective experience. The evocative dialogue between Minnie and Dr. Sherwood, is easily understood as the authentic experience of her inner and outer worlds, coalescing, integrating, tentatively and tenderly feeling into the soul of the study.

Yet, there is so very much more, other expressive avenues, that allow us to participate in Dr. Sherwood's encounter with the unconscious. The beautiful way in which she explores the alchemical process known as Solutio as it relates to her study is one such example. She titles this section, *Solutio: The Alchemy of Drowning and the 'Trauma-world.'* At once, we are drawn in. True to her pattern of quickly engaging her reader, we find that we are stunned, rewarded, and deeply informed. Instead of "learning about" this alchemical process, we with Dr. Sherwood, enter a state of reverie in which we find ourselves considering the relationship between water and the feminine or the idea of the great round that links birth, death, and rebirth in continuous cycle. As I read, I felt wonder, and awe. It is not easy to create an imaginal exploration, to tie so many moving parts to a dynamic whole. To see it happen through the able work of Dr. Sherwood is like hearing a resounding symphony for the first time. One feels part of a birthing, or an explosive mystery. The discoveries, the links, the meaning-making, all of it, becomes a new creation.

Dr. Sherwood's scholarly and experiential journey allows us to be present to the ongoing trust in the psyche that the work requires. Throughout, I witnessed Dr. Sherwood's capacity to, in Jung's words, "stay with the image with a self-reflective ego attitude," the stance required in the process of active imagination. She didn't look away, even though what manifested was at times, both viscerally difficult, and psychologically dangerous. Dr. Sherwood reports that she worked with a clinician as she progressed through the personal part of the study, bearing witness to the essential contribution of psychotherapy to such demanding work.

In my view, the inclusion of the imaginal archetypal in the study is groundbreaking, as much of what we know of the archetypes is theoretical. To ground an unconscious collective dynamic with individual human experience is no small feat. The potentially crushing havoc that accompanies such joining of the archetypal with the personal requires ego strength, and a capacity to hold multiple realities in consciousness.

The intimate nature of the subject matter being researched–personal encounters with the Death Mother, concrete adoption, and psychological infanticide–yielded openings to the mysteries within Dr. Sherwood's life and the cultural milieu out of which the research flowed. We see her talent in the act of bridging the almost impossible gap between soul's experience and the words that describe it.

That she allows us to witness the sacred transformation within the work, *her* transformation, is what I most cherish as her reader. A particular passage in which 19th-century baby farmer Minnie Deane speaks to Violet toward the end of their correspondence is illustrative. It shows that just as Dr. Sherwood is healing, owning her lovely transformation so too is the imaginal Minnie Dean. Minnie's shame and crime are no longer central to her imaginal identity. We see in the passage below that Minnie Dean too, has been transformed by the work. This animated imaginal figure has become Dr. Sherwood's inner, able partner and mentor. We hear this in the words below as Minnie instructs Dr. Sherwood:

> *You need to link more clearly the process of actual infanticide through baby farming & then to adoption so the reader has a clear understanding of what you mean & how it has occurred. The progression from killing to abandonment to the handing over to us baby farmers who hold a particular tension that mothers refused to hold for themselves any longer & then to the denials of adoption.*

In this passage, we are gifted to bear witness, to see first-hand that the compassion and attention Dr. Sherwood offered to the internal Minnie Dean throughout their ongoing dialogue evoked transcendence and healing *within* Dr. Sherwood, a woman we have learned, who has been deeply wounded by psychological infanticide and closed stranger adoption. Thus, the healed internal Minnie figure could assist Dr. Sherwood in her very important study. Minnie was no longer paralyzed in her historical reality, the woman who was hanged for murdering then discarding infants in her care. This particular moment in the study was powerful, evoking deep joy within me. I wish the same for you dear reader— joy, along with enlightenment, and healing—whether you are a psychotherapist, a mythologist, an adoptive parent, or whether your own history is that of an unwelcome child or a mother who at some point in time found yourself without the capacity to hold a precious child in your care. This is your book.

-Mary Harrell

Mary Harrell is a Jungian-oriented psychotherapist, and licensed psychologist who received her Ph.D. in Clinical Psychology from Pacifica Graduate Institute in Santa Barbara, California. She is Associate Professor Emerita in the School of Education, State University of New York (SUNY) at Oswego. Her chapters, in the areas of educational reform and imaginal psychology, appear in five books. In 2014, Syracuse University's *The Stone Canoe, a Journal of Arts, Literature and Social Commentary, No. 8* anthologized her poetry. Her first book titled, *Imaginal Figures in Everyday Life: Stories from the World between Matter and Mind* was published in 2015 (Chiron Publications). In 2018 Dr. Harrell completed a companion book to *Imaginal Figures*, titled, *The Mythmaker*, a Young Adult fictional account of the constellated Orphan/ Angel archetype in the healing process. Dr. Harrell lives with her husband Stephen in South Carolina where she continues to write and conduct a clinical practice in New York and North Carolina. She also conducts individual Jungian Seminars throughout the United States. She can be contacted through harrellpsych@hushmail.com or maryharrellpsychologist.com.

Dr. Harrell's blog posts are at http://www.maryharrellphd. com/. YouTube interviews include a conversation with Dr. Dave for *Shrink Rap Radio*, and with Bonnie Bright for Pacifica Graduate Institute's *Discussions in Depth*. Dr. Harrell's *Author Chat*, in which she answers readers' questions can be found on the Chiron Publications website at http://chironpublications.com/shop/imaginal-figures-everyday-life/.

Acknowledgments

I would like to thank the many people who have supported me in the writing of this book.

I thank Professor Keith Tudor and Dr Frances Kelly, for their astute, kind, wise, warm and creative nurturing of my ideas. Thank you to Dr Mary Harrell, and Dr Valerie Sinason, who legitimised the work with their loving and highly attuned attention. Thanks to Dr Lynley Hood for generous access to her archival research in the Hocken library collection, and for thoughtful conversations about Minnie. Thank you also to the team at Chiron Publications for wise guidance and nurturing of this book into being.

I thank both my families, who keep teaching me about compassionate relationship. Deep thanks to Lauren, Tania and Sharron – three graces in my life.

Deep thanks to Lesley, kin, who sat in familiar territory with me.

I deeply appreciate the loving support of Liese and Crea, who held and cradled the many songs of the imprisoned over the years. Thanks too, to Jill and Rachael who helped hone the Jungian perspective and listened to my dreams.

Thank you to all my friends and colleagues who encouraged, supported, and made a space for these ideas in their lives. To Helen, Mary, Leah, Paul, Rob, Joanne, and Penny for the gifts of friendship. Thank you to Rachel Pollack, tarot and fountain-pen friend.

I thank my clients, who teach me so much about experiences of psychological infanticide and infanticidal attachment.

I gratefully acknowledge funding received from the New Zealand Association of Psychotherapists, without which I could not have completed the research.

Much gratitude to Martin McRae, descendant of Minnie Dean, who gave his blessing.

Thank you also to Charlotte Brontë and Virginia Woolf (angels of the Victorian feminine consciousness); to baby Susan of the Oamaru cemetery; and Ashton, Autumn, and Margaux – guardians of the open heart.

Most of all, thank you to Williamina McCulloch (Minnie Dean) for her wise guidance and companionship, and her willingness to be all I needed to explore.

Finally, heartfelt love and thanks to my lovely Deb, and to Sophie and Jade, for being in my life and sharing your love. In memory of Sally, not forgotten.

Dedication

To the unsung.

Also, to Williamina McCulloch (Minnie Dean)
with deepest gratitude and compassion.

Prologue

I am haunted by a recurring dream:

My grandmother takes me to visit a dead baby in a glass shrine. We enter the place with reverence and a sense of mystery and holiness. My grandmother reveals to me a previously unknown piece of my ancestry. The little baby lies still and peaceful, enshrined in glass on top of a pedestal. I am curious about this little baby whom I know nothing about, yet sense she is connected tome. I want to know her history. My grandmother tells me nothing, only invites me to say a prayer for the dead infant. As I do so, I have a sense the child is listening and that I'm receiving some kind of grace. There's an aura of powerful presence emanating from her. How is it that nobody has told me about her before? Who is she and how is she related to me? Why do I feel such a strong and mysterious connection to her? Why does she seem so present when she is so little and dead? How did she die? Why are we venerating her?

In my waking reverie I realise the Dead Baby is a part of myself, and that in connecting to her I feel more connected to life. I look forward to these dreams when I am taken to visit this child who bestows grace through her death. She haunts my inner life with her mysteries. It is my curiosity about this dream that leads me to embark on a re-search for the Dead Baby in myself, which in turn leads me into an archetypal pattern of creation and destruction, the cycle of eternal return.

Introduction

When I was twenty-years-old, I had a breakdown precipitated by a relationship in which we had discussed marriage and the idea of children. The idea of becoming a mother terrified me. I became increasingly unwell, and as the relationship ended, I became a ghost, not allowed to exist, terrified of being snuffed out by an immense, powerful darkness. As I became more afraid of being killed, I paradoxically became intensely suicidal. I was preoccupied with the fear of being murdered by Mother. It was during this time that I began to write in a desperate attempt to continue to exist. Over time, writing, reverie and therapy revealed to me the symbolic nature of my breakdown as a psychological infanticide.

Years later, I began to witness infanticidal attachments and psychological infanticides in some of the people I worked with as a psychotherapist. I felt sharing my experience could contribute to the understanding of these devastating experiences of Soul murder, and provide hope and a map for healing.

I searched for evidence of psychological infanticide in social history, mythology and literature, hoping to make sense of what I instinctively knew was not just my personal story but an archetypal theme played out through time and culture. I combined methods of heuristic self-inquiry and imaginal psychology to explore the relationship between nineteenth-century baby farming, an early method of caring for or despatching unwelcome children, and my experience of psychological infanticide through closed stranger adoption, in which all right to information or connection between birth parent and child was legally removed..

Weaving through my personal journal material – images, art and creative writing – I discovered how my long imaginal relationship with New Zealand baby farmer, Minnie Dean, revealed, and worked through, themes of the Death Mother archetype. I linked my exploration of this archetype with infanticidal attachment theory and its foundation in the psychohistory of infanticide in the Western world.

Infanticidal attachment theory proposes that psychological infanticide contributes to serious mental disorders, notably schizophrenia and dissociative identity disorder. Drawing on themes of relationship with the Murderous Mother, I explored archetypes and myths, personal story, historical evidence and literature to illuminate both internal and external factors of psychological infanticide.

My focus on nineteenth-century baby farming revealed a pivotal historical time in which social conscience metamorphosed the literal enactment of infanticide into psychological forms – a Soul murder reinforced by closed stranger adoption laws.

What I discovered has the potential to enlarge our under-standing of prenatal infanticidal attachments formed in the situation of closed stranger adoption, or in any other pre-birth scenario in which the unborn child experiences its existence as threatened or annulled.

I aim to offer hope to people living through prenatal psychological infanticide, and guidance for the clinicians who work with them. The process of imaginal engagement with archetypal themes and figures enabled me to engage in a relationship with an archetypal Murderous Mother in ways that were ultimately profoundly transformational.

I also discovered that psychological infanticide as a result of the dynamic between unwelcome child and unwilling mother in closed stranger adoption is a controversial and difficult topic.

Most people avoid acknowledging or feeling into the infant's experience of adoption.

Structurally, each chapter covers a theme in the narrative of psychological infanticide. I have included examples from my creative writing, journals, dreams, poems, body symptoms, photos and art in order to present a vivid picture of the lived experience and inner world of psychological infanticide. The work is intended to offer a medium for Soul to speak directly – to have her own voice and her own say, as part of a healing process.

In Part One, I describe the methods and context by which I explored the nature of psychological infanticide and identified the themes of my inner life. I explore theories of psychological infanticide, infanticidal attachment and prenatal dissociation. I relate a psychohistory of infanticide in the Western world, culminating in a pivotal point in the nineteenth century when baby farming was suppressed and adoption legalised. I introduce the dynamic of unwelcome child and unwilling mother as an archetypal pattern that occurs throughout history, society and culture wherever women do not have the resources and support they need to welcome and care for a child. I identify this archetypal pattern as the Death Mother archetype – a result of wounding of the Sacred Feminine.

In Part Two, I delve into further detail of the nineteenth-century practice of baby farming, identifying the baby farmer as representative of the Death Mother archetype. I describe four means of child-murder – violence, abandonment, drugging and neglect – weaving the social reality of baby farming with the themes of psychological infanticide through closed stranger adoption, in order to illuminate their commonalities and relationship. I share more of my personal experience of psychological infanticide in order to show the themes and lived truth of the Soul-wound that results from possession by the Death Mother archetype.

In Part Three, I go further into the underworld journey of my personal myth, identifying themes through which I explore alchemical symbols and images resonant with psychological infanticide. I include aspects of my imaginal engagement with New Zealand baby farmer, Minnie Dean. In doing so, I illuminate a path for Soul-healing that may bring us more fully into life and wholeness.

As the individual and collective wounds in Western culture inflicted by the Death Mother are given loving attention in Psyche, there is great potential for resurrection from psychological infanticide. Writing about this archetypal wound, and its healing and transformation through attention to both personal and collective themes and symbology, is an act of witnessing, voicing and making visible. It is an act of creativity that is the antithesis of the life-annihilating destructiveness of the Death Mother archetype. As we collectively wake from annihilating forces in the psyche, we are released from the spell of paralysis, and freed to participate in the healing of the Sacred Feminine and our Mother Earth.

Note to the reader: During the writing process, as part of my healing transformation, I changed my name from Bron Deed to Violet Sherwood. Therefore, my personal and professional writing within this book is referenced under whichever name was chronologically correct.

PART ONE

SETTING THE SCENE
FOR A MURDER INQUIRY

Chapter One
A Haunting

*And what guiding intelligence weaves the threads of an
individual biography; what hauntings of the invisible
world invigorate, animate, and direct the multiple
narratives of daily life?*
James Hollis (2013)

As a result of my experience of psychological infanticide
under the closed stranger adoption system in place in New Zealand
between the 1950s and the 1980s, some of my questions were:
*What are the archetypal themes of the experience of psychological
infanticide? What does it mean to feel you must be dead in order
to be mothered? How does it alter the way you live and engage
with life? Can it be healed and, if so, how?*
I've allowed these questions to lead me, through this book,
into deeper personal and archetypal truths about psychological
infanticide as murder of the Soul by a Death Mother whose anti-
life mothering reflects a wound to the Sacred Feminine.

My story involves a long imaginal relationship with a
nineteenth-century New Zealand baby farmer, Minnie Dean
(1844-1895), who was hanged for child murder. This dialogue
sparked my sense of a connection between nineteenth-century
child murder and psychological infanticide, which I explore
throughout this book.

When I first conceived of writing about the Death Mother archetype, and felt the idea take root and begin to flourish inside me, I felt an intense terror that the work would kill me. This terror manifested in spontaneous suffocative attacks, often while driving, in which my airway became blocked until I was frantically airless.

Anyone who has experienced something similar will know the terror of driving on a motorway at high speed surrounded by other vehicles and suddenly having no air. Negotiating your breath, your instinctive panic, pulling over safely, assuming there is an open shoulder to pull over to, is no mean feat of survival in the three minutes available before you become unconscious due to lack of oxygen.

This might be interpreted as a panic attack or an asthmatic attack. I recognise it as a re-membering – a manifestation of the feeling I have had throughout my life that I am not meant to live. I say feeling, rather than belief, because it is an experience embedded in my body. I recognise my motorway breathing attacks as similar to the birth journey: full speed down the narrow and convulsing birth canal, experiencing suffocating pressures and a limited timeframe, arriving – not to an exhilarated and safe reunion with mother in another dimension, but abandoned to the terror of no-one there and no personal means to survive. Run off the road.

In this inquiry, I engage with a deep mythic and trans-generational wound in the psyches of desperate mothers and unwanted children – a wound that is dangerous to explore as it lies so close to the bone. My terror of being killed is a central theme of psychological infanticide. This mother-child wound is a dark aspect of the archetypal Feminine, which constellates as a Death Mother complex.

Reflecting on the terror that my inquiry would kill me, I thought about Minnie Dean, alone in her cell the night before she was hanged, imagining her terror at her impending death, and the panic she may have felt. I imagined being in the cell with her, holding her hand, and being a comforting presence in her last hours. This compassionate practice soothed my own fear and relieved my symptoms. It also points to an essential theme of this inquiry: it is through my ongoing imaginal engagement with Minnie, who has represented my conflicts about the Murderous Mother, that I have been able to connect with, reflect on, find compassion for and integrate these terrifying maternal forces inside myself. Becoming a compassionate presence to all parts of the mother-infant wound is both healing and transformational.

It may not be immediately apparent that the experience of closed stranger adoption could be one of murder – a sacrifice of the child for the individual and familial adult shame, and fear endured during an unwanted pregnancy. The effect of such a psychological infanticide generates vast emotions, primarily of terror and rage, in both its victims and in the clinicians who work with them. The concept also stirs powerful taboos against the idea of mothers having infanticidal wishes, thoughts or feelings about their children or pregnancies. Such a powerful taboo invokes the forces of denial against, and the punishment of, the one who tells the tale – in effect re-murdering the murdered. Such intense victim mythologies tend to pass blame and shame like hot potatoes around the trauma triangle of Victim-Perpetrator-Rescuer. (Karpman, 1968). This does not heal wounds. It deepens them and makes them more embittered.

It is not my purpose or intention to blame mothers for the way they survived an impossible situation. Rather, I aim to give voice to the 'unsung' truth of the experience of psychological infanticide, and to provide hope for the compassionate understanding and care of those people whose infant lives were sacrificed, and who dwell as tenuous ghosts in the underworld shadows of constant terror.

Literary Ghosts

Ancestry refers to those who have gone before, those who – while no longer present– shape and influence our culture, ideas and ongoing conversations about ourselves. Our ancestors begin the conversations that we continue to develop. In this way, the themes and myths of the personal and the collective continue to be worked on through time. Carl Jung (1989) described this concept as the dead continuing their work through us as we engage with what they have offered. This is extended by Greg Mogenson (1992) who wrote: "The dead are at work, making themselves into religion and culture, imagining themselves into soul" (p. xi). They become a part of us as we engage in imaginal conversations. By engaging with the stories and voices of the dead, we are part of an ongoing transformation. A significant part of mourning is to participate in honouring and experiencing the past, and what has died inside the self, what we have murdered or neglected until it faded away. Mourning includes allowing ourselves to be haunted by the ghosts of what did not come to life, of what might have been, while still holding an energy that has been hidden from consciousness. These ghosts are echoes of history, both personal and collective. Literature helps us to see them, and to hear them.

I write about mourning and haunting because they are essential to the process of healing trauma, and because they reflect the personal truth of my inquiry. The dead provide guidance, as I hope will be evident throughout this book. Of course, not all the writers that influenced me are dead. Contemporary writers, too, offer much. Each voice reflects different and connected facets of universalised themes.

My European ancestors were dislocated, alienated from wherever home might have been, to begin again in a new place called New Zealand. Because my right to my personal history was severed by adoption laws, I do not know their personal stories or identities, do not know their relationship to the myths and tales of their culture, and nor can I participate in the conversations handed down over generations.

Consequently, from a young age, books became my connection to self, life and history. My sense of being in the world was rooted in conversations with stories, myths, songs and poems. Without ancestral connections, I was both disconnected from my familial inheritance and free to create my own stories. Now, I feel fortunate to have found, and integrated into my being, stories and myths from many cultures – and to have discovered the universality of themes addressed by them.

Many paths of spiritual enlightenment or of psychological individuation are based on direct experiencing. Having insight about something does not lead directly to transformation. For transformation to occur, knowledge-based insight must be integrated with experience. True wisdom is not simply intellectual but an integration of mind with embodied knowing. I believe, therefore, that before we can truly understand the experience of those suffering the effects of psychological infanticide, we must first step away from the safety of theories and actually *feel* something of the experience.

When we read literature, watch a movie, listen to a piece of music or gaze at an artwork, something moves us. That emotional response is the part of us that resonates with the experience evoked. If we are willing to allow ourselves to feel, and to move more deeply into the experience evoked, then we integrate theory with embodied knowing, and we are more able to be with these feelings rather than banish them from consciousness.

Personal narratives based on deep self-inquiry are one means by which we can be moved and know something with more than just our minds. The literature I discuss below has moved me so deeply, and resonated so powerfully, that it was like a compass directing my exploration and a divining rod telling me I had discovered something precious: the literature kept me honed on authenticity. I draw on creative, therapeutic and life-writing theories. I include the voices of biographies, poetry and fiction to develop a richly complex (phenomenological) sense of the experience.

It is no accident that my inquiry weaves themes of pregnancy, childbirth and writing. It is through becoming creators that we repair the wound of thwarted creation. Learning to conceive an idea, gestate it, birth it into the world and continue to nurture it, is the alchemical task of living our full potential: a painfully difficult task for the psychologically infanticided child.

Soul Murder

Both psychohistory and psychobiography are primarily concerned with the emotional effects of childhood. Psychohistorians and psychobiographers both claim that attitudes towards unwanted children reveal that early infanticidal practices and modes of child-rearing have gradually shifted from literal infanticide to a psychological infanticide performed on the identity or self of the child, supporting my theory that literal infanticides perpetrated by some baby farmers developed towards a psychological form of infanticide in closed stranger adoption (de Mause, 1974; Grille, 2005; Shengold, 1989, 1999, 2013; Stone, 1977). The term Soul murder, which I use interchangeably with the term psychological infanticide, was originally coined by Feuerbach in 1832 to describe "the deadly and murderous abuse of children" (cited in Masson, 1996, p. 65), in respect to the notorious case of Kaspar Hauser (which I discuss in more detail in Part Two). Soul murder became a familiar psychoanalytic term through its use by Daniel Schreber (1911/1903) – one of Freud's more famous case studies. The term, as applied by Leonard Shengold, suggests all child abuse has some form of murderous intent, whether conscious or unconscious, toward the child's psyche. Whilst this includes infanticidal wishes, as discussed by Brett Kahr (2007a), the term psychological infanticide appears to be used by Kahr more specifically, identifying several unique aetiologies leading to infanticidal attachment.

Infanticidal Attachment

This term explores the attachment dynamic between unwelcome child and unwilling parent, *as it is perceived by the infant*. Infanticidal attachment theory traces psychological infanticide back to its roots in infanticidal child-rearing and demonstrates the ways Western culture and society has continued to evolve its approach to the difficult question of what to do with children who are unwanted or unable to be cared for. While the methods of 'solving' this problem have changed over time, the experience for the unwelcome child continues to hold the remnants of a collective infanticidal past.

Nineteenth-century Baby Farming

Nineteenth-century baby farmers are the most recent infanticidal ancestors of psychological infanticide. They provide the pivotal point in Western history where consciousness around abandoning infants to 'angel makers' shifted into legal and moral concern for the welfare of unprotected infants. In other words they demonstrate that pivotal point in social history where literal infanticide shifted into the psychologically infanticidal trauma of adoption.

As my own healing journey over many decades involved an imaginal relationship with a nineteenth-century New Zealand baby farmer, I felt parented (to varying degrees of comfort or terror) by my internal conversations with her and other baby farmers.

In New Zealand, Minnie Dean's story has the status of myth as a monstrous child murderer. Baby farmers in England and Australia also hold positions of infamous notoriety as figureheads of the Negative Mother archetype. I drew on the lives of these notorious women to illuminate the Death Mother archetype and the experience of psychological infanticide.

Closed Stranger Adoption

My personal journey through psychological infanticide occurred as a result of closed stranger adoption – the twentieth-century answer to the difficult question of what to do with unwelcome children.

Closed stranger adoption describes the process enacted under the New Zealand *Adoption Act 1955*, in which the adoption severed all contact with the birth family. Children were not allowed to know their original identity, based on beliefs that environment was more important than heredity, and that infants easily bonded with new caregivers. Research now clearly indicates the importance of identity and attachment, and acknowledges the severe traumatic effects of separating children from mothers. These are often denied, ignored or misunderstood by adults who attempt to prevent the expression of grief and its accompanying abandonment rage (Bowlby, 1980; Verrier, 1993; Winnicott, 1965, 1974).

The New Zealand *Adult Adoption Information Act 1985* acknowledges the need for adoptees to know their biological truth. There has been acknowledgment of the grief experienced by birth mothers who 'lost' their babies, but there has been very little acknowledgment of the devastating trauma to the adopted child (Verrier, 1993).

The legal term *nullius filius* – 'child of no one' – was applied to illegitimate children. Whilst the New Zealand *Adoption Act 1895* sought to provide identity and status for 'nobody's child' the unfortunate consequence of closed stranger adoption as a result of the *Adoption Act 1955* was to again nullify these children and turn them into nonentities with a legally imposed made-up life. It could be suggested this nulling and voiding of one's authentic self is a legally infanticidal act, enforced and condoned by unconscious socially infanticidal wishes to get rid of unwelcome children, and that this has the effect of psychological infanticide. The idea of living a fictional identity raises questions about continuity of personal narrative, the role of history and memory, and the fragmentation and inauthenticity of sense of self that are aspects of Soul murder.

Closed stranger adoption has been described as a devastating loss occurring at the separation of mother and infant and so creating a profound trauma that can be experienced as psychic death. Nancy Verrier (1993) and Betty Lifton (1994) indicated that 'integrity of self' begins while still merged with mother in the first year of life. When this bond is disrupted, continuity of self is also disrupted. These authors alert us to the 'nothingness' that occurs when trauma is too early to be remembered consciously. This is variously described in clinical practice as a void, abyss, chasm, black hole, being nothing, or not existing. Donald Winnicott (1974) described it as the nameless dread of annihilation experienced in phenomenal death.

I delve deep into the question of 'nothingness' when the child has perceived murderous wishes before birth, exploring the unconscious murderous or life-denying wishes of desperate mothers enduring unwanted pregnancies, reinforced by the legal killing off of original identity.

Imaginal Psychology, Archetypes, and Mythology

In the myths and themes of mother and child that Mircea Eliade (1954) described in *The Myth of the Eternal Return: Or Cosmos and History*, the deepest ancestral lineage of all is that of the Great Mother, goddess of the eternal cycle of life-death-rebirth. It felt imperative for me to get to know the Great Mother as the Greatest and First archetype who gestates all other archetypes in the collective unconscious through the fecundity of the void. Maureen Murdock's (1990) *The Heroine's Journey: Woman's Quest for Wholeness* and Anne Baring and Jules Cashford's (1991) *The Myth of the Goddess: Evolution of an Image* provided a feminine mythology – a connection with earth, body, matter and soul that literally helped me to matter, and to manifest a place to root and to flourish. They offered a new vision of the potentials of the abyss, black hole or great emptiness as a place where fruit could grow. They gave me a perspective of the wound as womb – in the dark emptiness of oblivion is a womb place where something might be dreamed into being. This creative feminine mythology was a necessary counterpoint to the dark or negative aspect of the Great Mother illuminated by Marion Woodman and Daniela Sieff

29

(2015) in *Spiralling Through the Apocalypse: Facing the Death Mother to Claim our Lives* and Bud and Massimila Harris (2015) in *Into the Heart of the Feminine: Facing the Death Mother Archetype to Reclaim Love, Strength and Vitality*. The traumatic world imposed by the Death Mother is further articulated by Daniela Sieff (2017) in *Trauma-Worlds and the Wisdom of Marion Woodman*. The Death Mother archetype resonated deeply with the figure in my psyche I had named Mother Death. This literature helped me to understand the negative power of this archetype and the infanticidal trauma that results when she is constellated.

In my personal writing, certain elemental processes and the language of alchemy and childbirth entwined. Literature on alchemy, the imaginal, and the psyche guided me to marry theory, the imaginal, and embodied experience.

Psychobiography, Biomythography, and Other Forms of Transformational Writing

I engaged with the healing aspects of writing as a transformational journey through the expression and exploration of personal and collective myths. The telling and retelling of a personal story is a journey into rebirth. We begin at our beginning and tell the story we believe we know about ourselves. As we explore further, we gain the strength to go more deeply into the darkness of our own selves.

Writing provides a womblike container in which to conceive of and gestate new ideas about ourselves, and new ways of relating to our inner processes, including thoughts and beliefs. Working on our original material, our *prima materia*, is a psychological alchemy that grows and refines us into our most precious possible selves. Through this alchemical process, new stories about ourselves and new ways of being are birthed into the world.

In my writing, I moved fluidly from the witnessing stance of the psychotherapist self, who is grounded in the present and looking back to the past, and the self, or selves, of the past reflected in creative writing material and journal material from different times and perspectives. Discovering the myths we may be living, through radical truth-telling and self-exploration, we reconnect with our more authentic self.

Trauma therapy also endeavours to reframe victim stories and uncover the courageous spirit who survives, and develop a compassionate witnessing stance to our own truths. We aim to hold and grow hope, face our own darkness, heal defensive limitations and allow the authentic self to really connect to life fully again as our whole selves.

Dennis Slattery (2012) offered an approach toward self-discovery through exploration of personal myth in his book, *Riting Myth, Mythic Writing: Plotting your Personal Story*. He invited a direct connection to mythic patterns through symbol and metaphor, claiming the relevance of eternal stories and archetypal patterns throughout our lives. Slattery helped me develop an ear for the archetypal and poetic echoes of myth within written work. His imaginal perspective engaged my poetic consciousness and anchored my sense of the importance of exploring eternal stories and how they unfold in the collective unconscious over time. This may reflect an imaginal explanation of intergenerational trauma. In *The Wounded Body: Remembering the Markings of Flesh*, Slattery (2000) engaged the embodied self with the intention of retrieving and reuniting "*biology* and *biography* – to get the story right – and to return home" (p. 23). This speaks to a need to restore a sense of psychic home and life, from a beginning of mythic homelessness and loss of life.

In *The Self on the Page: Theory and Practice of Creative Writing in Personal Development*, Hunt and Sampson (1998) explored the concept of fictional autobiography as having "a significant and positive impact on…self-understanding and sense of identity" (p. 21). This helped bridge a relationship between my fictional writing and the effects of adoption and psychological infanticide on my sense of identity and self. Hunt and Sampson explained that writing autobiographical fiction:

means that we are forced to enter into our own feelings and emotions in a way which we may not be able to do simply by writing about the facts of our lives. Thus fictionalising from ourselves...helps us to engage more deeply with our inner life, opening up possibilities for greater insight and self-understanding. (p. 33)

Writing what I call bio-fiction connected me with a deep emotional truth. It connected me to a source of knowing which poured out through images. Bio-fiction, or fictional autobiography, is a form of what Jung termed 'active imagination', clearly explained in Barbara Hannah's (1981) *Encounters with the Soul: Active Imagination as Developed by C.G. Jung* and Robert Johnson's (1986) *Inner Work: Using dreams and Inner work for Personal Growth*. Both these works developed my understanding of how bio-fiction, or biomythography, is an encounter with Psyche's truth.

Haunting

The ghosts and orphans of Victorian literature resonated with me, and so for many years I adopted the nineteenth century as a psychological home. In this sense, dislocated in real time, I began to haunt the nineteenth century, and to be haunted by nineteenth-century figures in my imaginal life. My interest in historical biography and the relative invisibility of women's narratives led directly to my imaginal engagement with Minnie Dean.

Biographer Richard Holmes was a tremendous influence, both in terms of validating my instinctive approach and in his choice of subjects, many of whom provide examples in later chapters. Holmes enabled me to link closed stranger adoption, with its lack of connection with identity and the past, with my deep interest in history and biography. In my writing, Holmes becomes almost a ghost in his own right, doubling as the (mostly) nineteenth-century subjects he conjures back to life in his biographies of historical figures. He drew attention to the nature of the biographer as haunting his subjects, and being haunted by them, and it is precisely this haunting, and his inner ear for the essence of his subjects, that haunted and taught me (Holmes, 1985). He described the development of a fictional relationship between the biographer and subject:

> a continuous living dialogue between the two as they move over the same historical ground, the same trail of events. There is between them a ceaseless discussion, a reviewing and questioning of motives and actions and consequences, a steady if subliminal exchange of attitudes, judgments, and conclusions. (Holmes, 1985, p. 76)

Holmes (1985) went on to describe the progression of this living fictional relationship towards a disillusion and "a growing awareness of psychological complication" which "awakens the necessary objectivity of the biographer" and that could be considered as a separating out from a symbiotically merged state into a more discerning self-hood. I have found no better explanation or blueprint for my method of engaging with Minnie Dean.

In all these layers of haunting, I recognised my own hauntedness and haunting as the territory of all forms of unmetabolised loss. James Hollis's (2013) *Hauntings: Dispelling the Ghosts who Run our Lives* addressed the Jungian psychology of this haunting; Jacques Derrida's (1993) concept of hauntology neatly intersects with Marlon's (2005) exploration of non-self and the black sun, along with my curiosity about the nature of absence-presence in closed stranger adoption, and in psychological infanticide generally.

Wolfrey's discussion of haunting and the Gothic interconnected with the profound influence of Charlotte Brontë's (1853/1993) novels on me, as well as the feminist theories of the female self in literature in Sandra Gilbert and Susan Gubar's (1979/2000) *The*

Madwoman in the Attic: The Woman Writer and the Nineteenth-Century Literary Imagination and Elaine Showalter's (1978) *A Literature of their Own: British Women Novelists from Brontë to Lessing*. All these works, and those of the Brontë family's many biographers, coalesced to help me think about the nature of haunting and the eclipse of the Victorian female mind that I had inhabited imaginally.

The Victorian era was one of extremes of idealisation and disempowerment of women. Through allowing myself to haunt and be haunted by the lives and works of nineteenth-century female writers, I understood the subjugated nature of the archetypal feminine wound more clearly.

Romantic writers offered much about the nature of Psyche and haunting. Samuel Taylor Coleridge (1817/1956, 1957) described the paralysed anguish of suspended animation in haunting memories, a result of childhood abandonment. Thomas de Quincey (1821/1971), also an abandoned child, educated me through haunting images of desperation and emptiness that fuelled his opium addiction, which I relate contextually to the history of opium use as an infant panacea, to the addictive self-soothing of unbearable pain by psychologically infanticided people, and to the opium-like dissociation of unbearable trauma. Throughout her life, Anna Kavan (writing in the twentieth century), also abandoned and opium-addicted, expressed her inner deadness, despair and struggle for aliveness, culminating in *Ice* (1967/1986). Through each of these addicted writers I heard the voice of the abandoned and psychically murdered child. They revealed their struggle with life and death as enacted through the passive suicide of opium addiction. Kavan eventually suicided by intentional overdose.

The Experience of Psychological Infanticide as Recorded in Stories, Myths and Personal Voices

Many biographies, histories, stories and myths give voice to the experience of psychological infanticide. They both personalise the experience and reveal its universality. Psychological infanticide is a metaphorical death associated with infanticidal acts or wishes by the parents, and/or by the extremity of the experience. Because the problem of children who are unwanted or unable to be cared for is ever present in social history over time, it is both archetypal and mythic. Referring to myths and stories of abandoned children, which is a form of psychic death, provides guidance on how to transform powerful wounds in the psyche. I explored three categories of children who experience forms of psychic death: the Orphan, the Feral Child, and the Bereaved Child.

The life histories of public figures who lost a parent early in life provided me with sibling-like conversations concerning the psychic territory of the abandoned child. Children experience and interpret these losses as a form of abandonment by the parent, without whom a part of them dies. These children are consumed by an inconsolable grief, a despair and outrage towards life that few emotionally, and some literally, do not survive. Such stories are inevitably filled with variations of heartbreak, mental breakdown, inability to connect with society, violence and aggression, suicide and murder in a parallel to the overwhelming statistical representation of adopted people in these categories. By engaging with these stories I felt companioned in my own eclipse, and able to engage my compassionate self. I realised the universal experience behind my personal suffering, and I began to think about how to live the story differently. To my ear, all these examples express the outraged protest and eventual despairing hopelessness that John Bowlby (1980) described as the inevitable effect on the abandoned child.

The Orphan

Charlotte Brontë's novels and life (revealed through countless biographies) have profoundly influenced me since I read Jane Eyre as a child, and for the first time had my own eclipse mirrored back to me. This classic novel speaks to something orphaned and murdered in generations of women. Brontë described the fate of orphaned Jane, barely surviving in the murderous and rejecting atmosphere of her aunt and cousins. Jane is exposed to terror-inducing and soul-murdering acts such as incarceration in the red room, said to be populated by a ghost, as a punishment. She is sent away to a brutal school for girls that employs starvation, neglect and cruelty as techniques to instil compliance, and to fit the girls (those who survive) for service. She is eventually employed by Mr Rochester as a governess and must face humiliation, the madwoman and betrayal before she reclaims herself, and life (Brontë, 1847/1993).

Brontë's Jane is an archetypal Orphan on a mythic journey. Jane is a heroine, gradually transforming herself and her life through connection to the authentic self – hidden beneath her false compliance – and by facing her demons. Jane appears meek, but her inner voice reveals a seething outrage at her truncated life, and a yearning for her passionate intelligence to be visible and accepted. Jane finally must choose between passionate Rochester and ascetic St John Rivers. She chooses life and is triumphantly resurrected from her perilous beginning.

The book draws on elements of Brontë's own life, but its archetypal nature makes the novel a work of biomythography, demonstrating the power of fictionalised biography to tell a greater emotional truth.

Another of Brontë's (1853/1993) novels, *Villette*, speaks eloquently to the experience of Soul murder and the imprisoned true self buried behind a compliant traumatised self. In the novel, Brontë's Gothic themes of ghosts and nuns bring to life the haunting and hauntedness of Soul murder.

Brontë's own life story was elevated to mythography, initially by her friend Elizabeth Gaskell (1891), whose *The Life of Charlotte Brontë* depicted the Brontës as a family of genius doomed by fate. Gaskell's biography and most of those that follow were critiqued by Juliet Barker (2010), whose own biography, *The Brontës*, claimed to demolish the Brontë myths. Barker's work is important biographical research in its own right, based on minute reading of Brontë manuscripts, and presenting a more factual than mythic truth. I argue, however, that myths are important. They tell us the stories behind the stories, the psychological truths that are just as, if not more, significant, than the literal truths. It is the myths that we resonate with, that touch on something personal in our psyches. Charlotte Brontë's life and works resonated with an aspect of the feminine wound that eclipsed the lives of women, and with the archetypal story of lost Innocence and the Orphan.

The Feral Child

The Feral Child tells us about life-destroying lack of human connection with ourselves and others. There are many myths and stories about children abandoned to fend for themselves – faced with the prospect of almost certain death by exposure to cold, hunger and wild animals. For example, Hansel and Gretel, abandoned to starve in the forest, are nearly murdered by the witch but saved by their own cleverness and collaboration. The poignant image of the trail of breadcrumbs, or in another version, a trail of white stones that gleam in the moonlight, suggests that the healing path out of our lostness lies towards returning to our psychological home. But when home is murderous where do you turn?

As a metaphorical outcast, I resonated with documented stories of feral children. What is murdered in the feral child is a sense of their own humanity, and the ability to trust human beings. According to Michael Newton (2002) in *Savage Girls and Wild Boys: A History of Feral Children*, feral children are deprived of their birthright as socialised human beings. To survive they must distrust, fear and avoid humans. In this sense, the feral child has been psychologically infanticided. His, or her, original human self has been murdered and a wild survival self develops. Newton related a history of feral children "through the fragmented and disrupted biographies of children whose histories are partially lost" (p. xiv) in an uncanny resonance of the experience of closed stranger adoption.

The attempts to resocialise such children through brutally enforced compliance, their status as objects, and their eventual re-abandonment once society has given up on them, reveal something of the misunderstanding, denial and mistreatment of the trauma of psychological infanticide.

Jeffrey Moussaieff Masson (1996) connected the feral child and the Soul-murdered child in his book, *The Wild Child: The Unsolved Mystery of Kaspar Hauser,* in which he included commentary on Soul murder by psychoanalytic psychobiographer, Leonard Shengold. Kaspar was the first in a category of feral children that includes children abused or neglected in ways that isolate them from human connection. He was allegedly kept isolated in an underground dungeon from early childhood until he was released as a young man. A figure of popular interest, he was rehabilitated enough to tell what he remembered before was murdered. Mystery surrounds his story. A second example is told in Russ Rymer's (Rymer, 1993 p. 24; p. 125; p. 127) *Genie: A Scientific Tragedy*, which heartbreakingly depicts the subjugation and dehumanising abuse of Genie, offering a visceral experience of psychological infanticide. Genie was rescued from more than a decade of isolated captivity from birth. Her parents had neglected several infants before her, all of whom died. Genie's story links directly to the infanticidal mode of child-rearing, and it echoes the experience of baby-farmed children in the nineteenth century, and the devastating destruction of humanness that occurs in psychological infanticide.

Richard Savage, a contemporary of Dr Samuel Johnson, was a feral 'adopted' child of the eighteenth century. We know his story primarily from Richard Holmes's (1993) biography, *Dr Johnson and Mr Savage*. Savage was a talented poet who lived a feral life on the streets, often involved in bouts of drunken violence. He was sentenced to hang for murder after a violent brawl, though reprieved by royal pardon at the last moment due to his status as a poet. Rejected by his mother at birth and brought up by adoptive parents, Savage remained furiously outraged and obsessed with his mother – visiting, stalking, taunting and blackmailing her – so creating scandal (Holmes, 1993). Savage would not remain a secret or be compliant. His story illustrates the murderous rage of the child abandoned by mother, and the paralysed chaos of a life that begins in infanticidal trauma.

The Bereaved Child

The bereaved child experiences early loss of a parent as a terrible rejecting abandonment. Something inside dies. The child seems frozen in the trauma of loss, haunted by the absence of the parent, and doomed to search endlessly to be reunited through death – resonant with my experience of longing for Mother Death. This *liebestod* is a seduction that promises death will reconnect the loved ones eternally. Lynda Schierse Leonard (2001b) described the dangers of this Romantic yearning in *On the Way to the Wedding: Transforming the Love Relationship*.

As depicted by Richard Holmes (1985) in *Footsteps: Adventures of a Romantic Biographer*, nineteenth-century French poet, Gerard de Nerval – whose mother died when he was five, and whose father maintained a critical, misattuned distance from his sensitive son – was haunted by his mother's absence throughout his life. He formed obsessive fantasy attachments with unattainable women, and gradually drifted deeper into a schizophrenic eccentric fantasy life. His poems weave fantasies of mythic love from ancient times. In particular, his poem, *El Desdichado,* speaks the anguish of the child abandoned by a parent's death. He longed for an idyllic time in the past when he was loved. Retreating further from reality into his fantastical life, de Nerval charmed others with his gentleness and poetic intellect, but he suffered paranoia and depression, and eventually suicided (Holmes, 1985).

De Nerval's rage is not outwardly expressed. His poem expresses his sense of extinction with the image of the black sun of melancholy, a poetic resonance with Marlon's (2005) exploration of *sol niger* and my experience of eclipse. De Nerval's psychosis – a deep haunting – and eventual suicide, reminded me how real and close the prospect of madness and suicide is, in the experience of psychological infanticide.

In all of the literature discussed above, personal voices and stories reveal insider experience in rich authentic language. It is as if we hear the murdered Soul speaking from beyond the grave, and in this sense these writers are a literature and legacy of ghosts and haunting.

Chapter Two
Researching Apparitions

Not only does an observer affect his observation,
but an observer gives meaning to what he observes,
thereby lifting it out of the depths of meaninglessness
and empty idle running or no running at all.
Miroslav Holub (1996)

In writing a personal story with Soul in mind, there is a process of development from the personal to the collective, an alchemical balancing of the personal subjective experience with the historical-social-cultural, and finally, a uniting of these opposites in a transcendent third dimension of the sacred, which contains, unites and holds all perspectives within its wholeness. Jung (1961/1989) wrote about the necessity of understanding the past through its art, myths, rituals and symbols – as well as its history.

Methodology and Methods

In fictionalised writing of self-experience, there is freedom to explore psychological truths without necessarily being conscious of them at the time of writing. There is room for Psyche to speak through images, symbols and narratives that present a biomythic truth – if we are willing to listen. In this book I offer excerpts of my personal writing from over two decades, much of it before

41

I studied psychotherapy, to illuminate aspects of my experience of psychological infanticide and the universal themes contained within.

Making the Invisible Visible

Initially I drew on the ideas of Clark Moustakas's methodology of heuristic self-inquiry as:

> a search for discovery of meaning and essence in significant human experience. It requires a subjective process of reflecting, exploring, sifting, and elucidating the nature of the phenomenon under investigation. Its ultimate purpose is to cast light on a focused problem, question or theme. (Douglass & Moustakas, 1985, p. 40)

I found this approach relevant because of its intention of researching into "*authentic accounts of human experience*" (Hiles, 2002, p. 2, author's italics).

Heuristic inquiry rests on the underlying phenomenological assumption that the structure of an experience may rest on hidden, invisible meanings that must be intuited (Grbich, 1999). This perspective aligns with depth psychology, which is an exploration of the invisible territory of the psyche and the individual meanings people make of their life experiences. I have valued the approach of Jungian-inspired depth psychology and its imaginal-archetypal descendants. In particular, I have felt drawn to imaginal psychology as offering what I intuitively feel is the right approach into the pre-verbal, unconsciously-memoried, embodied experience of psychological infanticide.

Essentially, phenomenology refers to a dual process of conscious awareness and reflectiveness (Grbich, 1999). Robert Romanyshyn (2007) invited us to re-engage with phenomena through direct experience in order to get to know them for, and of, themselves, inviting new world perspectives, which Romanyshyn explored as both a re-turn to the past and a process of re-visioning. The concepts of re-turn and re-vision are valid for any inquiry into a past experience, especially one involving loss and memory. As we re-turn to, and engage with, such material from our present perspective, we invite a fresh relationship with the phenomenon itself.

The idea that body and world are intimately engaged is a central tenet of phenomenology. French philosopher, Maurice Merleau-Ponty (1992, 2002), describing the phenomenological process of embodied experience, made a link between the lived body as a receptacle of past experiences and tacit knowing and culture as a collective body of lived experience. This implies that it is experiences, memories, images, intuitions, and body symptoms that can tell us much about our lived experience at a depth level. Goodchild (2001, 2012) suggested that in expressing embodied knowing through engagement in the arts, we are connected to deeper imaginal dimensions.

Phenomenological psychologies emphasise the idea of Soul (Psyche) as existing not just within us but both of, and in, our engagement and relationship with the world. This suggests that exploring an experience from the perspective of Soul can show us more than simply an individual experience. We discover how Soul relates to the world through the experience.

Soul represents the part of us that knows and reaches for the eternal, universal, and infinite; whereas the personal self is confined by its own self-defined limits. Jung (1967) describes Soul as a psychological reality, which mediates between the ego and the unconscious. Soul does this by receiving unconscious images and transmitting them to the conscious mind. Soul and the unconscious manifest and speak in symbols and images through dream and imagination. Soul also corresponds to the hidden side of the roles we live that holds our unconscious processes.

Soul or Psyche is therefore the inner realm. In using the term 'Soul', I differentiate from the logic, clarity and reasoning of the cognitive-analytic mind. Archetypal psychologist, James Hillman

(1994), differentiated between the clarity of the Apollonian mind, centred in Apollo's abstract daylight vision, and Soul – *anima* and *animus* – the shadowy and elusive aspect of mind that animates and moves us from within. Soul is the mind's psychic aspect – intuitive, deep, cryptic and mysterious – her 'logic' is spiralling, multidimensional, and mythic.

Imaginal inquiry lends itself to themes of Soul, Psyche, and transcendence in the sense of personal growth through inner work. For example, Dave Hiles (1999, 2001, 2002) elaborates on the transpersonal themes of human experience that emerge from heuristic inquiry. Hiles highlights here what, for me, has seemed a natural means of Soulful exploration of inner experience through written inquiry, bringing personal psychological development to greater transformational potentials.

Heuristic inquiry is therefore a process of making the invisible (inner) visible (expressed). Bringing the imaginal dimension into the inquiry contributes a mutually transformative relationship between matter and spirit.

Jung's concept of active imagination guided and developed my personal method of imaginal inquiry, and Jung himself was a warm presence and reliable companion on my inner journey.

A Containing Methodology for Personal Process

I found Jung's advice regarding the necessity of knowing our social-cultural history to be a valuable means of connecting with other examples of the collective story that resonated with my personal experience, expanding the process from feeling-into to feeling-with. This shift has powerful potential to open the experiencer out of a position of personal victimhood into a resonant compassion for others in a similar situation, rendering the situation both less personal and more connected with others. When we make the shift from victimhood (personalised trauma in which we seek to blame an other) to compassion and connection (the situation is no longer isolating and personal) healing transformation begins.

Neuroscience also describes the embodied or feeling self as one of several layers of self-experience and self-knowledge (Damasio, 2000; van der Kolk, 2014). I found it to be true that the body knows things of which the mind is not aware. In the practice of imaginal inquiry, it became possible to listen to and hear this embodied knowledge more clearly. This inner realm of embodied knowledge, the realm of Soul, expresses itself in images, sounds, bodily sensations, symptoms, and dreams.

Imaginal inquiry is internally focused, and process-oriented rather than result-oriented. The inclusion of the imaginal dimension opens up archetypal themes and resonances. The inquirer does not actively search for the archetypal so much as remain receptive to the imaginal experiences and archetypal presences within the energy field of the subject. In this way, matter becomes spiritualised, and the spiritual materialised in an alchemical process of transcendence. What I mean by this is that, through including the imaginal dimension, we witness the sacred light within ordinary experiences or beings, and the relationships between human and mythic realms.

The Methodology

Engaging in a personal inquiry, a re-search into lost, hidden or negated parts of myself, I realised I needed a depth approach, one that was able to reach down into, and work with, imaginal and archetypal aspects of the psyche and the experience of psychological infanticide.

Robert Romanyshyn's (1997) methodology of alchemical hermeneutics has a lineage extending from Jungian depth psychology through to Hillman's archetypal psychology. The term *imaginal* refers to the work of philosopher Henri Corbin, who explored the subtle realms of Sufi mysticism (Goodchild, 2012). The imaginal dimension is to be differentiated from the imaginary. It is considered a realm with its own reality, located somewhere between the realms of spirit and matter (Goodchild, 2012). One might describe it as the realm of Soul. Associated with the feminine Sophia, the imaginal realm is seen as a 'spiritually creative force', an 'interworld' of interiority and subtle energies whose function is to materialise spirit and spiritualise matter (Goodchild, p.17-18). This imaginal dimension aligned with my Jungian-inspired process of writing, reverie and imaginal engagement with personified figures of the psyche. Romanyshyn (1997) outlined clear methods for taking the inquiry into a deeper, imaginal field, accessing energies beyond the self, which he describes as the transference field of the work.

This deepens the level of self-inquiry to one that values the communications of an imaginal realm that includes the presence of collective and archetypal forces that could (and ought to) be engaged with through imaginal processes.

I invited dream material, reverie, dialogues, symptoms, visions, signs and synchronicities into my work, bringing self-inquiry beyond the personal and into the realm of the imaginal-archetypal. Several of the images I worked with are included in the illustrations reproduced in this book.

In heuristic inquiry, Clark Moustakas (1990) drew together phenomenology and humanistic psychology's belief in people's potential for creativity, growth and self-expression (Moustakas 1990). So, what is the difference between humanistic ideals of self-actualisation and those of Jungian individuation? James Hillman (1994) described humanism as limiting thinking to the realm of ego, whereas depth psychology, he argued, lies in the realm of Soul. They occupy different positions and means of experiencing. My personal experience felt aligned with the depth work of Soul, and I wanted to find a way to more explicitly include this dimension.

Hillman argued that Eugene Gendlin's (1969) paper on focusing exposed the limitations of phenomenological and body-oriented therapies in which self-examination does not go beyond its own consciousness (Hillman, 1994). What I think he meant by this is that rather than simply explicating a personal experience to include other's similar experiences – an externalisation of the experience – we go more deeply into the realm of Psyche in order to discover the archetypal presences involved and find a way to relate to them, thereby including these figures into a deeper, wider illumination that is beyond the personal.

Douglas and Moustakas (1985) identified the essential difference between phenomenology and heuristic inquiry as: "Phenomenology ends with the essence of experience; heuristics retains the essence of the person in experience" (p. 43). An imaginal-archetypal approach includes, and more explicitly addresses, the essence of Soul in the experience.

Imaginal Inquiry in Practice

In three clearly defined phases based on Moustakas's heuristic inquiry, imaginal inquiry first immerses in the question, problem or theme, using concepts of indwelling, self-search and internal frame of reference in an attempt to know and relate to the experience. It is a journey of one's inner depths. I thought of it as exploring the dark interior. Second, there is a collection of relevant information, beginning with the self and extending outwards to the universal aspects of the topic, using personal resonance or intuition as guide. Finally, information is synthesised and presented experientially, through dreams, poems, fiction and journal writing,

Moustakas elaborated his model into seven central concepts for the basis of inquiry. I integrated an imaginal approach into the process because it adds the dimension of Soul, potentially taking the work beyond the humanistic domain of self-inquiry, and the personal self into the inner realms and archetypal dimensions of depth psychology.

1. ***Identification with the focus of inquiry*** – aims to facilitate understanding of the experienced phenomenon from within through open-ended self-directed inquiry. Using an imaginal approach extends this inquiry beyond the known aspects of self and into the archetypal field, understanding the self as contextualised within this field.

2. ***Imaginal dialogue*** – the beginning of critical thinking through self-reflective questioning. Imaginally, self-dialogue becomes more than a conversation with parts of the self, and engages in dialogues with personified imaginal figures related to as their own selves, much as the characters in a work of fiction have a life of their own that the author engages with but does not control.

3. ***Imaginal knowing*** – from Polyani's term 'tacit knowing' (1966), which describes implicit knowledge: a perceptual knowing beyond our external or explicit experience. An imaginal approach might ask who knows what about the experience, and remains open to different perspectives.

4. ***Intuition*** – described by Moustakas (1990) as the bridge between implicit knowledge and explicit knowledge. Imaginal inquiry encourages recognition and following of clues, dreams and synchronicities that present themselves. In an imaginal approach, reveries, dreams, signs, symptoms and synchronicities are all valued and paid due attention as communications from Soul/Psyche.

5. ***Indwelling*** – describes a process of deep contemplation. Imaginally, this contemplation may be taken deeper, into unknown regions of the psyche.

6. ***Imaginal Focusing*** – listens with an inner ear for themes outside the sphere of the ego realm, of the known. Instead of aiming to clarify an experience, an imaginal approach descends into the depths and complexity of what is not known.

7. ***Imaginal frame of reference*** – goes beyond the inquirer's personal experience as the ultimate criterion of

authenticity. "The works of writers, poets, artists, spiritual leaders and scientists all invite participation, and all of these can be usefully treated as the creative products of heuristic inquiry" (Hiles, 2002). In imaginal inquiry, this is extended to include both the researcher's felt experience, and archetypal presences with their own perspectives. Resonance with myths and tales confirms the place of the personal within the universal.

Imaginal Psychology: Haunted by Archetypes and a Map for a Heroic Quest

As discussed earlier, Romanyshyn (1997) critiqued heuristic inquiry as a method that, on its own, does not go far enough into the territory of Soul and the collective unconscious. Yet Jungian analyst, James Hollis (2013), described Jung's self-actualisation method as heuristic research.

I resonated with an imaginal approach and the freedom it offered to transcend my personal experience into greater mythic themes. It allowed for a re-cognition of the relationship between the personal and the archetypal patterns of the collective unconscious. While Moustakas's (1990) heuristic methodology points in the same direction of extrapolating a personal experience into a universalised one, the imaginal approach enabled me to adapt some of Moustakas's methods to resonate more fully with my intuitive approach into my experience. In doing so, I felt a shift in the locus of control from myself as inquirer controlling and directing my experiment, to co-creator and conduit for the energies that wished to be represented by the phenomenon of psychological infanticide. This allowed for the voices of the self to be dialogued with, and the voices of the historical past and the archetypal energies of collective and cultural patterns to be engaged with, and so I was able to express a deeper truth embedded in a more complex context than just my personal story.

I made this shift into being a conduit by listening for the greater myths and truths of my story, and engaging in dialogues with personified presences. I began with my imaginal engagement with Minnie Dean (representing the negative mother) and the Madonna (the positive mother). Gradually I felt drawn into the energetic field of the archetypal Divine Mother, represented in various cultures as a many-faceted goddess or series of goddesses, representing the whole dimension of this great maternal Being. The Great Mother includes aspects of creation, nurturance, decay and destruction in an eternal round of birth, life, death and the space between lives.

I held a perspective that includes both a personal 'factual' situation in a context of legal, social and political practicalities of what to do with unwelcome children alongside a more deeply mythic personal story held within a *mythos* of the eternal themes and archetypes of the unwelcome child. I have also held a thread connecting the factual realities of baby farming and infanticide and the more subtle realities of psychological infanticide.

My aims and intentions were not to impose a linear logic for the experience of psychological infanticide, nor to analyse and develop a method for its treatment, but to let myself down into the depths of the subject and discover what Soul wants us to know about this experience. Essential to the truths of imaginal inquiry is the resonance between personal truths and more deeply universal themes, which indicate a relationship between *logos* and *mythos*. We cannot simply research such complex mysteries from the perspective of logic. They are inextricably entwined with more sacred and profound mysteries that urge us to inquire more deeply into ourselves as mythic beings in a world of mythic narratives. I was interested in the mythopoetic themes of the situation of the unwilling mother and unwelcome child, as expressed throughout time in Western society.

Embodied Research and a Theoretical Womb

Using an imaginal approach with some of the flavour of Romanyshyn's (1997) alchemical hermeneutics, linking the idea of embodied research with alchemical imagery, I imagined a theoretical womb within which to contain an alchemy of Moustakas's seven phases of inquiry:

Initial engagement. Moustakas (1990) stated: "During this process one encounters the self, one's autobiography, and significant relationships within a social context" (p. 27). I began with personal writings from several decades, and a passionate engagement with baby farmer, Minnie Dean, sparked by my dream of the baby in the shrine. In this stage, I felt compelled to explore baby farming – an historical situation that resonated with my inner knowing.

Immersion. The dream initiated a quest to know more about the dead infant in my psyche. I immersed myself in the question of psychological infanticide, allowing its themes and essences to unfold around and within me, paying attention to dreams, reflections, and responses to literature, art, history or any other engagement with the topic.

Incubation. This process, described by Moustakas as like planting a seed that provides creative integration, is congruent with the process of depth psychotherapy in which material comes forth from a spacious receptivity rather than an agenda. In this phase I detached from my intense focus, trusting the material was being worked on within. I did not actively work the material, but observed the dreams, images and associations that began to unfold. The incubation phase took me back into images of the womb – the hidden, hibernatory world of unseen life creating itself in readiness for birth. I intuitively named this mysterious aspect of the creative process 'growing things in the dark'.

Illumination. "Illumination opens the door to a new awareness, a modification of an old understanding, a synthesis of fragmented knowledge, or an altogether new discovery of something that has been present for some time yet beyond immediate awareness" (Moustakas, 1990, p. 30). For me, this step symbolised the process of birth. Many of the words related to it are to do with light, sight, the eye – and images. Images are internal visions, and dreams are narratives of illumination. Images may also be experienced through words, sound or through sensation in the body, as if tacit knowledge reveals its clearest knowings through the medium of the senses. I reflected on illumination as a way of looking, of penetrating into otherwise dark or hidden places. It may also be considered as the development of a kind of night vision or seeing in the dark, in which illumination has a receptive quality in which Psyche reveals herself, and light births out of darkness.

Explication. "The purpose of the explication phase is to fully examine what has awakened in consciousness, in order to understand its various layers of meaning" (Moustakas, 1990, p. 31). In this stage, the personal begins reaching toward the universal aspects of the experience. I resonated with the experience of psychological infanticide expressed by other writers, validating the authenticity of my inquiry through these archetypal patterns.

Creative synthesis. A creative synthesis invites the telling of a story, drawing together the main characters and themes; in my case, the story of a nineteenth-century baby farmer named Minnie Dean, an unwelcome child (myself) and the theme of infanticide. I wove a mythopoetic narrative evoking the themes, insights, patterns and illuminations of my process. The process of a life, engaging with life's experiences, is a transformative poetics of consciousness, something John O'Donohue (1992) called 'a poetics of growth'. Like poetry, life is engaged and processed through a working with, and weaving of, images and stories in ways that are creative or destructive. We are always synthesising the fragments of our experiences into a cloth woven of associations, meanings and progressions. The more poetic our consciousness becomes, the more our weavings include imaginal engagements, dreams, synchronicities and other liminal experiences beyond the more prosaic level of thinking.

John O Donohue used the term 'inner harvesting' (p. 223) for sifting what he called the fruits of experience. His metaphors are rich with life and organic process. Life is not static, and we are not static within it; rather, we are required to work with the material we have in order for its fruits to be tended well and harvested. I thought of this in alchemical terms, working a *prima materia* through levels of transfiguration until it is brought to its highest potential – the philosopher's stone. The key concept in these metaphors is that of growth, transfiguration and release of hidden riches through working with the material provided.

Much of my personal writing refers to dialogues with imaginal figures. Jung (2009) initiated and developed the concept of dialogues through his technique of active imagination, the key components of which have been extended and intensified in imaginal/archetypal psychology (Romanyshyn, 1997). I drew on Mary Watkins's (2000) comprehensive history and development of the concept of imaginal dialogues. The skill of personifying and dialoguing is one fiction writers use constantly, and the best writers are able to suspend disbelief and engage with their characters *as if* they have a life of their own. Our internal worlds are peopled, or figured, and the more we connect with these internal worlds of complex inner life, the more rich and engaged we are in ourselves as whole and engaged beings. Inviting the imaginal realm extends this to figures beyond the personal self, figures from the realm of Psyche, the collective realm of the World Soul.

I engaged in dialogues with imaginal figures that were also real historical figures. They are imaginal because they are figures of Psyche, not their actual historical selves. These figures, such as Minnie Dean and Charlotte Brontë – in personifying my attachment to their themes, issues and representations – enabled me to explore these issues from many perspectives.

Healing Fictions: Writing as a Process of Discovery, Illumination and Transformation

I translated the ideas of imaginal psychology, as outlined in the previous section, into an attunement to the personal and archetypal myths that were living themselves out through my experience. In this process I moved from an analytical and potentially pathologising psychobiographical stance towards a mythic stance that valued an archetypal understanding of the narratives of trauma (Kalsched, 1996).

Narrative has been described as the primary process by which we make meaning of our experience, and construct and maintain our identity or sense of self (Hiles, 2002; Hunt, 2000; Hunt & Sampson, 2006; Matousek, 2017). In his comparison of narrative and heuristic approaches, Hiles (2002) stated:

Narrative dominates human discourse, and is foundational to the cultural processes that organise and structure human behaviour and experience. Narrative is also fundamental to human reality and our understanding of human experience (p. 8)

My natural inclination for writing personal narratives led me to make use of writing methods as both a framework for understanding my experience (autopsychobiography) and as a transformative process for shifting perspective from the personal to a greater contextual meaning (biomythography).

Rather than trying to move the work in a particular direction, I revisited and reflected on my personal writings in order to discover what the story was already saying. I attempted to attune my ear to the resonances already present and presenting themselves through the narrative and the language. This is the same attunement that a therapist practises with their client, which Hiles (2002) called an authentic participatory presence, and which has been referred to as a receptiveness to the process (Hillman, 1994; Kelly, 2017).

Hillman (1994) reminded us that, rather than attempting to impose a new story on top of the original, we allow the original to reveal itself and allow it to work on us and through us. He implied that it is through shaping the story, in its telling in therapy and through artistic process, that the story comes to be internalised and processed into our experience, an alchemical process which transforms the original material, and integrates it as part of us. This suggests the required approach of transformational writing: we must be both focused on our approach and intent and receptive to allowing the work to work on us.

In the following sections, I explain and discuss three methods and processes of writing narratives that informed my self-inquiry: psychobiography, biomythography, and transformational writing.

Psychobiography. This interdisciplinary narrative research method uses psychological theories to illuminate lives through the telling of coherent stories (McAdams, 2011, cited in Cara, 2007; Schultz, 2005). In *Healing Fictions*, James Hillman (1994) described both Freud and Jung as psychobiographers creating psychological fictions presented as case history, as analysed through the lens of their respective depth psychologies. The art of psychobiography concerns itself with telling the narrative of an individual and their personal motivations, based on an analysis of the emotional effects of childhood.

I used elements of psychobiography to structure, develop and analyse my narrative from a depth psychology perspective. I explored the subtleties of presenting a narrative that included both an historical biography of Minnie Dean and my autobiographical material. I began to feel limited by the traditional psychobiographical approach. Psychobiography aims not to pathologise or diagnose, but it does make psychological statements about essential themes of a person's life that I found definitive and limiting, rather than expansive with deeper wonderings. I wanted to elaborate Minnie Dean (and myself) in her complexities rather than pin her down as a lifeless butterfly in some Victorian specimen cabinet.

My intention was to open out and reveal dimensions of the experience of psychological infanticide, leaving room for subtleties, uncertainty and complexity – and for the work to speak for itself in an ongoing conversation with the thoughts of others who engage with it over time. It seemed this re-imagining of the personal and collective past could bring something alive.

Margaret L Young (2008a, 2008b) described her method of autopsychobiography as a combination of psychological theory and biography that looks at a slice of life, bringing together personal recollection and universal human experience. This felt closer to my objective of weaving an engagement between my personal experience and the historic phenomenon of baby farming. I combined elements of traditional psychobiography, using the psychological theories of infanticidal attachment and imaginal/archetypal psychology, with Young's method of autopsychobiography.

Extending a personal narrative into a wider universal context takes it further – into the realm of the archetypal or mythic dimension. I therefore went on to consider biomythography.

Biomythography. This term refers to a narrative blend of biography, history and myth. With its focus on soulful reflection and inner life, Jung's memoir – *Memories, Dreams, Reflections* – is an example of biomythography.

Biomythography tells a personal story which aligns itself with the emotional truth and mythic resonances, rather than the verifiable facts of a life. Where psychobiography does this through interpretation of psychic events through the lens of a chosen theory, biomythography seeks to express the personal myth that can be traced in a personal narrative, or the archetypes that are expressed either consciously or unconsciously (Hillman, 1994; Hollis, 2000; Jung 1989, 2014; Lorde, 1982; Slattery, 2012).

So Biomythography – a telling of life story as personal myth – is therefore able to hold a broader resonance and attune the ear to the *mythos,* rather than the *logos* of the experience. Hillman (1994) suggested that *mythos* is its own form of *logos*. Mark Matousek (2017) describes the differences between *logos* and *mythos. Logos* is the rational, deductive, logical thinking. *Mythos*, on the other hand, is based on feeling, intuition, symbols, metaphors, and subtle distinctions in order to make sense of the depths and mysteries of our lives. I describe *mythos* as poetic sensibility, with its echoes of Samuel Taylor Coleridge's (1817/1956) 'poetic faith' – the willing suspension of disbelief – and Gaston Bachelard's (1971, 2005) 'poetic imagination' a key element of inhabiting an imaginal realm. *Mythos* inspires and invites a sense of resonance or heartfelt response.

Matousek (2017) suggested that *logos* is based on reason and contributes wisdom, where *mythos* is based on faith and contributes depth. Both types of thinking are important resources. Being able to use both capacities balances and broadens the view of research.

Dennis Slattery (2012) also offered an approach toward self-discovery through exploration of personal myth. His work developed an ear for the archetypal and poetic echoes of myth within written work – my own and that of others. To be able to recognise universal stories offers us perspective and capacity for self-reflection. Slattery's imaginal perspective engaged my poetic consciousness, and anchored my sense of the importance of exploring eternal stories (such as that of infanticide) and how they unfold in the collective unconscious over time. I learned to trust and follow my images and symbols, inviting them to reveal their hidden knowledge. Slattery (2000) engaged the embodied self with the intention of retrieving and reuniting "*biology* and *biography* – to get the story right – and to return home" (p. 23).

In offering a narrative that includes biomythic and imaginal dimensions, acknowledging the Souled rather than a literal truth of a psychological experience, my aim was to provide insights into infanticidal experiences buried deep in the heart of the adoption process. I wished to present the experience in its internal aliveness rather than analysing 'dead matter', which is paradoxical, given that the phenomenon itself is about death where there should have been life.

Biomythography is a method that has been used to tell the mythic narrative of an historical figure. People such as Minnie Dean become mythic figures in their culture, as evidenced by the continuing interest in Minnie through songs (Henderson & Hamblin, 1995; Williams, 2013), television representations (Catran, 1985), fiction (de Bazin, 2012), ficto-criticism (Kelly, 2011), and magazine retrial discussion (Braunias, 2013), as well as Lynley Hood's biography (1994) and Karen Zelas's verse biography (2017).

Benton (2005) argued that biomythography tends to be written according to the particular mythic theme most evident or attractive to the biographer. This is also of concern in the field of psychobiography. William T Schultz (2005), for example, cautioned that psychobiographers may become over-identified with their subjects' themes. Contrary to Benton's and Schultz's views about the potential for author bias, I suggest that, at least in the case of imaginal inquiry, it is illuminating to present the mythic themes that arise out of the data of a life, as these hold essential elements of both the subject and their context, and the link by which the author is drawn to them. It is, therefore, a means of discovering the resonances that are still sounding between one life and time and another.

Slattery (2012) argued that phenomenology indicates that no biography of depth and insight is without author bias, and further, that this subjectivity is what brings the engagement between writer and subject alive. He argued that mythic elements connect us to collective experience and the archetypal experiences in our personalised lives. We are, therefore, both individual and mythic in the sense of our personal stories revealing collective mythic themes. From this perspective, it seems evident that author and subject cannot be separated from the mythic themes that arise between them.

A fluid method of exploration emerged that included elements of psychobiography and biomythography, and made use of writing practices from the genre of transformational writing, which I discuss in the following section.

Writing as a Transformative Process

I wrote my experience of psychological infanticide, and my personal engagement with Minnie Dean, in the first person – transparently and openly exploring the experience and my ideas about it in a way that I hoped would make the experience 'real' and show the self-reflective process as it was actually happening. This process was informed by ideas about life writing – the bringing together of a life story and of bringing a story to life.

For writing to be therapeutic it needs to become a vehicle for transformation. In order to do so, it must lift out of the narrating of a literal experience into a working of the narrative into new perspectives (Hunt & Sampson, 2006; Matousek, 2017). Through the writing of personal stories as fictions, a greater range of perspectives and expressions of a subjective experience are enabled (Bolton, 2010; Hunt, 2000; Hunt & Sampson, 2006). Hunt and Sampson explained that writing autobiographical fiction:

> means that we are forced to enter into our own feelings and emotions in a way which we may not be able to do simply by writing about the facts of our lives. Thus fictionalising from ourselves…helps us to engage more deeply with our inner life, opening up possibilities for greater insight and self-understanding. (1998, p. 33)

Transformational writing refers to both a genre and to methods of transforming personal stories from trauma-based narratives towards more empowered narratives through which a greater context of understanding is achieved, and with it a greater sense of wholeness and self-coherence. Transformational writing aims to go beyond victim-identified narratives to illuminate greater truths that resonate with the universal experiences we all go through. I see these writing methods as parallel practices with similar aims to methods of trauma treatment that include a transcendent perspective (Kalsched, 1996).

Matousek's (2017) approach can be applied closely to models of trauma therapy and demonstrates how writing can enable us to witness the victim stories we live in and transform these narratives through a process of writing that leads to personal depth and growth. Matousek encourages writing from a place of emotional truth, and a willingness to face into the deep questions that underpin our personal stories. He also draws on depth psychology, attachment theory, and the language of personal myth and its relationship to concepts of identity and self.

Where Matousek offers a method for writing focused on self-transformation and healing, and Slattery explores a mythopoesis of personal biography – a consciousness of biomythography – Hunt and Sampson (2006) defined reflexivity as an engagement with an 'other' through:

> creating an internal space, distancing ourselves from ourselves, as it were, so that we are both 'inside' and 'outside' ourselves simultaneously and able to switch back and forth fluidly and playfully from one position to the other, giving ourselves up to the experience of 'self as other' whilst also retaining a grounding in our familiar sense of self. (p. 4)

This 'doubling' of the self (Hunt & Sampson, 2006) is analogous to the process of imaginal dialogues (Watkins, 2000) and to the self-dialogues of heuristic inquiry.

Each of the processes of engagement described in this chapter were material for the alchemical container, the theoretical womb, out of which transformation naturally occurs when given our receptive attention.

Chapter Three
Infanticidal Attachment

*If we can bear to read the writings of the
psychohistorians on infanticide, we will understand that
the very foundations of humanity have been constructed
upon the charred bones of dead infants.*
Brett Kahr (1993)

A Mythology of Infanticide

Carl Jung (1961/1989) suggested that the universalised,
common or archetypal themes evident in an exploration of history
and literature, strengthen, validate and add perspective to personal
subjectivity. This implies that a test of the validity of imaginal
inquiry is its resonance with historical and literary parallels. The
psychohistory of infanticide, in particular the history of baby
farming, can illuminate the themes of infanticide resonant in the
experience of closed stranger adoption.

Throughout my underworld journey, I learned to listen to the
mythic truth of infanticide represented throughout history, and
in the many tales of children abandoned or killed by parents or
archetypal wicked witches. Fears of abandonment, rejection and
infanticide are universal childhood experiences that reveal the
child's awareness of its vulnerability and helpless dependency
on the mercy of powerful adults (Bloch, 1979). For many
unfortunates, these innate fears become lived reality. The greater

story of infanticide as a human truth occurring throughout time, place and culture has something essential to teach us about the way we kill off the most vulnerable and creative parts of ourselves and others. Guided by this mythic consciousness, which might equally be named 'collective unconscious experience' or 'intergenerational trauma', I felt that exploring the psychohistory of infanticide had much to reveal about this dark recess of our collective and individual psyches.

Just as Freud built psychoanalysis on the Greek myth of Oedipus (Sophocles, 1947), and Jung's analytic psychology, according to Romanyshyn (2004), resonated with the myth of Orpheus (Ovid, 1567/1965) – I was looking for the larger story that supported my hypothesis of psychological infanticide. Robert Johnson (1983) said of myth: "If we learn to listen, it also gives us specific psychological information and teaches the deeper truths of the psyche" (p. 1).

Mythologically, infanticide relates to the plight of the archetypal Innocent, who is literally and/or psychologically sacrificed at the very beginning of life (Estes, 1997; Pearson, 1986, 1991). Freud (1930/2005) adopted Oedipus, the tragic hero of Sophocles's cycle of plays, as representative of the psychological trauma of the human condition. Oedipus is the archetypal Innocent who is abandoned in an infanticidal act by his parents, and survives after being adopted by strangers. Due to not knowing his true identity, he ends up killing his father and marrying his mother. This suggests that the central trauma of the human condition relates to the infanticidal acts or wishes of parents, and the potential for psychological survival through connection with caring others.

The trauma and destruction that follow from infanticidal beginnings, and the resulting internalised murderousness, inappropriate seductions, impulsivity and lack of insight that occur through loss of identity and authentic belonging make Oedipus a tragic hero. Because he cannot know himself authentically, he makes terrible mistakes for which he punishes himself harshly,

62

blinding himself as he himself has been symbolically blinded by the disruption to his self-knowledge and authentic familial context (Sophocles, 1947). Freud related the Oedipus complex to the development of guilt feelings and the superego, and identified the complex as intergenerational, related to the way parents parent (1930/2005, 1930; Young, 2001). The myth describes the situation and effects of psychological infanticide.

Freud's use of the Oedipal myth also suggests that the lack of connection to one's true self is the great trauma we face and work through on the heroic journey through our lives. What the myth describes is a general human trauma intensified to archetypal dimensions lived by people who experience psychological infanticide. Because it taps into universal infanticidal fears and feelings that most people do not wish to feel, there is tremendous denial of the experience of psychological infanticide and a corresponding lack of understanding of the experience – its causes, effects, and methods of healing.

Returning to archetypes that guide our psychological development, the archetypal Innocent represents the beginning of our life journey and self-development. The Innocent lives in an idealised womb-like world, but in order to grow, this false refuge and denial of reality must be sacrificed. Carol Pearson (1991) described the developmental tasks of this archetype as retaining a sense of faith and goodness during adversity, and maintaining trust and optimism "without denial, naivete or dependence" (p. 79). This is the psychic blueprint of the beginning of human development. We must all experience the disillusionment of the loss of the perfectly sustaining world of the womb, and grow towards a more complex and conflicted reality and independence.

It is also a truth that life sometimes brutally sacrifices our innocence through betrayals and breaches of trust. Archetypally, this leads to the next stage of human development, that of the archetypal Orphan who must grieve the pain of abandonment and betrayal and learn to rely on herself to survive (Pearson, 1986, 1991). The shift from Innocent to Orphan is also the archetypal pattern of trauma, in which sacrificed innocence leads to a hypervigilant, bitter and grief-stricken battle for survival, the healing of which leads to greater resilience, humility, compassion and a capacity to thrive – a trusting in both life and one's own resources. Pearson (1986, 1991) described the Orphan's developmental tasks as working through the cynicism and despair that result from loss and betrayal, learning to feel without blame, accepting help and developing interdependence whilst maintaining realistic expectations.

Archetypal systems such as Pearson's are useful in providing maps for universal human experiences, and guidance for how to work through our life experiences in ways that facilitate growth, wisdom and healing. In the case of psychological infanticide, these two archetypes of the Innocent and the Orphan are places that the psyche traumatised in childhood is likely to get stuck. Myths and stories offer symbolic ways to work through these developmental tasks, and highlight what happens when we do not (Bettelheim, 1976; von Franz, 1996b). It is also possible, as in my own example with Minnie Dean, to grow by engaging with the historical figures and stories that represent our archetypal patterns (Pearson, 1986, 1991).

However, there is a more sinister truth behind this archetypology. In earlier times infants were treated as disposable. Inconvenient babies and children were murdered, or abandoned to almost certain death. In the next section I discuss the psychohistory of infanticide: the literal sacrifice of the innocent.

At the other pole of the sacrificed infant is likely to be an infanticidal mother (or mother figure). Marion Woodman (2005) introduced the concept of the Death Mother archetype to describe the most negative pole of the mother archetype: a mother who wishes death upon her child (Woodman & Sieff, 2015). This Death Mother comes about through early trauma, is internalised by the child, and destructively drains vitality, paralysing the ability to engage in life (Harris & Harris, 2015; Sieff, 2017; Woodman & Sieff, 2015). According to Daniela Sieff: "The Death Mother energy feeds on humiliation and shame, powerlessness and the fear of annihilation", and "Ultimately the Death Mother carries the wish that we, or some part of us, did not exist" (Holmquist, 2015, cited in Sieff, 2017, p. 5).

Marion Woodman linked the Death Mother energy to not being welcomed into life, and to feeling unwanted or wrong in the womb (Sieff 2017; Woodman 2005; Woodman & Sieff, 2015). As with all Shadow material, it is important to identify the archetypal energy activated in a particular wound, in this case, the feminine wound that results for a woman in the situation of having an unwanted pregnancy. Identifying and naming of archetypal energies is the healing opposite of the dissociation that results for both mother and unborn child in such a conflicted situation. Naming and working with these archetypal energies consciously is transformative, as it takes the archetypal pattern out of unconscious repetition. Engaging with the Death Mother archetype helps activate and strengthen the warm and nourishing inner mother we all need.

The Psychohistory of Childhood

A comprehensive psychohistory of the actual sacrifice of infant life in the context of the development of child-rearing modes throughout history was presented by psychohistorian, Lloyd de Mause (1974) and revisited by psychologist, Robin Grille (2005). De Mause interpreted history through the lens of psychodynamic theory, combining insights from psychotherapy with research methodology of social sciences to understand the emotional (childhood) origin of social-political behaviour. These psychohistorians claim that early infanticidal practices have gradually shifted, along with attitudes toward unwanted children, into psychological forms of infanticide performed on the *identity or self of the child* (my italics) (de Mause, 1974; Grille, 2005; Shengold, 1989, 1999, 2000, 2013). A key understanding of my theory is that to remove an infant from all known reference points of identity, including biological connection with the birth mother – as occurs in closed stranger adoption – creates an experience of psychological infanticide. I explore this in more detail in the following chapters.

De Mause (1974) investigated the emotional effects of childhood and the resulting psychodynamic patterns that lead to family and socio-political systems. He exposed the brutal truth of the sacrifice of infants throughout human history. From earliest times, unwanted infants were exposed to the elements, or abandoned to almost certain death, carelessly slaughtered or ritually sacrificed. The general premise of the psychohistory of childhood is that we reap what we sow: violent means of child-rearing raise violent adults and create a violent world (the legacy of child abuse). Conversely, as we consciously practise more respectful modes of raising children, we raise more peaceful, less traumatised children, which offers hope for a more peaceful world (de Mause, 1974; Grille, 2005).

De Mause (1974) presented a timeline of 'the evolution of child-rearing modes' (p. 53) in which he proposed that the primary modes of child-rearing remained unchanged over fourteen hundred years. These modes, the infanticidal and abandonment modes, reflect adult acting out of child-rearing frustrations through murder or abandonment. According to de Mause (1974) and Grille (2005), the infanticidal mode was the first recognisable style of child-rearing, characterised by the exploitation of children and the discarding or destruction of them when they were no longer useful. More recent research argues that infanticidal modes of child-rearing are worldwide, occurring in part as a result of the development of agriculture and the effects of land desertification, scarcity, and the eventual developments in the valuing of commodity and land ownership, with the corresponding need to identify the lineage of children in order to protect property rights (DeMeo; 2006; Grille, 2005). This theory suggests an infanticidal mode of child-rearing is the result of trauma brought about by scarcity and imbalance of resources, leading to communities living in survival mode. This creates a situation where children become property of their parents and a possible drain on resources, objects for exploitation rather than valued for their unique selves. DeMeo (2006) contended that slave labour and the subordination of women also resulted from this shift to an agricultural mode of life. Regardless of whether DeMeo's connection with agriculture is accepted, rates of infanticide are directly related to the subordination and economic impoverishment of women (Allen, 1990; Dalley, 1999; Hood, 1994; Rattigan, 2012; Rose, 1986; Swain, 2005). I discuss this social context further in Chapter Four.

It was only after some development of the tolerance of ambivalent feelings and the rise of a moral conscience in the eighteenth century with regard to killing human infants that child-rearing modes began to develop some empathy and sensitivity to children. A new intrusive mode of child-rearing developed as mothers began to form greater attachments to their children (de Mause, 1974; Grille, 2005). Along with a greater attachment to their children grew methods of socialising children through manipulation of the attachment (through threats, fear and guilt) rather than murder or abandonment (de Mause, 1974; Francus, 2012; Grille, 2005; Stone, 1977). This development shows the transmutation from the literal enactment of murderous impulses into psychologised enactments of murderous wishes.

By the late nineteenth century, a further development led to the socialising mode of child-rearing with an increased focus on training and guiding children, for example through public education, rather than forcing them to submit to adult wishes (de Mause, 1974; Grille, 2005).

Eventually, in the mid-twentieth century a helping mode began developing, with an emphasis on child-centred parenting that respected the child's integrity, was emotionally responsive, and socialised children without force, violence or manipulation (de Mause, 1974; Grille, 2005). Of course this paradigm is a time-line of psychosocial shifts and, therefore, reveals general trends. As both de Mause and Grille pointed out, all the modes of child-rearing remain in use today, with parents tending to repeat the patterns of their own upbringing with their own children. It takes an effort of consciousness and personal transformation to break old cycles and move to more peaceful modes of child-rearing (Grille, 2005).

Infanticidal Attachment Theory

Attachment theory describes the effect of our earliest relationship with our caregivers, primarily our mother. The infant and mother bond to varying degrees, creating either secure or insecure attachment styles. Each style influences how we learn to relate to others and ourselves. It determines what we believe about ourselves, and our perceptions of others, their motivations, and the world. It influences our adult relationships with our partners and the way we will parent our own children.

Infanticidal attachment is a sub-category of disorganised attachment. It results from the relationship with a primary caregiver who is either, or both, frightened and frightening, creating a traumatic situation for the infant. It occurs at a very early stage of life, a time when experience is unintegrated and attempting to organise itself into patterns of identity and experience that must be regulated by an attuned mother.

A mother trapped in her own trauma is unable to offer the consistent, safe, attuned presence the infant needs to organise its self. When we are unable to acknowledge ambivalence and conflicting emotions, and we are in the situation of a double bind, feelings that are too difficult to tolerate, or even acknowledge, are acted out (de Mause, 1974; Pinzon, 1996). Pinzon (1995) referred to the contemporary example of unmarried mothers who kill their babies after the birth. "Out of despair and desperation, or a continuation of murderous rage being passed from generation to generation, this seems the only alternative" (p. 25). Here there is an allusion to the murderous impulses and acts that accompany the 'double bind' of the socially stigmatised unmarried mother, and the consequences for the illegitimate child.

'Double bind' is a term used to describe a situation in which someone must choose between two alternatives, both of which are unbearable (de Mause, 1974). In literature, this impossible choice was poignantly elucidated in William Styron's (1979) novel, *Sophie's Choice*, which is set during the Holocaust in Nazi Germany. Sophie, the mother of two small children, is forced by the concentration camp guard to choose which of her children to keep. The other will be murdered in the gas chamber. Under threat of losing both children if she does not comply, Sophie makes her choice. The novel follows her life, revealing how she is haunted, paralysed, and destroyed by her choice. Feeling complicit in her child's murder, something in her dies too, and the ability to live fully is arrested. The novel is resonant with the themes of infanticide, though its focus is on the effects for a grieving and guilt-stricken mother who remains haunted by her impossible choice.

Known as the Medea complex, mothers' death wishes for their offspring have been acknowledged at least since the time of this Greek myth by Euripides, in which Medea kills her children out of anger to spite her husband, Jason (Ovid, 1567/1965). The Medea complex continues today in the form of psychological enactments of unacknowledged death wishes against unwanted children in the womb, in the process of adoption, and by mothers who project their death wishes onto their children. Yvanna A G Sarmet (2016) linked the Medea complex with parental-alienation syndrome, arguing that women influenced by this complex kill their children out of hatred for the father. This suggests there could be an element of hatred by some mothers towards the fathers of unwanted pregnancies that contributes to death wishes against the unborn child, and to the decision to adopt.

Historically, when murder or direct abandonment were no longer morally acceptable, desperate mothers found other ways to dispatch their children, getting rid of them psychologically whilst rationalising that they had not abandoned the child but provided it with other care. In the nineteenth century this handover was to baby farmers or foundling hospitals, both of which had notoriously high mortality rates (Rose, 1986). Yet the double bind remained tightly in place – what other choices could a woman make without support and social acceptance?

As child protection and adoption laws came into being in the late nineteenth century, the principal handover of care to others was through legal adoption (Rose, 1986). At this point in history we can most clearly see how the theme of infanticide and abandonment transmuted from the literal to the psychological as mothers' murderous wishes – whether they recognised them or not – were enacted in adoption processes that enforced a psychological infanticide rather than the literal murder of former times. This is what Angela Pinzon (1995) referred to as the legacy of the collective unconscious – unspoken, unfelt or unremembered patterns that lead to the same responses – the historical memory of infanticide as the primary option for dealing with an impossible situation.

Infanticidal attachment theory describes the kind of relational attachment dynamic that forms when a child attempts to survive psychological infanticide. In the language of attachment theory, psychological infanticide describes the transfer of a death wish, either directly or indirectly, from caretaker to child. This emotional murder allows physical survival but leads to an internalised state of deadliness, infanticidal attachment with caregivers, and the terror of being killed (Kahr, 1993, 2001, 2007a, 2007b, 2012).

In his theory of infanticidal attachment, Kahr (1993, 2001, 2007a, 2007b, 2012) described psychological infanticide as the result of death threats towards, or attempts on the lives of, children. These murderous parental wishes may be conscious or unconscious, literal or psychological (Kahr). Sachs (2007) theorised that more concrete forms of psychological infanticide, for example, actual attacks on the life of the child, are more likely to produce presentations of extreme dissociation such as dissociative identity disorder (DID); whereas more implicit death wishes are more likely to result in schizophrenia and other psychoses (Kahr, 2007b, 2012; Sachs, 2007).

Drawing on my personal experience, clinical work with adopted clients, and adoption literature, it is apparent to me that the trauma of closed stranger adoption can result in significant levels of dissociation as well as psychotically organised states of distress. This suggests that each individual adoption scenario, and the unique personality and sensitivities of the child, orients the adoptee towards either psychotic or dissociative defences against the knowledge of their psychological infanticide.

Kahr (2007a, 2012) included the following scenarios as possible aetiologies of infanticidal attachment:

- actual or implicit death wishes received by the child
- being a replacement child for a previous child who did not survive
- death of a twin in the womb
- attempted abortion of the child

Infanticidal attachment theory seeks to understand psychological responses to infanticidal trauma. My inquiry contributes another potential aetiology: that of death wishes received by the unwanted unborn child, which are later reinforced by the process of closed stranger adoption. This hypothesis covers elements of the current aetiologies – an experience of deathly psychic trauma experienced in utero from which the foetus is helpless to remove itself and must, therefore, develop protective defences against.

The most powerful defence available between mother and unwanted foetus is dissociation. Both child and mother protect themselves from dangerous 'knowings' by dissociating into states of 'not knowing'. For the child, this may also become a state of 'not being'. Some mothers also dissociate into a state of 'not being' pregnant, which may result in nullifying the existence of the unborn child.

There is a significant correlation between high levels of dissociation in women going through unwanted pregnancies and harm to their infants soon after birth. Spinelli (2010) argued that the higher the mother's level of dissociation during pregnancy, the more at risk the child is of infanticide soon after delivery.

I offer a further clarification to infanticidal attachment theory here: that infanticidal attachment begins in the relationship between mother and foetus in the womb, and infanticidal patterns of relating are already established before birth. Whether the mother is actively hostile towards her unwanted child or whether she dissociates from her predicament may determine whether the child inclines more towards schizophrenic or dissociative disorders. While adoption offers a safety valve against actual infanticides, the high dissociation level of mothers in double binds, due to unwanted pregnancy, is likely transmitted to the unborn child. Such a child then becomes dissociative or psychotically defended before birth in order to survive psychologically.

The effects of psychological infanticide can include catatonia, frozen inertness, immobility, internal deadness, fear of petrification and engulfment (Laing, 1960; Kahr, 2007a, 2007b) and autistic and psychotic states in children and adults (Bettelheim, 1979; Bloch, 1979). Kahr (2007a) interpreted two purposes for these apparently bizarre symptoms: first, withdrawal from the obliterating world of relationships; and second, they are a desperate attempt to communicate the internal situation of deadness. These symptoms are actual states of abject terror, psychic death and hostage in the psyche to internalised murderers.

If infanticidal attachment begins in utero, then the effects of psychological infanticide replicate the state of helpless terror experienced by a being immersed in a sea of murderous intent from which it is helpless to escape. When the earliest relationship is of not being separate from annihilation and terror, all relationships are untrustworthy and dangerous.

Infanticidal attachment is a subcategory of disorganised and disoriented attachment (Yellin & Epstein, 2013; Yellin & White, 2012). The effects of this type of attachment have been described as including psychiatric illness, criminality, dissociation, aggression, loss and trauma, fears of catastrophe, and controlling or helpless behaviours (Kahr, 2007b). Researchers in the field of adoption have noted that adopted people as a population have much higher representation of these difficulties than the non-adopted population, indicating there might be some cause to compare the effects of adoption and infanticidal attachment (Brodzinsky, 1990; Feder, 1974; Lifton, 1994; Verrier, 1993; Wierzbicki, 1993).

Kahr (1993) made the stark claim, based on his clinical experience, that "life and death co-exist in a painfully intimate way in the biography of the schizophrenic person" (p. 269). The person who experiences schizophrenia lives in a personal myth of psychic terror, and the belief they are in mortal danger or have already died. It makes sense when we consider that infanticidal attachment generally begins before birth, so that the primary life-myth the child carries is of the double bind that to live is to be killed, so in order to live one must be dead.

In general terms, from my own understanding, the victim of psychological infanticide might have feelings of existing in a state of living death, of not existing, of terror of plots to kill them, of rotting or absent parts of the body or of having one's mind or Soul taken over by powerful, annihilating humans or aliens. They may hear voices telling them to maim or kill themselves or others. And they may act on these disembodied, archetypal commands or become frozen in catatonic terror.

In my journal writing I was able to record my version of these experiences from the inside, making sense of them later in a way I could not have explained at the time.

Exploration of Terms and Concepts

I use a number of psychological terms for the experience of psychological infanticide. Psychological infanticide, Soul murder, and phenomenal death are all psychodynamic terms that have been used to describe this death in the psyche occurring in childhood. Each is influenced by slightly different theoretical orientations and uses different languaging for similar concepts. Although both Shengold (1989, 1999, 2013) and Kahr (1993, 2007a, 2007b, 2012) are grounded in psychoanalytic thinking, Kahr's term, 'psychological infanticide', is more precisely anchored in attachment theory, influenced by Bowlby's (1960, 1980) studies on attachment and loss, by Winnicott (1965) who introduced the idea of phenomenal death, and by de Mause's (1974) psychohistory of infanticide. It is important to attempt to distinguish between the hauntings associated with grief and loss and the more murderous hauntings of internalised infanticidal threats. Both are integral to the experience of adoption.

A number of theorists express 'psychological infanticide' in terms of Soul, haunting, and possession by introjected (internalised) others. Jacques Derrida's (1993) theory of hauntology centres on notions of absence-presence, non/existence and gaps, which I explore in relation to adoption in Part Three. The language of haunting is used specifically by Lifton (1994, 2009) in her description of closed stranger adoption as a ghost kingdom full of hauntings. She described this kingdom of ghosts in order to reveal the complex, internalised dynamics between all members of the adoption triad.

James Hollis (2013) wrote of haunting as a metaphor for the effects of our internalisation of experiences and people through memory and introjection, particularly through un-metabolised loss. What of the un-metabolised experience of being killed off or wished dead? I suggest this gives rise to the archetypal dimension of infanticide – the Death Mother (Harris & Harris, 2015; Sieff, 2017; Woodman 2005; Woodman & Sieff, 2015).

To explain this idea of haunting by the past further, children internalise or introject their parent as a normal part of their development. When an attachment figure is murderous, these qualities become introjected, and this is known as an *infanticidal introject* (Kahr 2007a, 2007b, 2012; Yellin & Epstein, 2013; Yellin & White, 2012).

The birth mother of an adopted child may haunt both by her absence (loss) and her death wishes transmitted to the child (murderousness). Introjection or internalisation of the executor by the child is also a defence mechanism against their terrifying qualities.

Having identified my predicament as a psychological infanticide (infanticidal attachment theory), and lived the experience of Lifton's ghost kingdom (haunting), in the following chapters I favour Kahr's (2007a, 2007b, 2012) descriptor of psychological infanticide whilst using the metaphoric terminology of ghosts and haunting.

Shengold (1989) described Soul murder as a "deliberate attempt to eradicate or compromise the separate identity of another person" (p. 4). I have explained how the infant requires the attuned mother to organise and regulate their self/identity structure. Closed stranger adoption is a process that systematically seeks to eradicate any connections with the child's original identity and sense of self. This leads to psychic damage and the possession of, or haunting by, another.

The term Soul murder, as applied by Shengold, would suggest all child abuse has some form of murderous intent, whether conscious or unconscious, toward the child's psyche.

In contrast to ideas of murderousness, Winnicott (1965) introduced the concept of phenomenal death as the death of the psyche that occurs on separation of infant and mother, in which the infant experiences having 'died' in infancy as a kind of annihilation. Whilst there is an implication of some kind of murderousness (who is doing the annihilating?), Winnicott seemed to be describing the effects of devastating loss rather than overtly acknowledging infanticidal wishes. This raises a question about the nature and effects of the relationship between mother and unborn child.

If the child experiences a devastating loss on separation at birth, there must already be a profound attachment bond between mother and unborn child. Therefore, they must influence one another during the pregnancy. Indeed Winnicott (1965) claimed that in the first months of life there is no such thing as a mother *and* a baby; rather, they remain merged as they were before birth. The nature and quality of the attunement between mother and baby has profound influence on the child's sense of self in relationship with the world. Neither Winnicott (1965) nor Verrier (1993) explored the experience of having been 'murdered' in infancy. There is a qualitative difference between the felt experience of psychic death and psychic murder. Social and cultural taboos against admitting murderous feelings towards children serve to perpetuate dissociative denial of the child's reality of psychological infanticide. The very idea of mothers (or other caregivers) having non-loving feelings for their infants is rejected; yet the evidence of on-going child abuse and child deaths by violence demonstrates this truth.

To further differentiate between the experiences of phenomenal death and psychological infanticide, when a child loses a parent at an early age, the trauma is profound. When an infant loses a mother, what is lost is the very being who defines you, who gave you your body and ground of being. Without this, you are bereft, lost, and inconsolable. With shattered foundations and spirit, you live in darkness – lost to the light and without hope. The formidable task for such a child is to survive, to successfully defend against and resolve this trauma. Such traumatic grief is therefore related to psychological death. For a child, the loss of mother means loss of self and context for living. Very often, in children with early parental losses, we see profound depression, lack of identity, mental fragility, abandonment fury and suicidal ideation. There is hopelessness about the possibility of surviving.

For the adopted child, there is not just loss but the psychological reality of being abandoned by mother, leaving an infanticidal psychic imprint, since an infant is incapable of surviving without mother, and the infant instinctively knows this. This child is more likely to experience deeper levels of psychological disturbance and relational trauma. When this abandonment occurs via dissociation during the pregnancy, I suggest the trauma may be even more profound.

Pre- and Peri-natal Trauma

Pre- and peri-natal research reveals that mothers' feelings, admitted or defended against, have an effect on the unborn child, indicating that psychological death wishes before a child is born can have an impact throughout life (Grof, 1988, 1998; Irving, 1989; Verny and Kelly, 2001; Ward, 2006). Grof (1988) stated: "The memories of vital threats in the womb, during delivery and after birth represent important sources of fear of death" (p. 156). He suggested these impair our ability to be fully authentic in life, and recommended using methods of self-exploration to bring fears of death into consciousness and overcome them (Grof, 1988). Experiences before and during birth have significant impact and such memories are held in the body, influencing our life trajectory, health and wellbeing (Grof, 1988; Verny & Kelly, 1991). Grof wrote powerfully of the perinatal influence on our entire lives:

Individuals whose experiential self-exploration transcends biography and reaches the perinatal level of the unconscious typically make a surprising and shattering discovery. They recognise that the inauthenticity of their lives is not limited to certain partial segments that are contaminated by specific childhood traumas, but that their entire approach to existence and their life strategy have been inauthentic and misdirected in a very basic way. This total distortion of existential emphasis is based

77

on the fact that one's actions are dominated from a deep unconscious level by the unresolved trauma of birth and by fear of death that is associated with it. (p. 259)

In the experience of psychological infanticide, I surmise there is a collapsing of the potential space – the life – between birth and death. I explore this theme further in Part Three. Further, pre- and peri-natal research suggests that, even before birth, the foetus may feel its life to be in danger, or even that it has died before it is birthed, and this has an impact on the experience of living (Grof, 1988; Verny & Kelly, 1991).

Stanislav Grof described the ability of patients to recall foetal and embryonic experience through combinations of psychedelic therapy, holotropic breathwork and psychotherapy. He made an argument for the validity and accuracy of prenatal and perinatal knowledge, arguing that it has been reported frequently in psychoanalytic literature, but usually not taken seriously. He claimed holotropic therapy provides examples of recall that can be authenticated and verified. This is supported by Verny and Kelly (1991), who claimed that prenatal experiences are shared between mother and child, and the child may experience particular events, especially if traumatic, and more subtly nuanced "communications" (p. 74). For example, during holotropic therapy, patients accessed clear messages of feeling loved and wanted, or more traumatically, of being unwanted. Grof (1988) claimed that foetal traumatisation is a significant factor in emotional instability and the possibility of later psychopathology. He described the unwanted or emotionally deprived child as having "very few positive nourishing experiences" (Grof, p. 257) and stated that progress in these cases is slow and painful as it engages with deep traumas without positives to support the individual.

According to Grof (1988), the experience of a "bad womb" or "rejecting" womb (p.264) leads to feeling unwanted. People who experience this do not have the same sense of emotional and biological nourishing as people with supportive womb experiences, and this is a traumatic beginning to life. Grof suggested that, for these people, a move to wellbeing and trust in the world takes a long time and requires 'anaclitic' support to provide a corrective experience for rejection and emotional deprivation early in life.

The Child's Fear of Infanticide and the Nature of Infanticidal Trauma

The pre-verbal embodiment of very early trauma, also known as implicit memory (Fischer, 2017; Levine, 2010; Siegal, 2010; van der Kolk, 2014), means that for infanticidally-traumatised infants, their fear is reality: psychological infanticide is real and (potentially) mortally devastating. A traumatised child internalises their experiences in unprocessed archetypal form; they absorb the overarching thematic pattern rather than its limited human expression (Kalsched, 1996; 2013). Many writers, such as Bettelheim (1976) and von Franz (1996b), described the hidden symbolism of fairy tale and mythic content as close to the child's way of processing and digesting their world. My personal narrative presented in Parts Two and Three contains archetypal fairy tale and religious imagery. It has been suggested that birth and pre-birth imagery expressed in art alerts us to the presence of an archetypal dimension of uterine experience that continues to express itself and inform personal development (Grof, 1998; Irving, 1989).

An infanticidally traumatised child exists in a state of terror and must find a way to work through, successfully defend against, and survive this trauma (Bloch, 1979; Kahr, 2007a, 2007b; Yellin & Epstein, 2013; Yellin & White, 2012). Healing of infanticidal trauma is more complex than just rooting out an introjected mother. There may be many figures in the archetypal psychodrama of infanticide. For healing and integration to occur, all of these possible figures in the psyche of the psychological infanticide must be engaged with, and related to, as parts of the whole person.

79

This is where an awareness of archetypal dimensions of early childhood trauma is particularly useful.

Dorothy Bloch (1979) described the state for a child exposed to such murderous impulses of caregivers as existing in a state of terror that can lead to autistic and psychotic states in both children and adults. She affirmed that the fear of infanticide is a reality for many children. It is important for children to safely work through these fears in fantasy and play (Bettelheim, 1976, 1979; Bloch, 1979), as well as ensuring the safety of at-risk children. Without this safe processing of overwhelming terror, the child may succumb to being trapped in the fantasy of being killed with no resolution. Such children are prone to becoming adults who are psychotic or criminal (Bloch, 1979). Having worked to develop my capacity for imagination, my fascination with Minnie Dean became an opportunity to use fantasy to safely work through the power of the Murderous Mother in my psyche. Without knowing it at the time, I had embarked on an archetypal journey toward resolution of internal murderous conflicts.

Kalsched (1996) provided an excellent rationale for including an imaginal, archetypal dimension to research. His particular focus is the illumination of the *inner world* (my italics) of trauma as revealed through dreams, fantasies and interpersonal issues. Kalsched offered a non-pathologising acceptance of the "miraculous life-saving defences that assure the survival of the human spirit [threatened] by the annihilating blow of trauma" (p. 1). He understood the impact of trauma that occurs in early infancy before ego has formed, resulting in unbearable feelings of disintegration or annihilation, and the development of dissociative defences including "splitting, projective identification, idealisation or diabolisation, trance-states, switching among multiple centres of identity, depersonalisation, psychic numbing etc" (Kalsched, p. 2).

Kalsched's (1996) work referred to an archetypal drama that is played out in/by the psyche. These defences are described as archetypal in nature and meaning and are designed to protect the traumatised person from experiencing what is unable to be thought about or known. He claims the archaic defences associated with trauma are "personified as *archetypal daimonic images*" (author's italics; Kalsched, p. 2) and that dream imagery offers us a self-portrait of the traumatic archaic defence structure.

Kalsched (1996) described how the traumatised child's psyche splinters typically into a regressed infantile part and a progressed part that matures precociously, adapting to the outer world with a false self as described by Winnicott (1965). In dreams, the regressed self is expressed as a vulnerable or shameful child or animal, protected by the progressed part in the guise of a powerful benevolent being, or persecuted by a malevolent being. These archetypal figures represent the defences that protect the core self. These mythologised parts represent what Kalsched termed "the psyche's archetypal self-care system" (p. 4) because the defences are both archaic and typical. Because these defences develop before the ego is fully cohesive, he calls them defences of the self, distorting the self-regulation of a non-traumatised ego. These defences – developed to survive trauma that threatens the being of the self – become a source of major resistance to life, and seriously disrupt ability to function in relation to self and others. The self-care system becomes persecutory in its faulty attempts to keep protecting the person from further harm through isolation from reality. At its extremes, this can develop into psychotic delusion or suicide, as the protector/persecutor determines to kill off the host rather than risk further (perceived) harm to the core of the self (p. 4).

Translating this process to adoption, we can see how the unbearable and therefore unthinkable experience of being wished dead or gone by the mother initiates an inner world of trauma that is primitive, and relies on dissociative defences and the development of an archetypal self-care system designed to protect the child from further experiences of unsurvivable disintegration or annihilation of self. During times of separation or loss, the archetypal drama of the self-care system intensifies, with benevolent/persecutory figures doing whatever it takes to isolate the self from the reality of loss and dislocation. Added to this trauma are the traumas of dislocation where there is frequently a feeling of misfit that compounds the badness already experienced earlier. The legalised secrets of closed adoption all compound the original trauma of being exposed to pre-birth dissociation and/or death wishes.

The healing work of trauma involves relating to these archetypal persons in a way that both reveres them as powerful forces in the psyche and humanises them.

Myth, Trauma, and the Body: Embodied Experience as a Portal to Understanding

Myth is the container of archetypal patterns and truths through which we can understand our mythic selves, the selves beyond the facts of a life and more true to the essence of a unique self. Myth reveals to us the archetypal themes we resonate with, and our living-out of stories and patterns in our lives. By being open to myth we can catch the voice of deeper truths. We can open out the non-verbal and embodied stories preserved or frozen within. We can work consciously with myth as a process in which we purposefully live out or alter the mythic path in order to arrive at our deepest fulfilment and expression of a life.

According to Stanley Keleman (1999), Joseph Campbell intimated that our mythology is related to our biology, suggesting that mythology describes our collective and instinctive commonalities: that our experiences are rooted in our bodies and that our bodies are created in ways in which emotions and responses are recognisable as part of our commonality as human beings. Levine (2010) suggested that, in terms of trauma, humans are linked, not just by their common instinctive responses to trauma, but also by their capacity to transform these experiences. He suggested that through weaving the threads of heroic myth, and through an understanding of animal and human life (biology), we are able to comprehend trauma and its transcendence through the lens of "mythobiology" (Levine, p. 35). Levine went on to describe the function of mythology as teaching us about meeting life's challenges, resonating with archetypal stories and connecting with our deepest longings and strengths. He referred to myths as the maps that guide us to connect with our essential selves and with others and the universe (Levine, p. 35). In this way, myths help orient us within a greater context and offer a path of meaning and purpose that allows us to fulfil our own life journey.

Trauma derails the connection with the deepest self. It derails a sense of connection with others or to the wider world and cosmos. It disrupts the sense of a meaningful life of purpose and growth, leaving the traumatised person adrift in life, socially isolated and fearful, trapped within a trauma-world. The traumatised person no longer has a connection to their resources, and all focus is used up in surviving. Myths can help traumatised people to re-cognise their true selves and be guided in the process of healing.

Medusa: Face of the Death Mother

A myth that speaks directly to understanding and trans-cendence of trauma is the Greek myth of Medusa. Levine (2010) and Bright (2010) have both written about Medusa in the context of trauma. Levine said: "The Greek myth of Medusa captures the very essence of trauma and describes its pathway to trans-formation" (p. 36). He described the myth as a process for healing trauma in ways that are not re-traumatising and are transformative. He also explained: "The paradox of trauma ... has both the power to destroy and the power to transform and resurrect" (Levine, p. 37). He went on to say:

It is possible to learn from mythology, from clinical observations, from neuroscience, from embracing the 'living' experiential body, and from the behaviour of animals; and then, rather than brace against our instincts, embrace them. (Levine, p. 37)

Medusa is one of three Gorgon sisters. She is traditionally an archetype of the negative mother and an aspect of the dark goddess and can represent the disconcerting aspects of the feminine. Harris and Harris (2015) made use of the Medusa myth as a direct healing myth for the Death Mother archetype. Medusa is also known as a sovereign of female wisdom, the female mysteries, and cycles of time and nature. She is universal creation and destruction in eternal transformation, making her part of the cycle of eternal return (Eliade, 1954; Grof, 1988). She destroys to create balance and is a symbol of the potency of the triple goddess.

Bright (2010) embraced the Medusa myth as an alchemical and transformative process. She described the essence of the Medusa myth as teaching us that embracing death is the key to transformation and new ways of being. In particular she explored how the myth illuminates dissociation and disregard – key aspects of infanticidal trauma.

In the myth, Medusa was originally a beautiful woman who was transformed into a horrendous figure with hair of writhing snakes and whose stare turned people to stone. When we try to look directly into the pain of trauma without preparation and support, we are petrified, immobilised in our terror, our emotions and potential frozen. It is only when Perseus is advised by the wise goddess, Athena, and given some useful tools, that he is able to kill Medusa – using his shield to see her reflection and slice off her head. By learning through wise counsel and our own feminine intuitive wisdom, we can use the essential tool of reflection to look into the face of trauma without its petrifying effects. In doing so, the negative aspect of Medusa/trauma is destroyed, and she is flung into the sea – realm of the unconscious and of feelings. Her image returns to the collective unconscious, the sea of images, rather than the spectre of personal horror. Medusa, out of her death, gives birth in the myth to two children – Pegasus, the winged horse of poetry, and another child of golden light. Out of facing and reflecting on disabling trauma, we are uplifted by poetic clarity and the joy of creating beauty and healing images; and thus we receive illumination into our personal stories.

Medusa's story seems directly relevant as she presented herself in a dream I had about Minnie Dean at the beginning of my inquiry:

I am joined with Minnie in a dance. Periodically I leave her to go down into the basement level of the house, during which I pay close attention to the concrete floor with its emphasis on a strong foundation. I recognise it as my house. During these episodes underground I meet a number of odd figures, the last of which is a child named Medusa who half hides from me, believing she is hideous though she isn't at all. I feel a compelling connection with her. (Deed, dream journal, 2015)

The Orphan archetype also offers insight into the healing of infanticidal trauma. The essence of the Orphan archetype is a fight against death, which, if won, creates inner healing, power and strength (Estes, 1997). Through fairy tales, Clarissa Pinkola Estes showed that the healing journey involves surviving death, reigniting the flame of life inside the self, and growing a nurturing and wise inner mother who guides us through life and through which our creative potentials can be birthed and thrive. The journey involves facing into the fear, despair, and emotional hunger of the Orphan's precarious predicament, and becoming warmed by relationship with feelings, and building a sense of stability through a connection with the archetypal mother (Estes, 1997). Estes encouraged the unmothered child to live their personal myth in ways that foster new and creative outcomes.

This is essentially the process I have presented here. Through it, I wish to offer hope for other abandoned and unmothered children who are still in the struggle with death inside themselves. I offer a personal story that survives death and embraces life and reveals some of the ways this might be done and some of the difficulties that might be met along the way. On the other side of the darkness of infanticide is the warm and loving light of a mothering energy fiercely protective of life in all its intense aliveness.

Chapter Four
Nineteenth-Century Baby Farming:
A Crucial Link with Adoption

The history of childhood is a nightmare from which
we have only recently begun to awaken.
Lloyd de Mause (1974)

In his theory of infanticidal attachment, Brett Kahr described psychological infanticide as the result of death threats towards, or attempts on the lives of, children. His theory is founded on evidence of centuries of actual infanticide (de Mause, 1974). Understanding our history of baby farming makes the literal, or concrete, attacks on infants' lives more real, and establishes the connections between historical and psychological infanticide.

Baby farming was likely practised in some form throughout history. It comes into stark view in the nineteenth century as a result of shifting attitudes to child rearing and child welfare, which led to child protection laws and the criminalisation of child abuse. The common threads between baby farming and closed stranger adoption are the illegitimate child's position in society as the most vulnerable to harm by others and most likely to be disposed of by the mother, and the development of interest in child protection leading to adoption legislation (Rose, 1986).

As discussed earlier, there is a centuries-old Western tradition of the murder and abandonment of children. By the nineteenth century, infanticides by mothers, partners or family members had, to some degree, given way to baby farming (Allen, 1990; Dalley, 1999; Hood, 1994; Rattigan, 2012; Rose, 1986; Swain, 2005). The Victorian conscience was no longer comfortable with the abandonment or murder of infants, and made use of baby farmers and foundling hospitals to place the offspring they either could not care for or did not want (Rose, 1986).

Even during the nineteenth century, journalistic opinion held that baby farms were a convenient way to dispose of unwanted, mainly illegitimate children, and that mothers were complicit in murderous outcomes. It is difficult to separate out the dualities of 'complicit and selfish' motives versus 'naïve impoverished victims'. In psychological thinking, we can now accept that both are true: that mothers were likely to have been complicit in some way, even if only through the massive denial required to survive such a predicament emotionally, and also that they were naïve and in an economic and socially impossible situation (Brown, 2010; Rose 1986; Rattigan, 2012).

It is possible to acknowledge that, on some level, some mothers wished their children out of their lives, and also to have compassion for their denial of something they could not bear to think about or reconcile for themselves. Brown (2010) referred to cases where women had their children 'adopted' by baby farmers without their consent, or who genuinely wished to reclaim their children as circumstances allowed. Women, such as Evelina Marmon, who handed her baby daughter over to Amelia Dyer when she was temporarily unable to care for it, persisted in trying to find their lost (dead) children and took great courage in aiding police in arresting murderous baby farmers (Brown, 2010; Rattle & Vale, 2011). In the process, their shame at being unwed mothers was made publicly visible in court testimony. Such examples demonstrate an ongoing attachment by some mothers to their infant as a human being, which feels palpably different from the secretive disconnection of those women who did not want any reminder of their 'shame' to exist. Brown indicated that in most cases in the agreement between mother and baby farmer, "there was also a tacit understanding between the two parties that, in the harsh conditions of life in working class areas...the child's chance of survival would be extremely slim" (p. 2).

The practice of baby farming grew out of the need for short- and long-term childcare for children who were either unwanted or could not be cared for by their parents (Cannon, 1994; Hood, 1994; Rose, 1986; Swain, 2005). Baby farming provided some women a means of earning an income at a time when women's employment options were both limited and frequently demoralising (Allen, 1990; Hood, 1994; Rattigan, 2012; Rose, 1986; Swain, 2005).

Baby farming is a term that covers a range of practices from respectable small-scale domestic child-minding to large-scale farming of children for financial incentives that led directly to infanticide (Allen, 1990; Hood, 1994; Rattigan, 2012; Rose, 1986; Swain, 2005). According to Swain (2005), many women simply took in children for a small fee, and out of neighbourliness – not unlike contemporary babysitting. Others made a small and precarious living caring for children who may already have been bereft, ill, neglected, or poorly nourished if they were not breastfed (Rose, 1986). Another perspective is that baby farmers took advantage of the need for somewhere to place children who could not be cared for, exploiting them for financial gain (Cossins, 2014; Hood, 1994; Rattle & Vale, 2011; Rose, 1986). Brown (2010) supported this view, claiming that baby farming was viewed with suspicion "as an occupation which shuns the light" (North British Daily Mail, 2 March 1871, as quoted in Brown, 2010, p. 2) rather than as a necessary means of childcare. In another double bind, society expressed outrage that the profession was so visible, whilst continuing to stigmatise and exclude single mothers from support to keep and raise their children. Baby farmers advertised in respectable local, regional and national newspapers to acquire infants through 'adoption'. This generated the potential for substantial financial remuneration via an underground network of infant trafficking (Brown, 2010; Rose, 1986).

89

Not all baby farmers were child murderers. We know little of the many baby farming industries that quietly went about their business without coming to the attention of authorities. However, it is the infanticidal aspect of baby farming that is relevant to my inquiry as it reveals the literal enactments of death wishes against unwanted children. These later became banished to the unconscious (both personal and collective) as social conscience and moral values changed with regard to the value of infant life and the need for child protection. Marilyn Francus (2012) pointed out that infanticide goes against social beliefs about motherhood, the maternal instinct and the maternal "obligation to care (or arrange care) for her child" (p. 74.) This made death wishes against unwanted infants less able to be thought about or acknowledged publicly, and even personally, contributing to high levels of dissociation in infanticidal mothers and in mothers who adopted-out inconvenient children. In Jungian terms, such thoughts and wishes become part of the personal and collective Shadow (Johnson, 1991; Zweig & Abrams, 1991).

Having developed a conscience against killing their own infants, mid-nineteenth-century society now projected infanticidal impulses onto midwives and baby farmers who were judged as evil witches or monstrous women made accountable for doing the business that others could no longer bear to think about (Francus, 2012). Some child-murdering baby farmers were socially tolerated as long as they kept to themselves – a trend that continues today in social responses (or lack of) to child abuse.

In an unsupportive patriarchal and hierarchical society, women who 'got into trouble' required the services of abortionists, midwives who could kill newborns, and baby farmers who would take away children who were the evidence of 'fallen women' (Cannon, 1994; Rose, 1986). However, some baby farmers, such as Amelia Dyer discussed below, exploited the financial potential of taking in and killing large numbers of infants (Rattle & Vale, 2011; Rose, 1986).

As will by now be apparent, baby farming offers a pivotal historical link between infanticide and adoption. Through an investigation of baby farming, we can trace the progression from infanticidal acts within families, to the transfer of the infanticidal wishes of desperate parents to baby farmers and finally through to the infanticidal wishes (to have an unwanted baby out of the way) behind closed stranger adoption (Feder, 1974; Lifton, 1994).

Whilst individual mothers, midwives, and family members have been involved in infanticidal acts throughout history, baby farming was an industry, with the transfer of infants for financial exchange based on, and supported by, women's lack of choices over contraception and financial support. It has been pointed out that infanticide correlates with the sexual and economic vulnerability of women (Allen, 1990; Dalley, 1999; Hood, 1994; Rattigan, 2012; Rose, 1986; Swain, 2005).

In the following sections I illuminate the grim practice of baby farming through examples of convicted nineteenth-century child murderers, revealing the patterns between baby farming and closed stranger adoption. I take up these themes further in Part Two where I discuss the common murderous themes enacted in baby farming and felt by adoptees that experience psychological infanticide.

The Desperate Struggle for Survival

Figure 1. Emma Williams,
Public Domain

Figure 2. Frances Knorr,
Public Domain

Australians Emma Williams (1873-1895) and Frances Knorr (1869-1894) both vividly represent the desperate struggle for survival of mothers without support. Both these women lived in poverty after being separated from their husbands. Work options for working-class women were limited to domestic service, the drudgery of sewing or washing, barmaiding, baby farming and prostitution. Many of these occupations – as well as requiring sweatshop levels of physical work for little pay – also held a high possibility of sexual abuse leading to unwanted pregnancy (Allen, 1990; Cannon, 1994; Rose, 1986).

Michael Cannon (1994) described the life of Emma Williams, a Melbourne prostitute hanged in 1895 for drowning her two-year-old son (1994). Pregnant and forced to marry at aged 14, Emma was left penniless with a baby when her husband died suddenly. Unable to secure work or another partner, according to Cannon: "Her only alternative now to starvation or suicide was to turn to street prostitution" (p. 129). Emma was suddenly widowed and penniless with a baby to support, no widow's or domestic benefits available, and no acceptable way of making a living. At her trial, a neighbour testified she was trying to get work. Unable to find work she turned to prostitution against her will. Even so, she was unable to raise enough money to board her young son. Emma went from showing fondness for her child to urgently trying to hand him over to someone else, but he kept being returned to her when she could not pay for his keep. According to Cannon: "Emma Williams was [still] trying to dispose of the child to anyone who might feed him" (p. 131). At one point she asked Jane Daniels to hold the child while she went to get some things. She did not return. Jane took the child to the police station. Emma was tracked down and forced to take back the child. Finally she left him with a Mrs Wilson and disappeared. Six weeks later, Mrs Wilson traced Emma and returned the child. At her wits end, Emma drowned the boy in the Melbourne lagoon. Her description of the death suggests her dissociation from her guilt over the murder:

On the following day…Mrs Williams confessed to him that she had tied the stone to the boy. 'The child was looking down into the water and smiling, and slipped from my hands into the water,' she said to Martin (Cannon, 1994, p. 132).

Emma Williams was not a baby farmer. She committed infanticide after she ran out of options to both care for her child and earn enough money to survive. Emma was only twenty-two-years old when she was hanged. Emma's story is one repeated endlessly throughout history, most obviously by women in financial hardship. For example, Cliona Rattigan's (2012) doctoral research on Irish infanticide reveals endless stories of dire poverty and choice-less choice echoed in the title of her book, *What else could I do?* Even sadder, repeat offenders revealed that such luckless women, locked into cycles of endless pregnancy and impoverishment, sometimes murdered each new infant in order to keep surviving as best they could (Rattigan, 2012).

We may think infanticide is something from the past or committed by monstrous mothers who are psychotic or psychopathic (Francus, 2012) but Rattigan's (2012) research takes us into the 1950s, the generation of my parents and of closed stranger adoption. Modern baby farms also exist to impregnate women to provide babies trafficked for the adoption market (Clarke, 2006). Thoughts and acts of infanticide remain part of the human psyche in response to the burden of children who are unwanted or cannot be cared for.

Frances Knorr also turned to baby farming after giving birth to her first child while her husband was in jail. She returned home from the lying-in hospital with her daughter and another child whom she said the hospital had asked her to nurse. Wet nursing has many parallels with baby farming. Rose (1986) described how 'fallen women' were employed to nurse other people's babies, thus starving their own children. The deaths of wet nurses' children in order to feed other people's babies was barely alluded to during the time this practice was fashionable (Rose, 1986).

By 1893, Frances had taken in 12 or 13 infants in six months. Several murdered infants were found buried at properties she had rented. She was to testify at her trial: "I found that I could not make a living any other way" (cited in Cannon, 1994, p. 56). Whilst in prison, Frances attempted to gain false evidence through her boyfriend to show she had not killed any infants. When this failed, she attempted to implicate her boyfriend as the killer (Cannon, 1994, p. 56). As is so often the case with nineteenth-century crime reportage, there seem to be many aspects of the story that are not clear, especially with regard to the social and economic circumstances of the women.

Evidence was presented that Frances was epileptic, and probably mentally ill. One can imagine it was difficult for her to find other work, and difficult to manage so many babies. Despite her probable mental illness, which if taken into account might have led to a plea of insanity and a prison sentence, Frances was given a death sentence for infanticide. In her final statement she implored other women not to follow her path by becoming baby farmers (Cannon, 1994, p. 56).

The Makin Family

Figure 3. Sarah Makin,
Public Domain

Figure 4. John Makin,
Public Domain

A woman did not have to be alone to be desperate enough to get involved in prostitution or baby farming. According to Annie Cossins (2014), respectably married Sarah Makin likely turned to prostitution to make ends meet for her large family when her husband John was either jobless or imprisoned for debt and theft. Both John and Sarah came from freed convict families and were familiar with violence, exploitation, deceit and desperation.

Cossins (2014) suggested that Sarah Makin contracted syphilis through prostitution, which led to her chronic ill-health and the deaths of her last few babies from congenital syphilis, which in turn may have led the Makins to try their hand at baby farming.

Sarah had raised a number of her own children and may have wished to mother babies to assuage her grief over the deaths of her last few little ones. Or she may have been advised that the best way to get over the death of a baby was to adopt another one to mother. Like Minnie Dean, she appears to have begun compulsively taking on babies after the loss of a child, suggesting that loss of a child may be one possible reason women chose baby farming as employment. This scenario is similar to the idea of the replacement child, whose role is to make up for a child lost or unable to be conceived. The adopted child is one such form of replacement child. Being a replacement child is one aetiology of infanticidal attachment.

The Makins soon discovered that rearing other people's babies did not pay well, and the amount of work was exhausting. It was apparent that the only way to make a living minding babies was to charge a fee and then get rid of the child. John and Sarah's tendencies to manipulation and deceit were channelled into exploiting desperate mothers (Cossins, 2014).

Their sensational trial for child murder revealed a life of constant moves around Sydney, with a trail of babies buried in the garden plots of their homes, and probably in nearby parks or common ground. John and Sarah Makin represent the pattern of baby farming as a family business, which is also seen in the larger scale operations discussed below. Both John and Sarah were convicted. John Makin was executed, and Sarah Makin was sentenced to life imprisonment. Despite the Melbourne cases cited above, both the law and society were generally squeamish about hanging a woman.

The Makins appeared to have no qualms about exploiting parents and dehumanising infants. They drew their own children into the baby farming business. They showed no concern or remorse on hearing the distraught testimony of mothers whose children had died, and they attempted to manipulate the court with dramatic lies, accusations, arguments and 'histrionics' (Cossins, 2014). Given their own harsh and exploited childhoods, it is likely they were simply repeating an infanticidal mode of childcare that felt normal to them and to many others who survived the Australian penal system. What I mean by this is that when our own childhood vulnerability is not seen and respected but brutalised and exploited, we will go on to treat the vulnerability and helplessness of others in the same harsh ways.

Murder or Manslaughter?

In New Zealand, Minnie Dean (1844-1895), may or may not have been practising infanticide on a smaller scale. Her conviction for child murder seemed to have been influenced by the social scapegoating and the hysteria about baby farming that the recent Makin case in Australia had provoked (Hood, 1994).

Minnie began collecting babies after the death of her daughter, Ellen, and two grandchildren, in what appears to have been a suicide-infanticide. One can only imagine the grief she went through, which may have manifested in a compulsive longing to rescue other needy infants. However, Minnie was also in financial difficulty, and we can see in her story a recognisable pattern of a need to get babies as both a psychological compulsion related to loss and an economic necessity (Hood, 1994).

Minnie was probably herself an unmarried mother. She appeared in New Zealand history when she arrived at her aunt 'Granny' Kelly's house – pregnant and with a small daughter. She claimed to be the respectable widow of a doctor. However, her biographer's rigorous searches have found no evidence to support Minnie's claims (Hood, 1994). She is also absent from any records for several years between disappearing from Scotland and appearing in New Zealand. Hood speculated on a number of possibilities for Minnie's life in these early years. Most likely she was unmarried when she had one, if not both, her daughters. Without a home with Granny Kelly, Minnie might well have ended up like Emma Williams except that she had enough education to find work as a teacher.

With Granny Kelly's support with child-minding, Minnie later took work as a governess. She married Charles Dean, who was employed at the large sheep station where she worked. They set out to farm a property of their own and were beset by difficulties. It seems significant to Minnie's subsequent child-minding career that she and Charles had no children of their own, and that he soon proved to be a poor provider, which resulted in financial difficulties that led to Minnie looking for work (Hood, 1994).

Minnie had adopted a child, Margaret, the orphaned daughter of a friend who died of cancer, not long before her own daughter died with Minnie's grandchildren. Perhaps it is not surprising that the combination of financial difficulty, adopting a child, her own history of illegitimate children, and the death of her daughter and grandchildren led Minnie to take in unwanted children to make ends meet (Hood, 1994).

Minnie soon found that taking in and caring for unwanted children was not financially sustainable. She seems to have taken great care to feed and clothe the children well, and provide medicine and doctors for them when they were ill. She also discovered most families of illegitimate children did not want any responsibility for the infants (Hood, 1994). Minnie began taking on more and more babies to make ends meet, and developing ever more grandiose ideas about how she would care for them. After their house was burned down, Charles built a rough cottage that offered poor, cramped conditions for so many children and the new infants that kept arriving (Hood, 1994).

Local police began to be suspicious of Minnie's baby farming activities, harassing her with visits and warnings, and requiring her to register as a child-minder. This pressure drove Minnie to evasion and secrecy. She refused to name the families of children who had been in her care so they could be traced. She claimed this would destroy the confidentiality she had agreed to with these families, foreshadowing the later secrecy upheld by adoption laws (Hood, 1994).

Was Minnie deeply moral, rigid in character, or was she hiding the trafficking or infanticide of some of the children she took on? Minnie remained incorruptible about naming these families even in her final statement just before her death (Dean, 1895). What I notice in her story is the slide into (possible) infanticidal activity due to financial despair and prolonged stress. At the very least Minnie did traffic illegitimate babies, making a small profit by handing them on to another baby farmer for a fee – a common baby farmer tactic.

The deaths of the last two babies in her care raises the question, as it did at her trial, of whether she was deliberately murdering the children she claimed she was adopting (Hood, 1994). Minnie confessed to causing the death of Dorothy Edith Carter with an overdose of laudanum, but she insisted it was not intentional (Dean, 1895). The other infant, Eva Hornsby, was weak and starving when Minnie got her, and it is likely she died within an hour of being in Minnie's care. It is not clear what caused Eva's death. Dark bruises behind her ears would indicate to a modern coroner that there had been an attempt at suffocation, but by Minnie or someone else who had been with the child in the previous twenty-four hours (Hood, 1994)?

Minnie's death sentence for child murder was appealed and declined. There is still legal debate over whether the sentence should have been manslaughter, which did not carry a sentence of capital punishment (Thomas, 2014).

Minnie's case is full of complexities. It remains unclear whether she was another unfortunate woman scapegoated for trying to earn a living and getting into some trouble, or whether she was carrying out infanticides for financial gain at least some of the time. Minnie Dean took in twenty-six children (that we know of). Hood (1994) was able to trace eighteen. Of these, twelve survived. Six died. This leaves eight unaccounted for.

A Family Business

Figure 5. Amelia Dyer, Public Domain

Like the Makins in Australia, for Margaret Waters and her sister Sarah Ellis (known as the Brixton baby farmers), and for Amelia Dyer and her daughter Polly, baby farming was a family business. The Brixton baby farmers and Amelia Dyer highlight the high numbers of children murdered, a virtual factory of infanticide that Lionel Rose (1986) aptly named the massacre of innocents.

Figure 6. Margaret Waters and Sarah Ellis, Public Domain

Margaret Waters and Sarah Ellis apparently entered the business of baby farming due to economic necessity. Rose (1986) stated: "Her biography illustrates the economic pressures on unsupported Victorian women that could drive them into sordid means of livelihood." (p. 96). Waters specialised in abandoning infants by giving street children sixpence to hold the infants while they went to buy sweets. When they returned from the shop she had gone. Waters and her sister were also part of an underground network of baby traffickers in an elaborate system of baby-sweats (as in sweatshop), traffickers, sub-farmers and disposers (Rose, 1986). Alternatively, Swain (2005) suggested there were no sinister motives in the wide female networks of shared support. What may have originated as a relatively benign collective of local women sharing the care and feeding of children during hard times became, or included, a covert group of midwives, abortionists, doctors, and baby farmers who made children from all over England disappear for a fee.

When police searched Waters' house, they found ten infants. I quote extensively here to give a realistic image of the treatment of these infants:

> In a back kitchen…five three- and four- week old infants lying in filth. Three under a shawl on an old sofa and two stuffed into a small crib on a chair. The children were barely clothed; the few rags which clung to their bodies were saturated and stank of urine and faeces. The bodies were huddled in so small a space that none of them would have been able to move even had they wanted to; though they appeared to have no such inclination. They were ashen-faced and emaciated, their bones visible through transparent skin. They lay open-mouthed, in such a state of torpor that movement seemed impossible to imagine. They lay with eyes fixed, pupils unnaturally contracted, scarcely human. (Rattle & Vale, 2011, p. 37)

In another room lay five more infants. Older, cleaner, and somewhat better fed, these individuals were clearly favoured, their lives deemed worthy of being sustained a little longer. They were Waters' nurse children, lodging with her for a weekly fee. The longer she could keep them going, the more income she would receive. But these too were dying: one after another they would succumb to a death which was more drawn out but just as inevitable. (Rattle & Vale, 2011, p. 38)

Only half these infants survived once uplifted from the home (Rose, 1986). Baby farmers argued that they were trying to raise children that were frequently already compromised by illness and neglect, and who, if not breastfed, were doomed to die of poor and inappropriate nutrition. It was also true that the foundling hospitals established to ease the numbers of abandoned and murdered infants on English streets had horrendous infant death rates and were mere holding pens for unwanted children to die in (Rose, 1986). Margaret Waters was hanged in 1870. Sarah Ellis was acquitted on lack of evidence and imprisoned on a lesser charge.

Factory Farming

Amelia Dyer was an English contemporary of Minnie Dean. She was hanged in 1896. Her baby farming business spanned thirty years, and she was associated with the network of midwife/baby-farming women that included the infamous Brixton sisters (discussed above) who were convicted early in Amelia's career. A series of letters proved that Waters had been involved in a nationwide trade in infants (Rattle & Vale, 2011; Rose, 1986). Twenty of these letters referred to a midwife supplying unwanted newborns. This midwife was Amelia Dyer, though she was not drawn into police speculation at that point. This was unfortunate as baby-farmer arrests in England over the next two decades revealed that *all of them* (author's italics) had regularly received infants from Amelia, who was running a house of confinement.

Amelia trained and worked as a nurse. In 1863 she began working alongside a midwife named Ellen Dane who apprenticed her in the arts and networks of the baby business. When her first husband died, Amelia was already in the baby business, making a profit by taking in children who could not be cared for, and providing lying-in and midwifery services for women 'in distress' and then dealing with their illegitimate children for them (Rattle & Vale, 2011). While it could be considered that as a young woman she had no choice, Rattle and Vale argued that her background, training and experience made it possible for her to have survived financially without resorting to the murder of children.

Over time, Amelia took in vast amounts of children who were not seen again. She lived lavishly for her class, wearing expensive clothes, eating good cuts of meat, and spending freely. Clearly baby farming on her scale was a lucrative business.

Her daughter, Polly, was brought up around neglected and dying babies and as young as five was helping Amelia 'care' for the babies. Polly and her husband eventually went into the baby business with Amelia, at times operating their own independent baby-farming operation. Arrested at the same time as Amelia, they were acquitted. Amelia did everything she could to protect her own child from being convicted. Polly and Harold carried on the business after her death, and were arrested several years later for the abandonment of a child (Rattle & Vale, 2011).

Significantly, Amelia had actually farmed out her first child, Ellen, from her first marriage, when she was small. While it was common practice in pre-nineteenth-century society for children to be apprenticed for trades, working, or reared in another family where they might also do some domestic service, the census evidence reveals that Amelia sent six-year-old Ellen to a baby farm where she was described in the census details as an orphan (Rattle & Vale, 2011).

Amelia was a laudanum addict and alcoholic; she was violent, unstable and unpredictable in temperament. When crossed by the law or by upset parents she was hostile, threatening and blaming, presenting herself as the aggrieved party. Her methods with babies were brutal. While they lived they were drugged, starved, neglected in filthy and diseased states, and treated violently if they whined (Rattle & Vale, 2011). One child, of aristocratic parentage, and who therefore brought in large sums for her ongoing care, was treated better and grew up as an adopted child of the family. Others were disposed of as soon as they were no longer of use, many just hours after they were handed over by parents. Amelia pawned the piles of baby clothes caring mothers had made and provided for their infants (Rattle & Vale, 2011).

Infants who were no longer useful were strangled using tightly-tied white tape knotted around their necks and a handkerchief stuffed in their mouths. Amelia was also known for midwifing babies and suffocating them before they left the birth canal; this means being difficult to differentiate from stillbirth by Victorian coroners (Rose, 1986; Rattle & Vale, 2011). Amelia parcelled up her murdered babies and dumped them in the local river, or in the streets.

Amelia managed to escape detection until her live-in servant, an old woman named Jane Smith, disturbed by the events in the house, tipped off the local inspector of the National Society for Prevention of Cruelty to Children (NSPCC). The officer inspected the house and alerted police. At the same time, an infant body had been recovered from the Thames, and police were looking for the killer (Rattle & Vale, 2011). It was the courageous public evidence of Evelina Marmon, mother of murdered baby Doris, which led to Amelia's conviction. Barmaid Evelina had left Doris in Amelia's care, intending to take her back when circumstances were favourable (Rattle & Vale, 2011).

It is estimated that Amelia Dyer murdered hundreds, if not thousands, of infants and children over her three-decade career. This is based on the numbers of infants proved to have come and gone, many of them discovered dead, in the months of police investigation leading to her arrest (Rattle & Vale, 2011).

Amelia's crimes were described as the very worst in the scale of baby farming. She seemed to have no capacity for empathy for the infants she farmed. Neither did she have any empathy for her little daughter Polly who saw it all and was involved from an early age.

We could call this large-scale baby farming a factory farming of babies who were seen as non-human – merchandise to be used for what they could provide and then discarded, trafficked or destroyed. Amelia's treatment of babies reflected the attitudes of the infanticidal mode of child-rearing. Polly's early exposure to Amelia's infanticidal acts and neglect towards infants will have stimulated in her what Bloch (1979) claimed is a child's instinctive fear of infanticide, which in turn creates an infanticidal attachment with the caregiver. The internalised murderousness, which defends against the child's feelings of helplessness, continues the cycle of infanticidal attitudes towards children. This is evident in Polly becoming a baby farmer, and in her infanticidal, abandoning and neglectful practices towards her own 'adopted' infants, which I discuss further in Part Two.

Amelia Dyer's story represents the actions of one person, though we have just seen that her actions were perpetuated over time when her daughter also became a baby farmer. In the broader socio-cultural and ideological context of the time, the sentimentalising of Victorian childhood reveals a dark Shadow side:

> The systematic mistreatment of children was common-place in Victorian England, citing the National Society for the Prevention of Cruelty to Children's (NSPCC) record of assistance given by their organisation to 166,161 sufferers of neglect and starvation, 41,226 sufferers from violence, 21,916 enforced beggars, 7,053 female child prostitutes, 3,897 children enslaved in dangerous employment or performances, and 1,067 fatalities from ill-treatment. (1890s no date, as cited in Rattle & Vale, 2011, p. 13)

A Note on Language

The language of baby farmers, and in common use in much of Victorian society, referred to individual babies as 'it' rather than he/she or by name, thereby reinforcing the sense of a baby as an object or commodity rather than a sentient being with individual characteristics and sensibilities. The use of this language reflected, and made possible, the handing round of babies like parcels, as well as the violence, drugging, and neglect that some babies endured. Once people have been dehumanised, any kind of behaviour towards them is possible, as was demonstrated by the horrific violence to Jews in Nazi Germany. Once they were described as vermin, they were easily seen as needing to be eradicated (Brenner, 2014). Dehumanising language made practices of slavery, factory labour, and intensive farming possible, where people, time, or livestock were seen as units. Recently this has occurred in a new take on baby farming – baby farms in which women are impregnated to provide babies that are trafficked on lucrative adoption markets (Clarke, 2006). This is the language of an infanticidal mode of child-rearing, based on exploitation and power over the most vulnerable, and creating a deadening psychological effect in both perpetrator and victim. For example, dehumanised Jews in the war – who had lost any sense of humanness and vitality – were known as 'walking corpses' (Sachs, 2013). This illustrates the psychologically murderous effect of dehumanisation which is then introjected and perpetuates this deadliness in all other relationships, even being transmitted intergenerationally (Sachs, 2013). When done to infants, it causes psychological infanticide.

As is evident from court material and newspaper advertisements, the story shadowing the murder or abandonment of infants was adoption. Baby farmers either advertised as childless women eager to adopt a child, or they responded as such to letters offering a child for adoption. Before adoption was legalised it was simply a means of selling or buying a child for one's own purposes. For example, Margaret Waters advertised for children in the *Lloyds Weekly Newspaper*:

Adoption – a good home, with a mother's love and care, is offered to a respectable person wishing her child to be entirely adopted. Premium sum 5*l* which includes everything. (as cited in Rattle and Vale, 2011, p. 36)

Minnie Dean responded to an advertisement wanting someone to adopt a child:

I am well pleased with the account of the child's parentage, and I in return promise to do my duty to the child before God and man, and will try and train her to become a good, useful woman, when you wire me…please do not mention the child, as I do not wish anyone to know where the little one comes from. When she comes to me, I wish all trace of her parentage to be lost. I want the child to be mine and mine only. (letter by Minnie Dean, in Hanlon, 1939, as quoted in Shawyer, 1979)

These carefully crafted letters emphasise respect and good mothering, whilst also clearly stating that the child will be fully the child (or property) of the adoptive mother. Some naïve mothers may have believed, or refused to give up hope, that their child would be brought up well by a stranger. For others, such letters were code for despatching a child for a fee – and no questions asked. Similarly, when babies disappeared from baby-farming homes, servants and family members were often told the little one had been adopted, or sometimes that the mother had returned to claim the child.

Adoption legislation grew directly out of a desire to protect and benefit children who had no parents to care for them. The evidence of sensational infanticide cases such as those presented in this chapter placed the fates of unwanted children into social and legal consciousness. The present New Zealand history of adoption information website (Griffith, n.d.), provides a brief paragraph linking baby farming (1880-1920) and the *Adoption of Children Act 1881*, which intended to confer full legal parent-child status on adopted children who were previously described as *nullius filius* (child of nobody). This act was replaced by the *Adoption of Children Act 1895*. The *Infant Life Protection Act 1893* also sought to protect infants from unscrupulous baby farmers.

PART TWO
SUFFER THE LITTLE CHILDREN

The following chapters explore four infanticidal themes: violence, abandonment, drugging, and neglect. These themes are interrelated and, therefore, there is no significance to the order in which they are presented. Each of the chapters stands alone and also forms part of a whole. Each chapter reflects a method by which infants were killed by baby farmers. Together, the essays offer a vision of the grim realities of nineteenth-century infanticide and its parallels in psychological infanticide.

Each chapter invites a conversation in which the reader may engage in the personal world of the writer, following the uniquely intimate associations the writer makes. I have attempted to remain closely engaged with the spirit of the Victorian era, weaving my own intuitions and experiences with the history of nineteenth-century baby-farming and, where possible, with the voices and atmosphere described by the people who were there, who are the literary ancestors of the Victorian aspect of my work. My aim is to bridge the gap between the literal and the psychological through the use of metaphor, myth, and examples from my own experience, and from writers whose published works and biographised lives enable us to witness the effects of psychological infanticide, according to the themes presented.

In his work, *Symbols of Transformation*, Jung (1967) revealed the value of insights received through drawing parallels between mythology and psychopathology. By discovering the patterns by which we are living, we have the means to know how to heal. As Patricia Berry (1982) put it, the therapy of archetypal psychology is akin to the maxim 'like cures like': "That is, we treat it with itself – by deepening it, expanding it (so that it is no longer so narrowly fixated), and by giving it substance, body (so that it can now begin to carry what it is trying to express)" (p. 20).

In these chapters, I aim to deepen, expand, and give substance to the theory of infanticidal attachment discussed in Chapter Three. I implicitly and explicitly explore key aspects of infanticidal attachment: internalised murderousness or deadliness; homicide-suicide; terror of being killed; fear of death or belief that one has already died.

As previously discussed, violence to the identity of an adopted child through the social and legal systems, as well as the psychic forces enacted between mother and unwanted child – which threaten the infant's right to existence – are forms of Soul murder. This Soul murder creates a trauma-world (Sieff, 2017), perhaps even before birth, which is experienced as 'normal' because no pre-trauma existence for comparison is known. If a child comes into the world in a trauma state with defences against psychological murder already engaged, this 'normalised' murderous *mythos* will be enacted internally and repeated throughout life, unless the trauma can be resolved.

Each of the four chapters that follow illuminates a theme of psychological infanticide and how it might be enacted in actual life in the trauma-world of murderous forces directed both against and within the individual. This exposes a relationship with a Death Mother of archetypal dimensions (Harris & Harris, 2015; Sieff, 2017; Woodman & Sieff, 2015). It develops the child archetypes of the Innocent, the Orphan, and the Feral Child.

To contextualise the essays, I refer to the works of Rose (1986), Cannon (1994), and Rattigan (2012), because they offer a comprehensive social history of the social and economic plight of nineteenth-century women and the infanticide that occurred as a result of the double binds women were in sexually, culturally and economically. Rose described an alarming level of English infanticides by desperate mothers, and the midwives and baby farmers who created an industry out of relieving such women from their despair, leading to the development of foundling hospitals and eventual laws to relieve the societal burden of infant deaths and abandonment. Cannon exposed a vivid picture of the lives of five women hanged in Melbourne gaol, whom he argued had little choice but to commit the crimes of prostitution, abortion, infanticide, and murder in desperate attempts to survive destitution and violence in a society that did not support or protect women financially or otherwise. Rattigan presented a picture similar to, though wider than, Cannon's, based on her research into Irish women convicted of infanticide. Rattigan depicted the poverty and hopelessness that drove many women to infanticide, sometimes more than once. Her research spans the nineteenth century into the 1950s. Recent discovery of mass infant and child graves associated with an Irish Catholic care home that took in pregnant girls until 1961 reveals that the systematic murder or neglect of unwanted infants continued at least into the 1960s (Barbash, 2017; Grierson, 2017; O'Doud, 2017).

Chapter Five
Murderousness

This chapter explores infanticide, the murderous rage engendered by psychological infanticide, and its expression towards others and against the self. Murderous rage resulting from the infanticidal atmosphere of adoption can manifest in antisocial or criminal tendencies, self-harm, suicide and murder. The internalised Death Mother is dehumanising and without compassion.

Infanticide is a violent act: the destruction of new life.

Amelia Dyer and the Brixton baby farmers were part of a vast underground network of women that included midwives, abortionists, and baby farmers, who aided desperate women by ending their pregnancies or ending their children's lives at birth or in infancy (Rose, 1986; Rattle & Vale, 2011).

Amelia Dyer, known for her hardness and brutality to the infants in her care, boasted in an interview from gaol before her death: "I used to like to watch them with the tape around their neck, but it was soon all over with them." (Rattle & Vale, 2011, p. 238) As a midwife, Amelia was skilled at smothering babies before they took their first breath. This precise art reflected the legal question over what constituted the beginning of life. An important consideration when you are planning to take a life. The law of the time stated that a child was not a separate life until it was fully separated from the mother and had taken a breath. Infants who died before being fully birthed, or before taking a breath, were, therefore, considered stillborn rather than murdered (Rose, 1986; Rattle & Vale, 2011). Medical knowledge of the time was not able to detect evidence of suffocation if no breath had been taken. This provided a neat solution for both desperate mothers and the midwives willing to aid them in their need not to parent a child. Some midwives, such as Amelia Dyer, had perfected an art of murdering babies as they were born, and earned substantial fees for doing so.

It was popularly believed that baby farmers murdered babies by piercing the soft fontanelle at the top of a baby's skull, causing a death-inducing brain injury that was difficult to detect. In the Australian Makin trial, several of the infant bodies showed evidence of needle-sized perforations of the skin over the chest, along with bloodstains on infant clothing. It was inferred from this evidence that the Makins' had pierced the infants' hearts with long needles in order to induce death, though this was not proved (Cossins, 2014).

New Zealand folklore held that Minnie Dean murdered children by piercing them through the eyes or through the fontanelle with her hatpin (Hood, 1994). There is no evidence that Minnie did so.

I used to have a recurring nightmare of live crustaceans being pierced with long pins, the soft, visceral bodies writhing at the insertion of the needle. I associated the image with the torture of madness. There is a curious relationship between visceral piercing and madness in the use of lobotomy, a mental 'treatment' used from the 1940s to the 1960s. Lobotomy, or leucotomy, involved severing the connections in the prefrontal cortex through the insertion of a sharp instrument, such as a hypodermic needle, or a leucotome, through the eye and into the brain, which might then be injected with alcohol or formalin. The operation damaged the brain to the extent of causing a surgically induced infantile personality (Geller, 2005). That is, if the person survived. Lobotomy seems to have been a calculated means of Soul murder in an attempt to subdue wild expressions of madness and render the person docile and easier to manage. Is there something, I wonder, in the collective unconscious that remembers the murder of babies by needles, the destruction of the precious awareness of the original self? And is there something that remembers the state of helpless dependence in relation to a cold authority that seeks to destroy what is inconvenient and able to think for itself?

Returning to Minnie Dean, the evidence of her violence to children includes the coroner's report of deep bruises at the back of baby Eva Hornsby's skull, consistent with attempts to suffocate a baby. Minnie claimed the infant rolled off a seat when she was being changed, but Hood (1994) states the baby was not old enough to roll on her own. When handed over to Minnie, Eva was starving, weak, possibly fractious, possibly already dying. We can only surmise the circumstances of her death. Did Minnie unintentionally suffocate the crying Eva, trying to keep her quiet in the train carriage so as not to draw attention to herself, knowing she had a dead child in her hatbox? Did she intentionally suffocate the child? Or was the child so weak she died? Perhaps Minnie shook her to try to revive her, creating bruises with her panicked grip? Unlike today, the nineteenth-century coroner was unable to prove whether the baby had been suffocated.

Another child found buried in Minnie's garden died without clear cause. In her last statement, Minnie confessed she did not like Willie Phelan, and that she was sometimes violent with him (Dean, 1895; Hood, 1994). Such statements must be taken in the context of child-rearing of the time, which condoned physical chastisement. Minnie said that Willie was mentally deficient and that she did not like his dirty habits. She claimed Willie drowned in an outside water butt. She also claimed she tried at length to hand him back to his family because of her dislike of him, but

117

they had refused to take him (Dean, 1895). Was his death – like that of Emma Williams's child – the result of a desperation and frustration that got out of hand; the result of a murderous wish to get rid of a troublesome child whom she could not return?

Three children in Minnie's care, dead under suspicious circumstances, is concerning. There were also several children in her care who remained unaccounted for in her testimony written in gaol before her death (Dean, 1895). Were the children handed on, as she claimed, to adoptive families or other baby farmers, or were their 'adoptions' euphemisms for their deaths, whether by murder, neglect, or abandonment? Amelia Dyer, for example, frequently told her daughter, Polly, that infants she had murdered had been adopted or returned to their mothers (Rattle & Vale, 2011). This may have been a standard baby-farming ploy to explain the disappearance of murdered or abandoned infants to other children in the house and to curious neighbours.

Statistics on child mortality in Victorian England show high rates of infant death and infanticide linked specifically to illegitimacy. For example, in 1871 the Select Committee on Infant Life Protection (England) speculated that as few as 10% of illegitimate children survived to adulthood (Higginbotham, 1989; Rose, 1986). Illegitimacy and death went hand in hand.

High mortality was also linked with age. Babies under one year were more at risk of violent death than older children. Rose (1986) stated: "the more helplessly infant you were, the greater the chances of dying a 'violent death'" (p. 8). Statistics for 1870-71 showed that infants under one year were 2.5 times more likely to die violently than one- to two-year-olds, and more than four times at risk than four- to five-year-olds (Jones, as cited in Rose, p. 8).

The violent methods used by mothers and family members to kill infants reveal high levels of desperation and/or dissociation. Newborns were frequently smothered, beaten beyond recognition, knifed, flung against walls, dismembered, left to bleed to death

118

through the untied umbilical cord, abandoned to suffocate in privies or exposed in cold inhospitable places (Rattigan, 2012).

In order to murder a baby, it appears a high degree of dissociation from any feeling for the child as a living being is required. Baby farmers who murdered their charges must either have found ways to disconnect or were trained by their own childhoods to see children as objects, without feelings or needs. In order to exploit children as objects to be used or despatched, they must be dehumanised, much as Jews were treated during the Holocaust. Research based on Holocaust trauma may therefore have something to offer in understanding the psychological trauma of psychological infanticide – the denial of the right to exist unless you are useful to the more powerful other. Sachs (2013) made this link between Holocaust trauma and psychological infanticide when she described intergenerational Holocaust trauma as an infanticidal attachment disorder. She stated: "As the [second generation] child's main purpose in life was to heal the parents, failing to do that meant the child had no right to life." (Sachs, p. 31). The adopted child instinctively understands that it is a replacement for a child lost or unable to be conceived. The adopted child knows it can never meet the expectations of the parents for that other 'unattainable child' and that it is therefore the 'wrong child' (Lifton, 1994). As discussed in Chapter Three, objectification is a form of violence against the identity of the child, which Shengold (1989, 1999) termed Soul murder and Shaw (2014) described as the dehumanising subjugation of a person.

Whilst it might seem heretical to compare adoption with the Holocaust, Sachs (2013) poignantly argued that "the best yardstick for the enormity of trauma lies in our own incapacity to bear witness to it; or in the level of dissociation that listening to it inflicts on the witness" (p. 25). People have a great deal of difficulty listening to the distress of adoptees. They frequently refuse to hear or acknowledge the lifelong effects of being unwanted and wished out of existence. There is a culture of empathising with birth mothers for their grief and loss whilst expecting adoptees to be grateful for being taken in by a family (Verrier, 1993). Even the recommended ways of talking about adoption during the era of closed stranger adoption (1950s-1980s) denied the child's actual experience. Parents were advised to tell their child early on that they were adopted, that they were chosen by the adopted family and were special. I understand that these were attempts to bolster the esteem and security of a child coping with a non-ordinary family situation. However, these messages, creating a mismatch with the internal state of adopted children who experienced psychological infanticide, perpetuated the disavowal of such a child's reality, making it further impossible for the child's actual experience to be talked about.

Extreme levels of helplessness are an indicator of massive trauma (Herman, 1992). Putting together the combination of 'helpless, unborn child' and 'dissociated mother', we can begin to name and bear witness to the massive trauma the unwanted child goes through in this situation.

As we have seen in Chapter Three, desperation, dissociation, and murderous wishes against unwanted infants are themes of psychological infanticide that become internalised and continue to be enacted by adoptees throughout life while they remain unnamed, unwitnessed and out of consciousness.

Psychological Infanticide and Murderous Rage

Murderous acts, or wishes directed towards a child, instigate murderous rage in response. Bowlby (1960, 1980) described how, when separated from mother, the infant instinctively knows its survival is in danger and responds with outraged protest in a desperate attempt to be reconciled with the mother. He stated that there is nothing more likely to provoke intense and violent hatred for the mother than separation. Stevens (1982) has described this violent outrage as an archetypal attachment pattern innate in human beings, whose infants are born completely helpless and in an embryonic state, utterly dependent on the mother. Usually, the mother also fights instinctively and fiercely not to be separated from her child. Therefore, a mother harbouring death wishes against her child is a form of psychological violence that goes against moral constructs of what it is to be a mother (Francus, 2012). Unfortunately, these moral sentiments of motherhood cause the natural responses to desperate situations to be split off from consciousness in a dissociation of disowned murderous impulses that take on a life of their own outside awareness. As discussed in Chapter Three, this unnamed murderousness is introjected by the child, who experiences it as a psychological infanticide. What is happening internally when a pregnant woman must reconcile herself with the idea that she is not going to mother the child she is carrying? In Chapter Three I suggested that she must disconnect the innate instincts to bond, love, and nurture her child. In order to do so, she must disconnect her own biological instinct for mothering, if this has not already been disconnected by her own upbringing. She must also disconnect from forming a positive relationship with her child in the womb. Kalsched (2013) explained the establishment of early dissociative defences in the traumatised infant:

> With this traumatic splitting, aggression that should be available to the child to protect itself against its persecutors is diverted back into the inner world to attack the very vulnerability that threatens the 'old order' of control. (pp. 83-84)

And further:

> The child so worthy of preservation as a representative of the human soul and its aliveness, can be permanently exiled by defensive processes and the antilife forces that get established in the psyche after early childhood trauma. When this happens, the soul goes into hiding and its 'urge to release itself' may be all but extinguished (Kalsched, p. 85)

Giovanni Liotti (2012) pointed to evidence that the mothers of children with disorganised attachment styles have either experienced a trauma and/or grief in the two years prior to or after birth. Women going through an unwanted pregnancy experience unrelenting grief and trauma during the pregnancy and birth. The unborn child is immersed in this situation without relief, predisposed to disorganised attachments, fragmented self-states and dissociative responses.

The greater the mother's desperation and shame at her unwanted state, the more she is likely to dissociate from her pregnancy or to wish the child gone. Mothers who kill their children at birth are extremely dissociated, even to the point of being in complete denial that they are pregnant (Spinelli, 2010). Birth mothers dissociate in order to cope with the painful situation they are in and the impossible choices they have to make (Rattigan, 2012; Spinelli, 2010).

The link between actual and psychological infanticide seems to be dissociation from a positive relationship with the unborn child and from the murderous wishes for it 'not to be'. This suggests that dissociation – particularly before birth when the foetus is completely dependent on, and contained within, the rejecting mother – is the central process of infanticidal attachment and the disorders attributed to it.

Not all relinquishing mothers disconnect fully from their unborn child. Many birth mothers describe loving warm relationships with their baby, and wanting to offer the child more stability and love than they were able to provide in the circumstances. However, I suggest there is still some level of disconnect commensurate with the pain of knowing the child will be relinquished. A child is birthed, and simultaneously a child is lost, as if dead. It is simply unbearable to think about and perhaps unable to be thought about (Bollas, 1987; Reiner, 2012). This inability to think, I believe, has a psychological impact on the unborn child, who experiences not being able to be thought about as not really being able to exist. Any discontinuity of relationship suggests a disruption in the child's sense of some continuity of existence, the ongoing truth of themselves. Reiner (2012), commenting on Bion's concept of the 'truth-instinct', wrote:

> The desire for the death of the self is reflected in an unconscious preference for lies over truth, and the 'decision', often made in the earliest days of life, to live a lie which denies the mind and the existence of inner life. (p. 16)

Closed stranger adoption performs exactly this violence on the truth of original being. The adopted child, living a lie, is denied its own mind and existence in a kind of living death. As Reiner stated: "The battle between truth and lies is a battle royale between the death of the self and the possibility of being" (p.16). This comment perceives the intensity of pain that psychotherapeutic work may induce as it brings the dead to life and the deathliness begins to be felt.

When a woman copes with her impossible situation by wishing it were not so, by wishing she were not pregnant, or that the pregnancy would disappear, or by imagining she is not pregnant, the baby receives these messages as being wished dead. When a mother copes by not imagining a pregnancy, or a baby, or any relationship with what is happening inside her, the baby receives messages that it is not meant to exist – or does not exist. In my first novel, I expressed this horrifying lack of being:

> *She doesn't exist. There is an absence until his key in the door fills up the emptiness and he steps back into the space and makes her real again. Nothing exists outside of the house. If she were to step outside of the door the void would take her and she would be nothing. Yet when she is alone in the house she is the void. Utterly vacant. None of it exists. She doesn't exist.*

*Don't be silly says Monte when she tells him. Of
course you exist. You are sitting right here in front of me.
I can reach out and touch you. His hand squeezes hers.*

*But I only exist because you are thinking me she
says. I am a figment of your imagination.*

That's impossible he says.

*But it's true. When you go away I am not here. There
is nothing.*

*He doesn't understand because he is always thinking
her. When he stops thinking her she will simply disappear
and it will all stop.* (Deed, 1994a, p. 94)

Murderous rage is a natural outcome of feeling denied the
right to exist. Shirley Ward, (2006) who studied the unborn child's
rage, acknowledged that adoption is a factor that needs to be
worked with psychotherapeutically at a pre- and peri-natal level.

A mother who feels angry and frightened about her situation
transmits these feelings to the foetus, who may receive them as
terror and hate from which it is unable to remove itself. 'Shattered
states' are a result of such situations of fear without solution
(Yellin & White, 2012). The baby in these circumstances might
experience itself as at risk of death by the mother. This unborn
child is already traumatised, already reliant on dissociation, in
order to continue to survive such a frightening and irresolvable
situation. Receiving this start in life tends to create in a child a
perception that the world is dangerous, and they are at risk of
violence just by being visible (present) and at risk of disappearing
if not visible to others. This double bind makes living torturous.
One is not safe anywhere. This is evidenced in another example
from my second novel, in which the language described an internal
state of the terror of being killed:

*The house is my prison and my shelter. It squats over
me, breathing darkly and granting me temporary mercy
in its hideous blindness. The house is too fat and I hide*

here under the creak of its joints hoping to be spared. If I were to run, outside has become too naked, too large, and I am like a snail, vulnerable to the sky and all the possible predatory eyes in it. It will only be a matter of time before I am plucked off the pavement, snapped up by the carnivorous clouds. (Deed, 1995, p. 67)

This perspective reveals how, in the internal experience of the adopted child, nothing is safe. The house, symbol of safety and security from which the securely attached child steps out into the world, symbol of the womb from which the child is birthed into the world, is itself terrifying. Its containment merged with feelings of danger that could not be escaped, becoming both prison and shelter.

Adoption is a psychological experience of murder rather than its actuality. However, trauma research indicates that the body responds to traumatic thoughts as if the trauma were actually happening, and this sets the infant up for a life of embodied terror of being killed, of violent destruction, often without words to describe this preverbal state or a recollected experience to make sense of it (Levine, 2010; Rothschild, 2000; van der Kolk, 2014).

Murderous Rage Enacted Against Others or Turned Against the Self

While they remain disconnected from their true selves and their true feelings, adoptees re-enact their own murderousness and the death wishes they have experienced against them. Verrier (1993) described the rage of trauma being focused on adoptive parents (for being the wrong parents), or on the birth mother (for abandoning the child). She claimed troubled adoptees do not understand their rage and feel they have no control over it. They learn either to act out – leading to parental attempts to get treatment – or act in – becoming shut down and compliant, their psychic pain unseen.

Adoptees have much higher rates of suicide and attempted suicide than non-adoptees (Brodzinsky, 1990; Wierzbicki, 1993). Lifton (1994) claimed this is a subject that is avoided in adoption circles because it is seen as a personal, social or professional failure. Verrier (1993) linked suicidal thoughts to the adoptee's overwhelming sense of loss "characterised by hopelessness, helplessness, emptiness and loneliness" (p. 36), and suicide as an attempt to enact the psychic death that has already happened but is unable to be recalled as an experience.

However, Lifton (1994) went straight for the murderousness hidden behind suicidality, citing homicidal adoptees expert, Donald Kirschner, as saying: "behind every homicide there is a suicide" (p. 101). Kirschner (1992) contended that many adoptees who murder are more suicidal than homicidal, thus establishing an association between suicide and murderous rage. He claimed adoptees who kill have generally made repeated suicide attempts first (Kirschner, 1992).

The adopted child feels deeply outraged at being rejected by the mother, and also needs her to survive. The adoptee therefore is hostile to, and rejecting of, feelings of helplessness and need, and may attack others perceived as dangerously rejecting.

A vivid illustration of the relationship between suicide and homicide in adoptees is eighteenth-century poet, Richard Savage, a contemporary of Dr Samuel Johnson. We know his story primarily from Richard Holmes's (1993) biography, *Dr Johnson and Mr Savage*.

Richard Savage was adopted out at birth. Although not fully proven, he believed his parents were upper class and that his birth mother had conceived him during an affair, adopting him out to protect her marriage and reputation. Savage resented being deprived of his true entitlement – and the status and money that went with it. We could suggest his smouldering rage related to being outcast from his own worth as a human being. The adult Savage, a talented poet whose status was expected to rise successfully through patronage of his poetry, lived a feral life on the streets –

sleeping rough, hanging out with prostitutes, drinking heavily, and brawling. He impulsively killed a man with a knife in a senseless altercation and was sentenced to death. He received a royal pardon due to petitions by influential friends who invoked his status as a poet. Perpetually outraged and publicly provocative, Savage provoked his alleged birth mother by stalking, blackmailing, and libelling her. He even intruded into her home, intimidating her in her room where she was unable to raise help. She later claimed she was terrified he would murder her. Savage would not remain a secret or go away quietly. To quote Holmes (1993):

> Savage began to exploit the tortured psychology of the rejected 'bastard', cruelly deprived of maternal affections. He suggests his misery, as an unrecognised son, might almost be a form of madness. (p. 71)

We can see in Savage's life how murderous rage leaks out in his violent lifestyle and relationships, and in the unchecked impulsivity that led to his senselessly murdering a man. Descriptions from witnesses suggest that Savage was bewildered and perplexed when he came out of an altered state after the killing. While such impulsive and/or dissociative murders are by no means exclusive to adoptees, Kirschner (1992) testified in US courts that "the adopted person is particularly at risk for extreme dissociation under stress" (as cited in Lifton, 1994, p. 107).

Suffering bouts of crippling depression, Savage also wrote about his relationship with Suicide, whom he personified as a *female* figure (author's italics):
From me (she cries) pale Wretch thy Comfort claim,
Born of *Despair* and *Suicide* my name!
(Poetical Works, 114-15, as cited in Holmes, 1993, p. 90)

Savage died in Newgate prison – an ill, drunken debtor. His inability to move beyond violent outrage and despair, and the haunting fantasies of what might have been, stopped him from embracing life, despite many attempts by friends to rescue him from himself. His life is representative of the arrested life of those adopted people who seem unable to move beyond their overwhelming grief, anger and introjected murderousness. They have known nothing else. Savage's relationship with the female persona of Suicide is recognisable as an infanticidal attachment with the Death Mother archetype that destroys both the will to live and compassion for self and others (Harris & Harris, 2015; Woodman & Sieff, 2015; Sieff, 2017).

According to Kirschner (1992) and Lifton (1994), there are two types of murder specifically relevant to adoptees: serial murder and parricide.

While adoptee serial murderers are at an extreme end of a continuum of killers, adoption is a significant contributing factor in serial killings (Kirschner, 1992; Lifton, 1994). Adoptees are far higher represented in serial murder statistics than non-adoptees. Interviews with adoptee serial killers reveal their motive is frequently to 'murder the past' in order to prevent others from going through the pain the adoptee suffers. Such serial murders are often focused on young women, who may represent the birth mother: in their dissociated minds they are murdering the abandoning or life-negating mother (Kirschner, 1992; Lifton, 1994). Such murderous acts seem to parallel the dissociative death wishes of the unwilling mother for the unborn child.

Parricide refers to the murder of parents. A significant proportion of murders of one or both parents are committed by young adoptees, up to 15-20 times more so than non-adoptees (Brodzinzky, 1990; Lifton, 1994). Similar to Verrier's (1993) description of the child who externalises their rage, Lifton (1994) referred to the combination of uncontrollable rage and powerlessness that occurs as a result of being rejected at birth. Powerful forces threaten to annihilate any sense of self, and murder is often an externalised attempt to resolve a "catastrophic conflict" (Lifton, p. 104.) This catastrophic conflict results from dissociative splits to manage "genealogical bewilderment, emotional trauma, depression, anger and rage" (Lifton, p. 104). Lifton powerfully stated that closed adoption forces a child to dissociate in order to live an as-if life, creating an unrecognised form of abuse she described as cumulative trauma, preferring this term to Kirschner's term 'adopted child syndrome' (Lifton, p.104). The adoptee is forced to split off parts of the self in order to survive.

We may be tempted to deny the murderous potential of adoptees, arguing that serial murder and parricide are both rare, and may be due to personality or biochemical faults unrelated to adoption. However, adoptees are statistically over-represented in both serial murder and parricide statistics. It is important that we do not continue to deny the tormented murderousness implicit in the experience of closed stranger adoptees. Both Kirschner (1990) and Lifton (1994 claimed that the adoptee is under particular risk for extreme dissociation when under severe stress, in particular that of real or perceived rejection, which may result in a brief reactive psychosis during which the murderous part of the self may act autonomously. They have also claimed that some adoptee murderers may in fact suffer from dissociative identity disorder (DID), in which separate personalities may act without the main personality being aware of them. Extreme dissociation is frequently a result of trauma before birth. Both Kahr (2007b) and Sachs (2007) have written extensively about the links between psychological infanticide, infanticidal attachment, DID and crime.

By assuming unconscious murderousness within the psyche of the adoptee, and remaining aware of the ways this murderousness may be enacted, we may discover many small or large ways adoptees destroy aspects of their lives and relationships that activate feelings of longing, loss and frustration. One example of this is the desire to euthanise pets when in suicidal frames of mind.

In the psychotic moment of murdering their parent/s, an adopted person believes that they are fighting for their life (Lifton,

1994). As I explored in Part Three, during my breakdown I experienced the delusion of needing to murder Mother before she murdered me. In my later fictionalised writing, I found ways to creatively and symbolically kill off mothers in my imaginal world. In doing so, I found safe channels for accessing and expressing my murderous rage at mothers:

> *Once when a child was slicing oranges she wanted to kill her mother and the knife slipped. This is a way of saying it. The knife floating through the terrible air like an old movie. She will never again eat oranges or try to kill her mother.* (Deed, 2006)

In the following series of extracts from my first novel – which related the story of my breakdown – the themes of suicide, murder, and the (internalised) Death Mother develop as the delusion evolves. Through the character of Helen, the pieces illuminate how the themes are passed between self and the hallucinated or internalised mother. I wrote this semi-fictional autobiographical account long before I trained in psychotherapy, so I find it thought-provoking now to see how clearly it weaves the themes I explore in this book. In particular, I believe these excerpts reveal the infanticidal attachment to a mother who is terrifying, murderous, necessary and longed for. The yearning for closeness combined with utter terror of being killed is indicative of infanticidal attachment (Kahr 2007a, 2007b, 2012). It is noticeable in these extracts that the language becomes disorganised and it frequently becomes difficult to tell who is murderous to whom, revealing how the infanticidal mother is internalised, and a deathly battle is played out within the self:

> *The mother. Dead hands reaching out to smother her. Taking her white throat out of the air and seizing the living part of her. It is not okay to be alive. The rituals and incantations she must go through for it to be safe.* (Deed, 1994a, p. 76)

In the following excerpt, it seems inevitable that death will overwhelm her. Helen's death is an invisible occurrence. She is helpless to act, like an infant. We see in this piece the threads connecting murder/suicide, drugging, and the helplessness of infancy that are themes of infanticidal attachment and the methods used by baby farmers:

> *The snow is falling into her mouth and over her eyes. There is a coverlet of snow and her hair is plaited with icicles and her feet are far away in green glaciers. But she is too far away in the frozen casket of sedatives to ever come back. Helen will never wake up and they will never find her body.* (Deed, 1994a, p. 96)

This excerpt reveals the frozen, numbed and dissociated territory of the Ice Queen. It brings to mind Estes's (1997) telling of the story, *Warming the Stonechild*, which addresses the situation of the unmothered child. In this story, the abandoned child attaches to a cold stone and is frozen to the point of death. He is saved by the warmth of a wise mother figure, or from a mothering presence that develops from inside of the freezing stone, activated by the tears of the dying child. The story teaches the need for warm, real feeling connection and the development of an internal nurturing mother. In contrast, the infanticidal mother, representative of the Death Mother archetype, is a cold, life-depriving mother.

As Helen's delusion continues, the link between Death and infancy recurs:

> *The nurse gives her a christening gown that she laces up the back so she will have a decent burial* (Deed, 1994a, p. 105).

Helen begins to experience her own murderous rage and her longing for a comforting mother. Death of self and death of mother become merged:

131

Wars, child abuse, serial killers…The only way to get out of the burden and the guilt is to murder herself.

The mother standing over the bed with the little wooden cross in the other room by the samovar. Putting her hand out into the air over the sleeping child and taking it back again. She will never be good enough even though she has come back from the dead and learned secrets there she can never tell.

The mother is holding her hand out. Touching her arm. You must be quieter she says…But that is a different mother. The one that is dead. The one that she killed with the knife. (Deed, 1994a, p. 109)

When the hallucinated or introjected mother denies Helen's pain, she feels abandoned and responds with rage just as the abandoned infant does:

The tears rolling out from under the gold coins on her eyelids. Beads of ice slithering across her dead face into the light.

Crocodile tears says the mother. You always were good with words. See if you can talk your way out of this…

The cup crashes against the door with a fury of sound out of the silence. (Deed, 1994a, p. 113)

Note the dissociation, as if the cup breaks itself, rather than Helen breaking the cup.

Helen, bereft of mother and mothering now begins the murder of the mother in herself. Who is murdering whom becomes increasingly unclear as Helen loses any sense of separation between herself and the persecutory mother. In becoming her own mother, Helen will repeat her infanticidal experience and abandon, and murder, herself:

She is dead. She believes this. She must murder herself. The stars are powerful again. She will never eat oranges or feel the juice drip down her chin or spit pips onto the back lawn from the verandah.

I must be my own mother says Helen lying in the white bed. She must look for compassion and piety and unjudged love. The hand reaching out across the dark over the sleeping child. Pleading the hand will come down on the unquiet brow. The hand of maternal goodness and the clean line of its simple expression that could bear to touch her and smooth back her hair.

I am my own mother says Helen.

She must murder herself in order that the mother cannot do so. They will not keep her away. The terror of eyes. Mother dead crawling from under the woodwork. Eyes glittering and dangerous like broken glass. Eyes inaccessible and flat and hard like shards of chalcedony. Eyes splintering and agate and terrible. Topaz glowing under cruel light. Wax-white and moon-coloured. Perilous and unseeing. Eyes that pull you under to drown. She does not blink. Nothing they can say can make it safe again. (Deed, 1994a, p. 151)

This is an internalised Infanticidal Mother with death-dealing petrifying eyes, not a compassionate mother with a soft, attentive, mirroring gaze. It is an image of Medusa, whose terrible gaze turned people to stone.

In the following passage, Helen believes she has died and equates this with finding her way home. The search for mother and home is a familiar adoption theme. Now Helen is afraid of having the safety of death taken away. Home, mother, death and suicide are linked in an infanticidal attachment:

It is time she says when they bring her back. Following the dead mother down the passageway.

The mother has stitched up her mouth and sewn over her eyes. She has turned her around once and twice and a third time for luck with her eyes sewn shut. There was just a glimpse at the end of the passageway. How else would she find her way home? But if she does not go to her the gates will be closed and she will be found wanting. They will take the sandals away from her feet and throw rose petals. They will not allow her to mourn. There is no way to jump from the window. Glass sealed all the way round. (Deed, 1994a, p. 152)

Throughout this next sequence of infanticidal enactment there is a focus on eyes – not the soft mutual gaze of the bonded mother and child, but the merciless cruel stare of a persecutor, or the blind unrecognising stare that sees through and dehumanises.

The terror of eyes. She would gouge them out if she could. No longer wishing to see through the splinter of conception. Hailstones falling deep as pockets under the mother's finger. I will separate myself. Mother bloodless and unstoppable. Mother culling the light. (Deed, 1994a, p.152)

In these Medusa-like images, we can also sense Helen's dissociation, her unwillingness to see. Mother is equated with the power to destroy in an image of eclipse, which will be explored further in Chapter Nine.

Eventually Helen becomes deluded that she is pregnant. Having become her own mother, she now imagines she is carrying her own child. She has indeed become the murderer of herself. This passage holds an echo of the predicament of the birth mother who wishes she was not pregnant. There is also the poignant knowledge that, for her own mother, there must not be a child:

If she is pregnant she must kill herself before she can kill the child. There must not be a child while she waits for her hair to be smoothed under the samovar. While the sky stretches under the eye of the sun and the words beating at the back of her head. (Deed, 1994a, p. 164)

Finally, the longing for mother becomes too painful. At this moment Helen is deemed to be well enough to leave the hospital. In reality she has reconciled her terrible struggle and resolved to die. Her compliant demeanour is an acceptance of her fate:

The mother almost lays a hand on her arm. Ice-cold. The pain of it lingering. Dinosaur swinging its way back from the ice-age. Black frost. Taking a demented bite out of her. (Deed, 1994a, p.165)

Helen kills herself at the end of the novel. The struggle is over. I felt at the time of writing that this was the most authentic outcome. In the process of writing, this part of me sacrificed her self, leaving the rest of me freer to grow towards life. Writing, like psychotherapy, has tremendous potential to safely enable and contain the exploration of the enactment (in this case of both suicide and murder) rather than enacting it concretely. It provided a space for me to work with my murderous rage, to explore the ways I killed off the mother in myself, and to work towards resurrecting a positive internal mother.

Chapter Six
Abandonment

Human beings, seeking at every stage of life,
from birth to death, to give and take love, are at risk of
significant destabilisation (lost-in-space fragmentation;
psychic death) in the absence of feeling loved.
Daniel Shaw (2014)

Here I discuss the literal abandonment of infants and the experience of psychological abandonment resulting from being separated from the mother in infancy, identifying key themes of the Orphan archetype. These themes relate to the denial of the right to exist, and to the related subjugation and exploitation of the infant to the needs of adults (Shaw, 2014).

Healing the psychological abandonment of the Innocent and Orphan archetypes requires moving from states of objectified non-being (isolation, fear and shame, invisibility and disconnection) to states of being a person (human connection, truth and acceptance, empowered presence). As discussed in Part One, Pearson (1986, 1991) stated that the developmental tasks of the Innocent (whose trust and innocence are betrayed in psychological infanticide) and the Orphan are to survive difficulty, balance caution and hope, to grieve and accept suffering, to feel what is there, release blame, open into compassion for the suffering of others and reconnect with faith in the goodness of others.

The examples that follow have the potential to illuminate the journey for healing from death by psychological abandonment – by facing into the dehumanised aspects of self with compassion and reconnecting with the qualities of being human and part of the human race.

Literal Abandonment

Within the context of the psychohistory of infanticide (Grille, 2005; de Mause, 1974; Stone, 1977), an emphasis on abandonment over infanticide was the result of a new phase of moral consciousness. Socially it had become unacceptable to kill unwanted children, but something still had to be done with infants who were not wanted or could not be cared for. Mothers who would once have killed such a child now surreptitiously left them in the streets, in doorways, on riverbanks, in fields, in public conveniences, railway carriages, or outside homes, churches and foundling hospitals. Some left notes imploring people to take in the infants they could not keep. Others left their babies exposed to almost certain death from cold, hunger, predation (from animals or people), or from injuries such as bleeding from an untied umbilical cord (Rose, 1986).

Abandonment arguably gave such children a chance of rescue, of life, and relieved a parental sense of responsibility or guilt for death. The experience of the abandoned child, however, is not adulterated by any intended hope for their survival. The abandoned child is engaged in a struggle against death, helpless to survive without help. At first the child protests loudly, seeking reconnection with mother, the only hope of survival. When she does not appear, protest eventually gives way to despair and a turning away from life (Bowlby, 1980). Abandoned infants in care are known to die from 'failure to thrive' due to the depth of hopelessness and terror from severing of the primary attachment.

Baby farmers abandoned infants and children – who had already been abandoned by their mothers to baby farmers – as if they were parcels. Baby farmers such as Amelia Dyer and her daughter, Polly, were not squeamish about leaving a child without care.

According to Rattle and Vale (2011), Polly and her husband, Arthur, took Queenie, their newly 'adopted' four-year-old with them to the seaside. While they explored and enjoyed holiday sightseeing, they left the child locked in the house. "Day after day she spent lonely hours locked in a small downstairs room, with little water and no food, while her new parents went out and left her alone" (Rattle & Vale, p. 130). Later, she was told they were moving again. Arthur walked Queenie through the streets into an area that was unfamiliar. "He told her she was to stay put until he returned. And then he was gone. It is not known how long the child wandered the streets before she was taken to the police station by a stranger" (Rattle & Vale, p. 130).

Polly was involved in another abandonment incident in 1898. Railway workers heard a faint cry coming from a disused railway carriage and decided to investigate. They found a brown paper parcel tied with string with a three-week-old baby girl inside. She had been there since the previous evening, approximately 24 hours. The woman who had left the child was identified as Polly Dyer. Polly and her husband had received the child by applying in a letter to the newspaper for a child to adopt: "The little one with us would have a good home, would be brought up well and have a parent's love and care" (Rattle & Vale, 2011, p. 248). This familiar approach by baby farmers exposes the chilling relationship between adoption, abandonment and exploitation that underpins the experience of psychological infanticide.

Less callously, Minnie Dean left Dorothy Edith Carter, whom she had only just taken from her mother, alone in her hotel room while she ran errands. The child was sick, distressed, and drugged with laudanum. Minnie let the staff know that she had left the child asleep in her room. She had also attempted to feed the child some of her own meal (Hood, 1994). In the nineteenth century it was usual for a woman travelling alone with an infant to leave her 'safe' in a room while she attended to business. Little Dorothy would still have experienced it as abandonment. She'd been left unwell and drugged in the care of stranger Minnie, so she was probably already very traumatised. These examples show how routinely infants were handed over without consideration of their infant needs, and how vulnerable they were to the whims of strangers.

Left for Dead: The Orphan and the Feral Child

Carlile (2016) described loss as a natural disruption of the 'space/time continuum' (p. 237). She was referring to breaks in continuity of life and sense of self that occur in grief. When abandonment through loss or separation happens early in life, we experience some part of ourselves as lost, helpless and abandoned in the world. Breaks in continuity are a dissociation that protect us from experiencing the full impact of a devastating trauma or loss before we are capable of handling it. Adoptees may experience profound levels of dissociation due to abandonment trauma that is so early they are unable to verbalise it or cognitively remember it (Lifton, 1994; Verrier, 1993).

Abandoned children, if they survive, feel orphaned. They are disconnected from family and life, and in this sense they are entombed in a living death, their connections with life killed off. Although for the actual orphan it is the parents who are lost, abandoned children experience themselves as being lost; although the parents are dead (or seemingly so), the experience for orphaned children is that they themselves have become dead to the world. This is psychological infanticide through abandonment rather than through violence.

The orphan feels, and is, particularly vulnerable to exploitation and abuse. Alone in the world, without support or foundation, the orphan must make their own way and has no-one to turn to when others take advantage.

Orphans who survive dying on the street may be 'taken in' in both senses of the phrase. They may be absorbed into a new household (where they may be expected to be grateful and to hand over wealth, to offer service, or be exploited in other ways). Or they may be naively 'taken in', conned by those human predators who recognise the orphan's particular vulnerability. Child orphans may easily disappear without any carer to notice their absence. For example, Thomas de Quincey (1785-1859) discovered a child living alone in the dark shut-up home of a wealthy man. De Quincey, himself a psychological orphan and vagrant, had also been offered a place to squat there. The child, described by de Quincey as "hunger-bitten, cold and friendless" (de Quincey, 1821/1971) was retained there as a kind of servant when the owner was in residence, though she was banished from anyone's sight and was locked in the house on his absence. De Quincey was obsessed by her ghostly status, as he was even more so by his other abandoned friend, Ann, who had become a child prostitute. Ann failed to meet him one day at their usual place, and he was never able to find her again. Haunted, he returned to her image with regret throughout his life.

The adult orphan, particularly a female orphan with some inheritance or property, has traditionally been extremely vulnerable to exploitation in a patriarchal society where marriage signifies that the woman and her wealth become the property of the husband. In the nineteenth century, a popular plot of novels was that of the orphaned woman who was manipulated into marriage and then exploited for her inheritance, often locked away as a madwoman and stripped of her identity, personhood and legal rights. Examples include Wilkie Collins's (1860) *The Woman in White*; Anne Brontë's (1848) *The Tenant of Wildfell Hall*; and Charlotte Brontë's (1843) *Jane Eyre*.

This experience of becoming dead to the world is not unlike that of closed stranger adoption. This madness is not simply about injustice to women. There is madness in the lament of the bereft child, whose continuity of attachment and sense of self are erased. This is a state of profound disorientation, grief and loss. It encompasses the loss of security, the loss of a place in the world and in the community of others; the loss of the right to dignity and standing in the world. The orphan becomes disinherited from society.

In his poem *El Desdichado* (The Disinherited), French poet, Gerard de Nerval (1808-1855), described this anguished disenfranchisement and desperate yearning through a world of mythic longing. De Nerval's mother died when he was five. His stern father was misattuned to the needs of this sensitive child. As an adult, de Nerval suffered mental illness characterised by retreat into an active fantasy world. His frantic appeals for the approval and emotional support of his abandoning father and his increasing incapability in the 'real world' led to his retreat into the lost place of madness in which he could endlessly pursue his elusive lost mother/lover. Abandoning hope, he eventually committed suicide. The first stanza of *El Desdichado* reads as a desperate protest giving way to despair:

> *Je suis le ténébreux – le veuf, – l'inconsolé,*
> *Le Prince d'Aquitaine à la tour abolie:*
> *Ma seule étoile est morte, - et mon luth constellé*
> *Porte le Soleil noir de la Mélancolie...*
> (de Nerval, cited in Holmes, 1985, p.211)

I am the man of shadows – the man in the shadows – the man of darkness – the man lost in the dark – the shadowy man you cannot see. I am the widower; I am the un consoled, the disconsolate, the grief-stricken man. I am the Prince of Aquitaine... I am the Prince with the abolished, shattered, stricken or blasted tower, or the Prince standing by that tower. My only star is dead, burnt out, extinguished (the noun is feminine). And my star-studded lute, or my lute marked with constellations, or the zodiac signs; my lute carries, or is emblazoned with, the Black Sun of Melancholy or Melancholia.
(transl. R. Holmes, 1985, p.211).

This black sun is the alchemical *sol niger* I describe in Chapter Nine, referring to the obliteration of any right to exist. De Nerval's poem resonates deeply with my own experience of early loss. I have returned to the poem frequently for its resonance with the legacy of adoption. This first stanza reveals a shattering of his foundation in the world, followed by stanzas of memory and fantasy that centre round a lost idyll. Holmes (1985) suggested the poem symbolically tells the story of de Nerval's life. His interpretation reflects the journey of the Orphan archetype.

The poem has a haunted mythology about it that does not feel anchored in reality. That first stanza illuminates clearly how grief and loss obliterate the sense of one's self. He becomes lost in the shadows, bereft of relationship, inconsolable and unloved. His identity and status in the world have been destroyed, and he no longer has any foundation. His star —any sense of illumination or light – is dead. There is no hope. The lute, constellated with stars, and therefore heavenly, is burdened with melancholy. This image is richly, densely packed with ideas centred around Orpheus, the lute player – with his ability to go into and return from the underworld with the birthright knowledge of the signs of the zodiac (knowing your place in the heavens is vital to navigating a life journey), and with the alchemical *sol niger*, the black sun that represents a process of putrefaction in which all is destroyed. All de Nerval's lights have gone out, and his heaven (the time before loss) has been wiped out by this depressive black sun. We have here an image of the black hole, the dark matter that enfolds stars and is an entry into the underworld from which de Nerval strove but failed to escape. This *sol niger* is the experience of non-being.

De Nerval's paired themes of the solace of memory and a glimpsed elusive woman are central to his work. Yet again we see how separation from mother causes haunting or hauntedness that never heals. The loss of a mother, by whatever means, instils in the psyche a relationship with death as mother figure, which we can now recognise as the Death Mother archetype, who seduces us into believing that the only solace for our misery is death. This psychic death by abandonment destroys a sense of the possibility of life and may be enacted through suicide and a ghostly connection with the dead parent (or lost parent, which for the child is the same as dead). It may result in depression, psychosis and suicide.

The Feral Child

The Feral Child is an expression of literal and mythic experiences of the Orphan archetype and reveals key annihilation-survival themes of the experience of psychological abandonment. The feral child, like the adopted child, is forced to survive without their biological family, culture or history; no rootedness or grounding of memory, no legacy of heritage handed down, and no beloved mirroring in which to feel one's existence. This child stands outside family, history and culture – without language, without narrative and story with which to weave a solid and stable sense of self. The feral child – feared, rejected and unloved – retreats into an *other* reality for survival – a literal or metaphorical wilderness, a regressed world of isolation that cannot be communicated with others.

Historically, some abandoned children survived, living a feral existence, having been nurtured by wolves, bears, and other creatures (Newton, 2002). In modern times there is evidence of abandoned children surviving with domestic creatures such as dogs and chickens. (Newton, 2002). Some feral children are abused children who were kept in isolated imprisonment. Examples include nineteenth-century Kaspar Hauser in Germany (Masson, 1996) and twentieth century Genie in the United States (Rymer, 1993). The essence of feralness is the terrible consequence of the deprivation of human connection. The feral child is the extremity of the Outcast aspect of the Orphan archetype.

According to Michael Newton (2002), feral children are deprived of their capacity to reason or communicate as socialised human beings. They learn that to survive they must distrust, fear and avoid humans. Something vitally human has gone and seems unable to be fully repaired. The original innocent human self has been murdered, and a wild survival self develops.

Newton (2002) set out to compassionately relate a history of feral children "through the *fragmented and disrupted biographies of children whose histories are partially lost*" (p. xiv) (author's italics). He related the tragedies of their lives after their capture in the wild and return to society. What is most apparent is the brutality and misunderstanding involved in attempts to re-socialise such children through subjugation of their will, and their subsequent status as exhibits, not unlike zoo animals or carnival freaks. They are eventually re-abandoned to poverty, misery and isolation, once society has given up on them when they are deemed unable to be adequately re-socialised or to retain their novelty status. There are echoes in this of the treatments and incarcerations of the severely mentally unwell. This includes our well-meaning, but perhaps misguided, attempts to understand; and our perhaps equally misguided expectations and judgments.

The feral child in history either died quickly when placed in human care, languished in despair, or lived the liminal subjugated life of a part-human part-beast with a keeper-controller. This, I argue, is often the fate of the infanticidally attached child who has no safe connection with humanity and so retreats into a ghostly world of schizophrenia or a splintered world of dissociated identities. Formerly banished for decades to the back wards of asylums, those who suffer beyond the range of our understanding and tolerance are frequently abandoned or neglected, even now.

Masson (1996) made the link between the abused feral child and Soul murder in his book on Kaspar Hauser. Both Masson and Shengold (1989, 1999) gave voice to the Soul murder inherent in child abuse, which warps and destroys the child's original self. We have the benefit of Kaspar's conversations – written down by his carers – and his writings, which relate his experience as an isolated captive child. Kaspar's brief life reveals an experience of psychological infanticide. He claimed to have been imprisoned in an underground vault with almost no human contact for most of his life, until he was sent out into a world he did not know. He had apparently led a normal family life until perhaps four-years-old, which made him uniquely able to learn and communicate to a degree that feral children, who have never known language, are unable to achieve. Once able to communicate his story to others, he explained that he had entered a living dream state – an internal world in which he was part of the dream. Nothing seemed real (Masson, 1996). After his imprisonment ended, Kaspar remained vulnerable to manipulations and violence by people who exploited his naïvety and perhaps wanted him dead. He was stabbed to death only a few years after he was removed from his childhood prison. In Kaspar we witness the docile compliance and vulnerability to further abuse that comes of being dependent on an abuser in childhood. This is a tactic of the survival self when it is too dangerous to express aggression. It implies a lack of a conscious sense of self or autonomy of thought.

Genie is the other well-known example of a child reared in severe neglect and social isolation. Rescued from thirteen years of solitary captivity from birth, Genie is modern proof of the effects of the psychologically infanticided child. She never became her fully human potential as her own self, and was vulnerable to exploitation by academics and carers who appear to have used her to experiment and advance their own theories.

As Newton (2002) and Rymer (1993) described, what stands out in the histories of feral children, especially evident in the lives of Kaspar and Genie, is the attachment dynamics that occur between the children and their carers. At first an intense attachment forms, with a deep wish to rescue the child from their inner darkness through education and socialisation. Brutal or coercive attempts are made to determine how much the child can be 'humanised' from their 'savage' state. There are often disputes between carers, who seem to wish to possess and exploit their charge for their own purposes. Finally, when the child grows recalcitrant, difficult, reaches the limit of their capacity to learn, or regresses, he or she is handed on to other carers where they may be pushed, punished or experimented on, and handed over again. Eventually such children – re-abused, repeatedly rejected, and denied long-term attachments – are put out of the way, in custody, or in back wards or lonely sheltered care as Genie is today. This pass-the-parcel attitude is similar to the handing on of babies from baby farmer to baby farmer for financial gain. It also reveals something of the exploitative nature of adoption in those situations where birth parents abandon a child and adoptive parents adopt a child, both for their own purposes and gratification, without awareness of the child's experience. The child experiences their subjective self as subjugated to the need to be a particular kind of object for their parents (Shaw, 2014). This is the 'object use' I referred to in the infanticidal mode of child-rearing, in which the child is seen as the parent's property to be used as they see fit, and discarded or destroyed when not of use.

We can learn from histories of feral children that being rejected and having to survive in the wild (metaphorically) deprives us of ability to trust, to develop safe human connection, to grow our finest potentials, and to feel human and therefore worthy in our humanness. On a mythic level, the Feral Child teaches us what it means to be human.

For nineteenth-century scholars, scientists and philosophers, feral children raised questions about the nature of civilisation, personality and language development (Newton, 2002). As Christian theologians debated whether animals had Souls, feral children occupied an uncomfortable liminal space in which they were neither fully human nor animals. Given that Enlightenment thinking allowed the exploitation of anything not Souled, we can see how the feral child easily became the captive and exploited child. It is when we are separated from our Soulfulness that our actions are no longer human, lacking humanity or human compassion, and yet, paradoxically, it is our Soul aspect that escapes to survive in the wilderness rather than relinquish its true essence. It may take engaging with the beast in our selves to reconnect with the human compassion for the world, contained in an instinctual life.

Philosophers such as Rousseau idealised the *noble savage* and the *child of nature*, romanticising the idea of a return to Eden before the Fall (Newton, 2002). This Romantic yearning to return to a state of bliss can be recognised as the Innocent archetype (Pearson, 1986, 1991) and the seductive regressive pull back to the womb discussed further in Chapter Eleven.

Feral children were associated with the so-called 'forbidden experiment' that was based on the question of how a child would develop if reared without human contact. The experiment was forbidden as ethically wrong. Feral children survived in a similar state to the proposed experiment, and so were eagerly observed (Newton, 2002).

I suggest that closed stranger adoption was also a kind of forbidden experiment, one that touched on the question of nature versus nurture, and the question of the effect on a child of being reared in a different family from its biological one. In other words – are personality and potential predominantly biological and genetic, or more influenced by the environment? What is not voiced in this questioning is the impact of trauma on the developing child. In Chapter Nine, I refer to what Lifton (1994) termed *cumulative trauma* to describe the pervasive traumatic effects of closed stranger adoption, because the effects persist and are re-experienced throughout life.

As it happens, such an experiment was carried out on identical triplets, now the subject of a movie, *Three Identical Strangers*. In what appears to be a coldly calculating experiment, the three boys were adopted out to three different couples as part of a long-term study of siblings separated at birth. None of the couples knew about the research or that the boys were part of a triplet (Nevins, 2018).

Adoptees I have talked with have corroborated my own experience of feeling like a Feral Child, cast out into the wilderness in a form of abandonment one survives but with the loss of one's connection to others or even to the humanity in oneself.

The Feral Child symbolises the displaced child, whether orphaned, rejected, adopted or otherwise abandoned. Falling between the realms of animal and human, feral children symbolise the severed link between the sensate or animated self and the ability to think, imagine and reason. We may consider that they occupy the position of the fleeting, wild aspect of the feminine consciousness that is dissociated from the orderly and rational logic of masculine consciousness in a society with patriarchal values.

The Feral Child also represents something about the capacity for language that distinguishes humans from animals. Language offers us a means of shared human connection. We require language to articulate our inner world, our thoughts, feelings, memories and imaginings. When traumatic experience is unable to be named, it is unable to be processed and remains locked in the body, enacted impulsively, unable to be thought about. Christopher Bollas (1987) talked about the development of language coming out of the earliest relationships between mother and infant. In her research on representations of infanticide in literature, Aimee Pozorski (2003) "draws on the figure of the *infans* – 'without speech' – as something befalling language in order to emphasise both the incommunicability of these events and the sudden foreclosure of futurity in modern narrative forms" (p. i). The abandoned infant and the feral child are unable to communicate their trauma and remain trapped within.

Documented and anecdotal cases of actual feral children tell us much about poverty, neglect, abuse, and the low value of the lives of infants and children. They also reveal the consequences of the incredible will of some children to survive against all costs. These stories symbolise for us the experience of the survival of the Soul-murdered child. The feral child is also the child captured and brought back into civilisation, whose responses mirror those of the adopted child by either becoming excessively docile and compliant, or rebellious and aggressive in a traumatised fight flight freeze response (Verrier, 1993).

The psychologically infanticided child may go into a cocoon or coma-like state. Marie Louise von Franz (1996a) wrote, with regard to the symbolism of a spider, that it is not good to be weaving imaginary worlds too early in the day. A child needs to connect threads to the outside world and relationships to be secure and grounded. If the imaginal life gets woven too early without connection to the outside, the child becomes the spider's victim, an image I explore in Chapter Seven. The spider traps the lost one in the threads of imaginings from which one cannot escape, and instead is suspended in a living trance until eaten (drugged, exploited and killed). This is the world of the psychotic, or the severely emotionally deprived. As Donald Kalsched (1996) described, the world of childhood trauma is a realm of fancy of archetypal dimensions.

Joseph Campbell (1968) pointed out that the heroes of mythology are very often orphans. Mythology acknowledges that the path of the orphan is a quest for survival and wisdom, and that it is a treacherous, life-risking path. Orphaned children, if they survive their fate, are capable of reclaiming their power and moving beyond fear of life.

Similar to the adopted child, the feral child is adopted by another species and grasps this opportunity for survival, no matter what the cost. An example is Charles Dickens's (1837/1997) Oliver Twist, who is adopted by Fagin's gang. They find survival together in the vicious London streets by creating their own community and culture. Like Oliver, the adopted child learns to adapt, to be what is necessary, in order to be tolerated, accepted, approved of – maybe even loved. This inability to be your true self is the essence of Soul murder.

The adopted child's survival lies in remaining invisible, like the feral child whose existence depends on not being seen. Yet this invisibility reinforces the belief that they do not exist. Charlotte Brontë's (1847/1993) *Jane Eyre* offers an example of the orphan child who must find another way in the world. Jane is persecuted by her aunt, and in school, for her wild impassioned nature. Like the recaptured feral child, Jane is rendered docile, compliant and invisible as a governess, until she is seen by Rochester, and sees (becomes aware of) the madwoman in the attic (her captive distorted wild self). She survives in society through self-restraint and knowing her place. Inside herself, however, Jane never gives up on her authenticity, eventually choosing a life of integrity over conformity.

Many myths and fairy tales tell the heroic journey of the Feral Child and the healing of the Orphan archetype. Oedipus, on whose myth Freud based psychoanalysis, was left exposed to die (a common early practice with unwanted infants). He survived when taken in by strangers. As an adult he killed his father and married his mother because he did not know who he was. One point to observe here is that being brought up by kind people does not save the adopted child from the consequences of infanticidal abandonment, or from disconnection from their history and true identity.

The inability to be your true wild self, as opposed to the survival self, is the essence of Soul murder. The adopted child's survival lies in the true self remaining invisible. Estes (1992) spoke to the concept of the predator in the psyche who is out to maim the instinctual self. She described the need to reconnect with the wild (self) within who is not domesticated or compliant, and is therefore free to live their wild original truth. A reverie on wolves led me deeper into the ways a feral child is always cautious, and the relationship between predator and prey:

I have a vision of wolves, circling and spiralling, fearful of the trap or the gun, broken bones, shattered bodies, assassinations, wrongful deaths. What we have done to wolves we do to our own wolf children, the wolves in ourselves. No wonder the feral child is so often a wolf child: the wolf as beast, the wolf at the door, the wolf as child stealer and child killer, the wolf in ourselves that we cover with our veneer of civility – the wolf who is our hunger and our desperation. The loup-garou – *werewolf – the shadow side of the wolf in the human, the one who is out to kill, bloodthirsty and menacing, the deceptive wolf hiding in grandma's clothes – who can we trust? We cannot really trust the smiling granny, she'll eat you as soon as look at you. As I was musing on this, a homeless man stopped me on the street, pointed to my red shoes and said – you're red riding hood. I said I'm trying to stay one step ahead of the wolves. Living his own precarious wolf-like existence I'm sure he knew what I meant. He walked away laughing. It seemed the wolf was stalking me.* (Deed, journal, 2016)

Like the caged bird that will not leave once the door is opened, the Feral Child may cling to her only known means of survival rather than risk trusting humans again. She may continue to live in a world of intensity and precariousness, always on the edge. She may not know any other way to be. We need tolerance for the need to be free, to live on an edge and to give expression to the fragile, damaged, mad self who holds so much creativity and sensitivity. In order to integrate our Feral Children, we need to be there with them on the edge and not force them into conventional compliance. Engaging with the Feral Child – the one who does not trust society or humanness at all, the one who lives like a wild beast, scavenging on the edge of society for enough sustenance to survive but terrified of being trapped or driven off – requires gentleness and respect.

Chapter Seven
Opium

What was it that did in reality make me an opium eater?
Misery, blank desolation, abiding darkness.
Thomas de Quincey (1821)

The Use of Opium to Relieve Pain and Subdue Children

Laudanum is an alcohol-based tincture of opium that was in common household use in the nineteenth century. Baby farmers used laudanum in two ways: to subdue babies who were distressed and to drug babies whose lives were no longer useful for financial gain. These babies, often known as 'paid-ups', would not provide further income. It did not make economic sense to continue to feed and care for a paid-up baby. Frequently, no one was interested in following up on the welfare of unwanted babies. Paradoxically, it was often due to the strenuous efforts of distressed parents to trace their farmed-out offspring that led to the arrest or conviction of baby farmers for child murder. This was the case for Minnie Dean (Hood, 1994), Amelia Dyer (Rattle & Vale, 2011), and the Makin family (Cossins, 2014) as well as others. Attached mothers went to great lengths to find their children when they had farmed them out due to difficult circumstances and expected to visit them and to take them back when they could.

We need to consider the social context of household opium use in the nineteenth century to explain why some baby farmers drugged infants into oblivion with opiates. Laudanum was a common household anodyne used for pain, gastrointestinal ailments, nervous distress and to pacify infants. To pacify suggests an intention to soothe, calm, appease and placate. These are attributes of the 'good enough' mother attuned to her infant in a securely attached relationship (Winnicott, 1965). This suggests that laudanum was used as a substitute for attentive mothering rather than genuinely relating compassionately to the child.

To pacify may also imply the subduing or suppressing of a natural expression. It has been mentioned that abandoned infants go through discrete stages of outraged protest, acute anxiety, withdrawal and depression – in some cases followed by death (Bowlby, 1980). Baby farmers dealt with inconsolable infants whose protests and anxieties would have been disruptive and intense. Social convention encouraged the pacifying of children so as not to disturb others. The frantic distress of babies handed over to baby farmers was generally 'pacified' with laudanum, with its combination of opiates and alcohol making it extremely sedating. Such babies were so shut down by drugging that they were insensible, unable to communicate, or possibly even unable to feel their distress as long as the dose was kept up.

Babies given laudanum were quiet, slept deeply (or were comatose), did not feed and did not react to wet diapers, hunger, pain or infestations of vermin. They could be left for long periods of time without causing trouble. If persistently drugged, they eventually grew dehydrated, malnourished and unconscious, and could be kept in this state of living death for a long time if needed, or could easily die. If dosing was not regular, babies would have experienced the horrors of withdrawal as well as the return of their hunger, pain, and feelings.

Opium numbs and dulls sensation and expression, slows down and paralyses organ motility, and blocks appetite. Children dosed with laudanum wasted slowly. Laudanum suppressed infants' distress while they slowly starved to death. Even children rescued from this treatment frequently failed to survive. See for example in Chapter Eight the outcome for two-year-old Harold, removed from the care of Polly Dyer after her arrest for baby farming.

When I think of drugged babies, I have the image of spiders paralysing live insects and wrapping them in shrouds of silk to store in the spider larder for future meals. In a similar way, the innocent baby handed over to the wrong baby farmer might be drugged up with laudanum and left alive until it was no longer advantageous to do so. A cocooned fly paralysed with venom is not dissimilar from a swaddled baby dosed with opium.

What does this have to do with adoption? Early infanticidal trauma creates a state of psychological paralysis and a sense of living death similar to the cocooned fly, reminiscent of the disconnection of Holocaust survivors who were known as walking corpses (Brenner, 2014). Archetypally, these images direct us to the presence of the Death Mother who destroys rather than nourishes aliveness and who kills the archetypal Innocent psychologically through denial and dissociation from what is true (Harris & Harris, 2015; Sieff, 2017; Woodman, 2005; Woodman & Sieff, 2015).

The pain and trauma of psychological infanticide in adopted children has for many years been denied and shut down – or shut up. Adopted children not only had their experiences denied, they are, according to Verrier (1993) the only traumatised group who have been expected by society to be grateful. But as she stated: "They are not grateful. They are grieving, and the original abandonment and loss are the source of many other issues for the adoptee" (Verrier, p. 65). Most people not only do not understand this, they are unwilling to hear the pain and disturbance adoptees experience. This leaves many adoptees with no avenues for a healing expression of protest and grief, perpetuating instead dissociation, self-denial, suppression and despair, and/or intense and disconnected expressions of anger. Denial is a major defence against the emotional pain that comes up repeatedly in the adoption scenario. Each member of the adoption triad holds its own secrets and denials – of their own pain or of the other.

Alice Miller (1998) is one writer who challenged societal blind spots and moral commands against the child's awareness of abuse done to it. She described the psychological effects of such dissociations on the child. Denial of psychic truth can express itself through addictions to substances or food. It may also express itself in attention difficulties (spacing out), anxiety (in response to feeling nothingness), and dissociation. In Chapter Five, Sachs (2013) powerfully illuminated the effect of being unable to witness what we find unbearable, and the effect this has of killing off the truth of what is denied.

Victorian society suppressed its passions under the weight of denial, convention and duty. It favoured sentimentality whilst denying brutality, which was acted out particularly against women and children. This is evident in two examples: the extreme corseting of women, echoing the restrictive swaddling of infants, which is an embodied metaphor of psychological imprisonment (Reich, 1974); and the extensive number of (female) child prostitutes in a society that sentimentalised childhood (Rose, 1986).

Baby farmers were not unique in using laudanum to sedate and control children. They simply extended the common practice of sedating children to pacify them in order to control the lives/ deaths of children who were of no further value and therefore not worth keeping alive. Stone (1977) wrote about the common practice of Western labourers up to the nineteenth century dosing infants with laudanum, swaddling them tightly, and hanging them on a peg on the wall while their parents were out labouring in the fields. This kept children 'safe' and quiet, their breathing seriously restricted from the effects of opium and the postural suppression of the respiratory system, combined with tight wrapping causing inability to move. It also relieved the need to feed or care for children during work hours. Stone has also written about the dangerous use of laudanum for children's ailments and as a general panacea to such an extent that it was commonly known that children died from such practices.

Hood (1994) reproduces Crabbe's nineteenth-century poem on the effects of quieting children with laudanum in her biography of Minnie Dean. It remains powerful:

The boy was healthy, and at first expressed
His feelings loudly, when he failed to rest;
When cramm'd with food, and tightened every limb,
To cry aloud, was what pertained to him;
Then the good nurse (who, had she borne a brain,
Had sought the cause that made her babe complain)
Has all her efforts, loving soul! applied
To set the cry, and not the cause, aside:
She gave the powerful sweet without remorse,
The sleeping cordial – she had tried its force,
Repenting oft: the infant freed from pain,
Rejected food, but took the dose again.
Sinking to sleep; while she her joy express'd,
That her dear charge could sweetly take its rest.
Soon may she spare her cordial; not a doubt
Remains, but quickly he will rest without.

This moves our grief and pity, and we sigh
To think what numbers from these causes die.
(Hood, 1994, p. 48)

Crabbe was an opium addict, as were many children brought up on laudanum. The poem, and Stone's examples, enable us to imagine Western culture built upon the intergenerational transmission of childhood developmental traumas which were denied and suppressed with laudanum and alcohol, and which were perpetuated by adults who never learned to deal with traumatic stress in any other way. We can see how attachment difficulties and parenting modes are so tenacious.

Opium use by baby farmers should therefore be viewed in the social-historical context of the time (Swain, 2005). Parental use of laudanum to pacify children has a social-historical context. Laudanum was cheaper than alcohol and was used extensively by the poor to relieve the awfulness of their lives (Stone, 1977). It was not seen as a criminal or dangerous drug, and the risks of addiction were not well appreciated, despite Crabbe's portrait of its harmful effects on infants and the confessions of notorious opiate addicts: Samuel Taylor Coleridge (as cited in Holmes, 1989, 1999) and Thomas de Quincey (1821/1971).

Many women were also addicted, having been treated with laudanum for nervous conditions or painful ailments, often related to childbirth. Rattle and Vale (2011) indicated that murderous baby farmer, Amelia Dyer, was addicted. During several police arrests, Amelia broke down mentally and was sent to asylums where she quickly recovered. Rattle and Vale suggested that her temporary insanities could have been due to opiate withdrawal while in custody, which was relieved by laudanum treatment in the asylum. During one police inquiry and imminent arrest she attempted suicide, ingesting a near fatal laudanum overdose (Rattle & Vale). High levels of dissociation are required to be able to kill an infant (Grille, 2005; Spinelli, 2010). Amelia may well have used laudanum to suppress her own feelings at destroying infant lives. Or perhaps she was already dissociated and addicted from her own upbringing? Awaiting her hanging, Amelia was haunted by what she had done, suggesting that without regular laudanum and alcohol, her awareness of her actions and her feelings could no longer be suppressed. This is speculation on my part.

We can also consider that parents were actually soothing their own distress at having to deal with inconsolable infants. At a psychological level, fractious children are hushed up or shut down either through bribes, threats or devices such as pacifiers (dummies). In the modern context, I have heard stories of mothers dosing their children with sedating cough mixtures at times when they need their children to 'behave'.

Thinking about Minnie Dean

While I lived in Oamaru, I tried to make sense of the motives behind the overdosing of Dorothy Edith Carter with laudanum that led to her death. Opium poppies grew in my garden. I observed them closely, feeling my way into the secret life of opium:

Opium. The dark black specks of seed. Resinous brown fluid. The green orb of the seedpod with its domed architecture, its vast internal spaces, its vaulted ceilings. It attracts like a false promise. Did Minnie Dean ever grow a poppy plant in her garden? Did she ever cut the scarlet flowers to grace a scrubbed kitchen table? Did she ever stop to admire the green pleasure domes? The green and gold world of a chrysalis. Opalescent. Embryonic. Did she understand?

The poppies lie secretly under the fence in the now wild garden. They are beginning to send up blooms, silver green heads with the lips of tulips, a chrysalis growing silk petals. Between the ghost green leaves they speak already of shadow, glimpsed visions, momentary glances. (Deed, 2003b)

Dorothy Edith, according to Minnie, was unwell and hard to settle when she picked her up (Hood, 1994). It is not hard to imagine she gave laudanum both to relieve the child of her discomforts and also to help her sleep. But travelling with an upset child was also likely to draw attention to Minnie, something she wished to avoid as she was already under police surveillance and was not registered to farm children. Perhaps extra dosing was a precautionary measure to keep the child quiet enough not to be noticed. Perhaps also, and this is pure conjecture, in the stress of the situation Minnie administered some pacifying doses for herself and was therefore less able to judge how much or how frequently she was dosing the child. It is also possible the child was in a frailer physical condition than Minnie could know, and that her constitution could not take the dosing. Yet the pathologist's report indicates Dorothy Edith died from a serious overdose of opium, not a normal dose that a frail child might not cope with.

I began to wonder how aware Minnie was of the effects of laudanum, and whether she knew how to manage the dosing of the variable strengths of laudanum. Surely, mothers and nurses had a reasonable idea of how much of this common household medicine was too much, and what might result from too much. Yet it is also reasonable to assume that significant numbers of infants did die of unintended opium poisoning, as claimed in Crabbe's poem. Either infants wasted from chronic drugging when they stopped feeding and parents did not know the cause, or large single doses caused them to die in their (comatose) sleep. In my reveries on opium I began to sense its hidden themes:

In my vegetable garden the poppies drowse amongst the lettuces. Wild lettuce, Lactuca virosa, *contains opiates and was used as a soporific and as a narcotic for use in surgery prior to chloroform. All lettuces contain amounts of narcotic fluid, garden lettuce,* Lactuca sativa *contains the least. The poppies have reared up on their hairy stems and opened out. I have watched the bud swell and fatten over the days and the swirl of scarlet silk unfold in a crush, a butterfly's new wings unfurled from the cocoon.*

The cocoon or chrysalis is another opium metaphor, the life in suspension, the half-dead, the living dead, the slumbering, soporific, emblem of the unconscious, the workings of the hidden labyrinths of the imagination. The creativity that either grows and opens or twists on itself and shrivels and dies in the womb turned shroud. It is the struggle of life over death. The very essence of opium, the ultimate questions of opium being: how do I live with this death? How do I struggle with this living death? How do I survive waking briefly and knowing the truth?

By morning my scarlet silks are shredded, their severed heads gone, borne away in triumph, trophies to the vanquished dead. The stalks stand upright, pliant in the wind, a slash of petal bleeds on the ground. (Deed, 2003b)

A Romantic Sensibility of Opium as a Creative-Destructive Persona

When I lived in Oamaru, actively trying to understand Minnie, and therefore myself, I thought a great deal about the precariousness of infant life in Victorian times. I was grieving a recent loss, and reconnected with the deeply felt experience of abandonment, loss and the experience of being a child whose hold on life was tenuous. The mother-child relationship felt shrouded with potential losses.

Immersing myself in reading about women's and children's lives in the nineteenth century, I came across a list of infant elixirs and their dangerous ingredients – in common use to pacify or fortify babies:

Children's pharmaceuticals and their active ingredients in use up until 1905:
Children's Comfort ~ Morphine
Dr James's Soothing Syrup Cordial ~ Heroin
Dr Moffet's Teething Compound ~ Opium
Dr Grove's Anodyne for Infants ~ Codeine
Victor Infant Relief ~ Chloroform & Cannabis
Dr Fowler's Strawberry & Peppermint Mixture ~ Morphine
Mrs Winslow's Soothing Syrup – The Mother's Friend ~ Laudanum/Morphine

> *There were many deaths and many addicted children. I ask again, did Minnie really understand?* (Deed, journal, 2000. Original source not noted).

As I reflected on opium, the main ingredient in many infant elixirs and childhood pacifiers, it became a powerful metaphor for the ways that life, self and creativity are numbed and devitalised by trauma. I decided to personify Opium in the tradition of Romanticism, in which such concepts as Fancy and Imagination – two psychic functions that were considered in depth by opium-addicted writers (Coleridge, 1817/1956; de Quincey 1821/1971; Hayter, 1968; Roe, 2013) – were likewise personified and reified. By personifying Opium, and applying a Romantic imagination to Opium, as John Keats (2011) did in his poems, I could relate to her in personal ways.

This development of Opium as a personified metaphor uses two concepts from imaginal psychology. First, it developed from an imaginal dialogue with the spirit or essence of opium. Second, I drew on tacit knowing and intuition, what I call 'dreaming into' the opium state. This was then amplified by researching opium through many facets: historical, medical, chemical, mythological, opiate abuse, poetry, literary criticism and drug literature, homeopathic and trauma literature. I did not take any opiates myself.

Repeated themes supported my intuitive portrait of Opium as a passive feminine sensual image of fantasy, seduction and subterranean depths. As such, she represents the Queen of the Underworld, a realm that is now reduced to a term for organised crime and vice, particularly associated with drug trafficking and abuse.

Through this intuitive exploration of the spirit of Opium, I found her a useful ally in intuiting the feminine aspects of self that are traumatised by psychological infanticide:

[Opium] becomes at various times, through many shape-shiftings and disguises, the image of neglect, the grey lady ghosting through galleries, the maiden aunt, forgotten spinster, the godmother bestowing blessings or curses, the drowned woman, ministering angel, the mother's friend, the glittering glamorous courtesan, and – throughout – the heroin(e) if you will pardon the unavoidable pun, on a quest to find and rescue the inner self from certain death. (Deed, 2003b)

Relationships between Pain, Trauma, Dissociation and Addiction

This quest to rescue the inner self from death is the essence of the healing journey in the case of psychological infanticide. Using an archetypal approach to understanding trauma, we can see Opium personifying a fragmentation of parts of the traumatised psyche and the quest for restoration of wholeness and engagement with life (Kalsched, 1996, 2013). This particular quest holds serious risk of getting stuck in the suspended animation (living death) of psychotic fantasy, addiction or dissociative trance.

Opium has themes related to pain, trauma, numbing, entrapment, paralysis and death. Considering her as a female aspect of death, her role as Queen of the Underworld includes a relationship with night, sleep and dreams, as well as altered states, dying, and the hidden or unconscious aspects of the psyche. Opium is, therefore, a relevant personification for exploring the infanticidal relationship with the Death Mother archetype.

Opium seems to entrap the mind in seductive layers of soothing fantasy, much like Gaston Bachelard's (1983) Ophelia complex in which there is an infantile regressive desire to return to the womb where one is contained and supported in a watery underworld. My reverie of Opium took me into such an underworld:

Opium takes you into a timeless zone. Layers of experience wash over you and you either go with them,

floating on the surface, or plunge deep into memory,
old losses and griefs, the subterranean creatures of the
depths. (Deed, 2003b)

I discuss Bachelard's Ophelia complex, and its relevance to psychological infanticide in more depth in Chapter Eleven.

Thomas de Quincey's *Confessions of an English Opium Eater* (1821/1971) described opium as a panacea for physical pain (toothache; gastralgia) and the psychic pain of starvation, grief, exile, abandonment and homelessness. Both de Quincey and Samuel Taylor Coleridge (Holmes, 1989, 1999) – two of the most famous laudanum addicts of their time – were caught up in opium's initial tendency to produce wonderful visions and dreams. Yet, both de Quincey and Coleridge found their opium-enhanced delights were not able to be fully realised. Opium seems to block the capacity to manifest ideas in the real world, to bring them to birth and nourish them to fruition. It is as if in the opium cocoon, the caterpillar dreams so deeply that it forgets to complete its transformation and leave the cocoon, remaining in the suspended animation of living death. This idea of suspended animation, paralysis in a living death, is a pronounced Opium theme, which correlates with the experience of dissociation. The caterpillar turning to mush inside its chrysalis before reconstituting as butterfly is a powerful image of transformation. It is also a perilous state of non-being in which one may not make it through. One may stay suspended in the confused or vegetative state of decomposition or disintegrate entirely.

Retreat into soothing fantasy is the child's dissociative protection from abuse. Often the psyche produces an imaginal figure such as a wise feminine spirit or fairy that explains how they are putting the original self to sleep to protect her from further pain. This creates an every-day-life self who continues with life while the true self is buried in a trance like Sleeping Beauty. Whilst protecting the original self from further violation, this trance also arrests development (Fischer, 2017; Kalsched, 1996). My opium reveries revealed the themes of fantasy and arrested life that result from infanticidal trauma. Opium personifies dissociation – the survival of overwhelming trauma by burying the somnambulant, hypnotised and amnesiac selves in an encapsulated underground world. In the words of St Colette, founder of an enclosed order of nuns: "You have holy enclosure to hold onto, enclosure in which you can live for forty years either more or less, and in which you will die. You are, therefore, already in your sepulchre of stone, that is your vowed enclosure" (original date unknown, cited in Boston Catholic Journal, 2019). In response, I wrote in my journal:

> *Living a life within a sepulchre of stone, of isolation, of enclosure within the walls of the self. A holy person lives in a cell, as does a prisoner, as does a honeybee. A place of enclosure which is the stone sepulchre of a dark cold mind, building up its own walls to keep out the light. And I think of other architectural concepts – the cornerstone where a life was sacrificed for a building, beings walled up, sometimes to live, sometimes to starve, like some house spirit.* (Deed, journal, 2000)

Alethea Hayter (1968), in her work, *Opium and the Romantic Imagination*, analysed the creativity of opium-addicted Romantic writers and artists, concluding, as did de Quincey, that opium accentuates what is already present in the psyche. Both Coleridge and de Quincey were abandoned children, and their trauma is eloquently rendered in the heightened sensibilities so characteristic of the Romantic perspective. De Quincey's (1821/1971) opium reveries and nightmares were haunted by griefs, images of lost orphans and in particular, Ann of Oxford St – a forlorn child prostitute whom he felt close to, and who disappeared one night. He anguished obsessively over what might have happened to her. These images and his anguished responses are like the flashbacks of post-traumatic stress disorder, in which unintegrated aspects of trauma continue to haunt the sufferer. This poignant image of the lost and doomed child, never fully to bloom, is also an aspect of opium.

Eventually opium's soothing visions turn into tormented haunting, endless images of desperate striving without completion, images of devastating loss and bewilderment as the trauma underlying the seductive fantasies can no longer be denied. Heroin-dependent writer, Anna Kavan, took this psychic devastation to new depths in her autobiographical novels, revealing the tormented conceptual prisons and mental illness that are the consequences of cumulative childhood trauma self-medicated by addiction. Kavan died in her sixties of an (apparently intentional) heroin overdose, having been an addict for all her adult life. Her science-fiction novel, *Ice,* depicts a bleak and terrifying vision of psychic coldness, exile and rejection, in which the protagonist seeks warmth and connection from an unattainable figure, without which she will not live. (Kavan, 1967/1986). The traumatised child self's biography of her desperation to form an attachment to a Death Mother is heart-breakingly apparent. Kavan worked through this theme in her writing throughout her life.

Addicts including Coleridge, de Quincey and Kavan all described nightmares and visions of Escher-like or Piranesian prisons, torturous scenes of unreachable or unattainable endpoints or vanishing perspectives. Whether endless flights of stairs, changes of room or echoing corridors, they all hold a quality of haunted and inconsolable despair similar to my haunted obsession with finding the elusive lost mother:

The crypt lay beneath the disused chapel where the odours of death and incense crept up the walls. I sat on the step that led into the dark vault, lit by her candle, and watched as she sat amidst the remains of her relatives, laid out on their tombs in various states of decay. I wondered why she should choose to sit here amongst the dead instead of amongst her children, why she should see them so much more clearly than ourselves and so much enjoy their company. I wished myself dead as she clasped their bony hands, murmuring consolations, smoothing the ancient brocades with her fingers and stroking the dusty gems. (Deed, 1995, p. 23)

Opium, like the archetypal image of the seductive predator of the psyche (Estes, 1992) or the Demon Lover (Leonard, 2001a), seduces her victims with the promise of warmth, peace, refuge and greatness. In this she is the fantasy of the Ideal Mother:

Although most of my memories of her concern her moving away from me, apparently unaware of my presence as I struggled to make her notice me, there were times when I have an image of her that is beautiful and still. Mother sat at the open window on moonlit nights, her eyes open but with a far-away look, her face tilted and young again. (Deed, 1995, p. 25)

She is a false refuge whose gift is actually a petrification of spirit, body, outer life. Opium is an idealised mother who cannot nurture, who offers false love without genuine care. As her soothing dose wears off, or the body becomes tolerant over time, a torturous agitation and heightened sensibility of the nervous system occurs, necessitating an increase in the dose. The abandoned infant revisits the terror of annihilation. In this aspect, the Queen of the Underworld and the fantasy mother merge into Death Mother, whose only care is the solace of being dead.

By suppressing pain, rather than accepting and inviting its expression, we shut it down, kill it off and something dies inside us. We become numb to our true embodied selves and begin living an underground life. Opium is a metaphor for the underground life that occurs when the overt message is that you are not allowed to exist.

Opium is also the metaphoric mechanism by which denial of pain and trauma works. Pain that we deny or ignore eventually corrupts the bodies we have learned to ignore – our biography becomes our biology (Mate, 2003). Clear correlations are now being made between developmental trauma and chronic illness, in particular auto-immune disease (Brenner, 2001, 2014; Mate, 2003; Van de Kolk, 2014). Brenner (2001, 2014), for example, referred to the significant level of autoimmune disease in patients with childhood trauma, speculating on the possibility of a traumatically induced genetic susceptibility to autoimmune disease. When we banish trauma to the underworld, its pain continues unabated and grows secretly in the dark until we are forced to experience it through the eruption of dis-ease, via illness or overwhelming emotions:

> *Opium best expressed the signature of my inner state at that time and place. And I used that metaphor of opium as a stepping stone and compass, an orientation point. The body does not lie. One is revealed through one's person, the body, how the bones, muscles, contours and lines weft and warp to express the self in all its truths and deceits. And here I am expressing an inner journey, revealing the signature of a fluid emotional tide, telling the truths that are unique to my self, my version, my body through the voice of opium.* (Deed, journal, 2000)

Separation of the infant from the mother at birth has been identified as a situation of cumulative traumatic stress that frequently becomes a post-traumatic stress syndrome in adopted children whose trauma was not acknowledged (Lifton, 1994; Verrier, 1993, 2003). It is now established that misattunement between mothers and infants leads to developmental trauma that includes unstable sense of self, self-damaging impulsivity and addictions, intense inappropriate anger and recurrent suicidality (Grille, 2005; van de Kolk, 2014; Yellin & White, 2012). The devastating loss of the original mother is experienced as psychic death (Verrier, 1993; Winnicott, 1965). Yellin and White (2012) claimed that such "shattered states characterise the human response to unmanageable helplessness and terror when facing the possibility of psychic or physical annihilation" (p. xiv). We can see from this how infant abandonment leads to inevitable fragmentation as the infant faces "a situation of fear without solution" (Yellin and White, p. xiv). The shadowy body memory of this threatened oblivion is so terrifying that many adoptees rely on drugs, alcohol, food or other compulsive behaviours to fill themselves up and "hide out from grief and pain" (Lifton, 1994, p. 96; Mate, 2010).

Verrier (1993) made an interesting comment that "[separated] babies have been administered phenobarbital [in the hospital] in order to quiet the anguish and rage as they cry for their missing mothers" (p. 32). A ghastly echo of the drugging of farmed babies with laudanum.

In an article on brain circuitries and trauma, Hopper (2015) discussed the key brain circuitries of fear, seeking satisfaction, and embodiment. He described the satisfaction circuitry as "the opioid brain chemicals and receptors involved in feelings of satisfaction, contentment and connection with others" (p. 189). Our opioid circuitry is engaged during feelings of pleasure, contentment and love. He stated: "Such experiences, of course, are minimal or missing in the lives of many traumatised people" (Hopper, p. 189). This explains the link between trauma and potential for addiction as our seeking-brain circuitry and satisfaction (opioid) circuitry seek external means of experiencing states of content and bliss, or relief from constant anxiety and distress. Hopper linked satisfaction experiences with embodiment, in the sense that our bodily experiences can either reinforce addictions (avoidance of pain or negative body experience) or relieve addictions (pleasurable sense of embodiment relieves the need to find this externally).

Addiction to experiences of bliss, or avoidance of distress, might not always refer to physical substances. Whilst many traumatised people self-medicate with drugs or alcohol, others achieve similar temporary relief through self-harm (inflicting pain can release opioids, as in the example of the endorphin 'high' athletes experience after pushing their bodies hard) or through habitual dissociation and altered states.

Remaining in thrall to the seduction of fantasy is the psychological prison of the victim. The psychological task is to be freed from the spell of past trauma, and re-engaged in the enchantment of everyday life (Kalsched, 1993). As noted earlier, the pleasure of addictive highs that release natural opioids mimics the feelings that occur in the secure attachment of relationship with a warm and nurturing mother. Addicts may be considered as trying to soothe and comfort themselves in a bleak internal world where no comfort was offered or able to be received.

Another addictive tendency noted in adopted children is compulsive stealing (Lifton, 1994; Verrier, 1993). Winnicott stated: "The child who steals an object is not looking for the object stolen but seeks the mother over whom he or she has rights" (as cited in Lifton, 1994, p. 93). Adopted children may have the fantasy, actually a reality, of being the stolen child, who has been displaced from their rightful position and family (Frankiel, 1985). I have noticed a parallel between stealing and collecting in the rescue fantasies of adopted clients, and in wishes to possess and restore objects to their 'rightful' homes. The collecting of objects can be identified with childhood longing and the need of the traumatised infant self to be rescued or restored (Farrell, 2011; Stewart, 1993). During my breakdown, I began to collect images of the Madonna. I expressed the feeling of compulsive desire and the longing to be reflected by the other in my journal:

It seems Donna's work haunts me. In a café in Thames St I'm pierced with the dangerous allure of her icons on the whitewashed wall. I can barely breathe with desire. A particular madonna speaks to me with heavy-lidded sensuality, her cruelty betrayed in her narrow smile. She affects a pious look, but this madonna has thorns if you don't know how to approach her. I know to interpret this language in layers, this looking glass world where nothing is as it appeared on the surface, all the fragmented complexities of a Byzantine mosaic held in such initial simplicity.

For some time I have been collecting madonnas in my mind, a whole repertoire of madonna-ness that is the internal language that helped me interpret myself to myself. Here was an outward expression, a dialogue rather than a soliloquy. (Deed, journal, 2000)

I began to reflect on the way Minnie collected (rescued) unwanted babies after her own daughter and grandchildren died in a suicide-infanticide. The enormity of her loss, and her longing and inability to save her grandchildren and daughter, seems to have become enacted in a repetitive compulsion to rescue babies, even when it was no longer financially or practically viable to do so while also putting her in a difficult position with the police (Hood, 1994).

Chapter Eight
Neglect

It speaks of cold neglect, averted eyes,
That blindly crushed thy soul's fond sacrifice.
Mary Shelley (Holmes, 1985)

For someone with an infanticidal attachment, anything life-giving feels wrong. Neglect is essentially a passive form of suicide. When worthiness of existence has been denied, you do not care enough about your life to meet your needs, and you are dissociated from the body that you have been unable to relate to, or through. This explains why many adopted people do not feel they were physically born and may not feel fully incarnated in life (Lifton, 2009). To survive psychological infanticide, they have to dissociate from their bodies and feelings from, or before, birth. Many adopted people dissociate from their emotional pain and neglect their health and wellbeing in passive suicidal negligence because they (consciously or unconsciously) do not want to prolong their profound distress.

The person with an infanticidal attachment has been dehumanised and learns to dehumanise themselves, to treat themselves as a machine rather than as a being with both body and Soul life. Or, as Estes (1992) put it, they are instinct-injured and no longer know how to nourish or protect life.

Suicide by neglect can occur in various ways – through behaviours that damage or deny the body, or contribute to serious health conditions, and by avoiding medical care of conditions requiring treatment. Passive suicide by neglect is one of the legacies of the Death Mother archetype. The Death Mother archetype is also present in baby farmers who were able to neglect and otherwise harm the babies in their care.

Baby Farmers and Intentional Neglect

In describing the neglect and starvation of babies by some baby farmers, I refer to the deliberate and systemic abuse and neglect of babies whose situations presented a financial incentive to dispose of them. These unfortunates were drugged with laudanum and warehoused in dark unventilated rooms, unclothed, unattended and unfed, slowly dying from starvation and the illnesses and effects of squalor and neglect (Cossins, 2014; Rattle & Vale, 2011; Rose, 1986).

Such babies, if seen in public (rare) or in a coroner's inquest at their death, might be labelled as sickly babies, succumbing to marasmus or 'failure to thrive' as doctors and coroners either were unable to differentiate between intentional starvation and wasting due to illness, or did not care to stir up trouble. Rose (1986) tracked the overwhelming lack of interest in care and protection of infant lives in both politics and the medical establishment, despite devastating statistics provided by some concerned advocates for policy on infant life protection.

Rattle and Vale (2011) vividly described what was actually meant by the term marasmus:

> ...the cause of death is recorded, as so often in the past, as marasmus – "wasting away". Prior to her death little Emma Clara would have weighed less than 80% of what was considered normal for her age. Her skin would have fallen in folds over wasted and withered muscles; she would have been fretful, irritable and voraciously hungry.

Dr Deane was forced to state that death was due to natural causes; being unable to prove that the child was denied nourishment. (p. 151)

Some children were kept alive in a pitiful state of starvation and drugged for a longer period of time. An example is Polly Dyer's 'adopted' child, Harold. Polly was Amelia Dyer's younger daughter. She was brought up surrounded by her mother's severely neglected baby-farmed infants who constantly died or disappeared. Having learned from her mother the art of appearing solicitous towards children whilst starving, drugging and ignoring their distress, Polly appeared the tender, caring mother, desperately doing what she could for her sickly child whilst depriving him of nourishment.

Harold is a sad example of infants being exploited as dehumanised objects, which is a hallmark of the infanticidal and abandoning modes of child-rearing discussed in Chapter Three. Harold was an extension of Polly – a means to get her own needs met and to manipulate and exploit others for her own ends – rather than a human being in his own right. Polly was also 'caring' for her child in the only way she knew, as taught to her by her infanticidal mother in childhood (Rattle & Vale, 2011).

The plight of such children is starkly outlined by Rattle and Vale (2011) on the outcome for baby Harold after Polly's arrest for baby farming:

He was already seriously ill and on 11 July, aged just two years, he died of a condition known as *stomatitis*, or *cancrum oris*. The gums and linings of his cheeks would have been severely inflamed and ulcerated, the infection spreading until his lips and cheeks were slowly eaten away by the gangrenous disease. The most common cause of *cancrum oris* is severe malnutrition and very low levels of hygiene. Polly, it seems, had perfected the art of slow starvation and neglect. (p. 221)

Harold's brief life demonstrates the powerful repetition of experiences occurring so early in life that they are normalised and unquestioned. Polly was trapped in an infanticidal trauma-world she could not see outside of and went on to repeat what she had experienced. This link between childhood abuse and adult perpetration of violence that mirrors the child's experience has been well argued by Miller (1983 in her psychohistories of the childhoods of dictators.

Polly considered Harold to be her own adopted child and was attached to him in a different way than she was to the other farmed babies who were merely fodder for income. Children like Polly are victims of their parents' infanticidal urges disguised as care. In this situation, care and abuse become dangerously entwined in the mind of the child (Kahr, 2007a, 2007b, 2012; Sinason, 2013; Yellin & Epstein, 2013; Yellin & White, 2012). Polly seemed to have had no concept of an infant needing food and care for survival.

It was not only 'paid-up' children who were neglected. Sometimes children were neglected and starved simply to increase the financial gain from the regular payments made by those parents who intended to eventually collect their children – or who at least expected that their children were being maintained long term. Such children, shown to their parents when they visited, were passed off as sick and receiving care and medical support (Cossins, 2014; Rattle & Vale, 2011).

Sometimes a substitute child was shown to the mother when her own was too ill to be presentable or had died. I am reminded here of European tales of human children stolen by fairies or goblins, and a changeling child left in its place. Adopted children are also substitute children. As Lifton (2009) pointed out, they are replacements for the children who died or who could not be conceived by the adoptive parents. Being a replacement child is an aetiology of psychological infanticide and infanticidal attachment (Kahr, 2007a, 2012).

Compared to obviously murderous baby farmers, such as Amelia and Polly Dyer, or the Makin family in Australia, Minnie

Dean did not systematically dehumanise and despatch countless babies for profit. There is no evidence of neglect, starvation or systemic drugging of the children in her care. Court records described the children uplifted from the house after her arrest as well clothed, well fed and of good spirits. However, Hood (1994) described one baby that Minnie picked up and handed on who was hungry, wet and distressed. It appears Minnie had not fed or changed her in all the time travelling with the infant. This seems to have been an isolated incident, which Hood suggested was probably due to stressful circumstances rather than intentional neglect, as Minnie was travelling with a new baby and was not paid for another, so she didn't have enough money for accomodation for her and the child. She ended up desperately handing on the baby to another farmer and sleeping in a garden in wet weather, after having been turned away by acquaintances who did not approve of her vocation.

I was struck with how babies were frequently handed over to multiple baby farmers like parcels, as if they were without any human need for attachment (Cannon, 1994; Cossins, 2014; Hood, 1994; Rattigan, 2012; Rattle & Vale, 2011). I noticed parallels in the assumptions of early closed stranger adoption theory that babies would automatically attach to an adoptive mother without recognising any difference or noticing the original mother had gone (Lifton, 1994; Verrier, 1993).

The other incidence of neglect in Minnie's story is the death of baby Eva Hornsby, who, the coroner said, had the emptiest intestines he had ever seen (cited in Hood, 1994). The baby had not been fed for some time before it even got to Minnie. Minnie was outraged at the condition of the child, and the bottle of icy cold milk handed over with her (Hood, 1994). This scenario provides a glimpse of the broader shadow of the neglect of unwanted infants. The baby's own grandmother had not fed her, despite what must have been terrible anguish for the infant. The infanticidal mode of child-rearing, with its dehumanising of infant life, was apparently still in practice in the average household (Hood, 1994).

Institutional Neglect

A further dimension of neglect of unwanted babies is the evidence from the foundling hospitals that took in abandoned babies from the seventeenth century onward. These, and workhouses, were alternatives to baby farming for those mothers who believed in the charitable intentions of such institutions, which were founded to prevent infants being abandoned in the streets or murdered (Rose, 1986; Styles, 2010). However, so many babies were left with foundling hospitals that some initiated a lottery system. Mothers were given a numbered ticket and only those with the numbers called on the day were permitted to leave their children at the hospital (Styles, 2010).

The belief that children would be better cared for in a foundling hospital than with a baby farmer was not accurate. The hospitals were overcrowded; resources and food were scarce. The staff employed there were often workhouse women with no nursing skills, dealing with their own impoverished degradation and brutalisation. The food was a watered-down gruel, inappropriate for babies. Many children died from malnutrition or the overcrowded conditions. Children who were not breastfed had a tremendously high death rate in this era (Rose, 1986; Stone, 1977). Emma Donohue (2014), in her novel *Frog Music*, which contains a baby-farming subplot, described it succinctly:

> Baby farms were a paradoxical institution. You could describe their function as infanticide by neglect or as child care, without which many parents (working, single and unsupported, poor), could not have managed to keep custody of their children at all. (And the death rates in municipal institutions such as foundling hospitals were so astonishingly high, you could call them de facto infanticidal too). (p. 380)

It is clear, historically, that if you were a child born to parents who did not want you, or were unable to care for you, your prospects were dire. If you were lucky, you were farmed out to a baby farmer who looked after you as best she could in order to survive herself. This might mean, at best, overcrowding, lack of attachment, poor food and conditions. Or you might be cared for by another member of your family, and stigmatised as the carrier of the family shame. Or you might take your chances in the foundling hospital – facing disease, crowding, and malnutrition – or with a more murderously inclined baby farmer who might terminate your life abruptly or slowly at the whim of their preferred method.

Psychological Neglect and the Adoption Solution

In contrast, adoption laws from the late 1800s sought to address the protection and care of children without families who could care for them, and the situation looked good compared to the practices of baby farmers (Hood, 1994; Rose, 1986). I suggest that it is from this moment in history that literal infanticidal practices were transformed by social and legal opinion into experiences of psychological infanticide. The murder or abuse of infants was no longer acceptable, but unwanted infants continued to be psychologically destroyed in the many ways I have referred to throughout this inquiry.

Unfortunately, evidence exists to show how closely literal infanticide continued to underpin ideas about adoption and illegitimacy. In 2017, a mass infant and child grave was discovered in Tuam, in a former Catholic care home for unmarried pregnant women operating between 1925 and 1961 (Barbash, 2017; Grierson, 2017). Local historian, Catherine Corless, discovered that 700-800 infants and toddlers died in the home and were buried in unmarked graves there. The high infant mortality rate at the home was said to be due to malnutrition, neglect, and gastroenteritis (25% of children died in the Tuam home compared to 7% of the general population, significantly similar to, though not as high as, the appalling death rates in foundling hospitals). Corless revealed that eighteen of the death certificates recorded death by starvation (O'Doud, 2017).

Dr Ella Webb is quoted as saying: "A great many people are always asking what is the good of keeping these children alive? I quite agree it would be a great deal kinder to strangle these children at birth than put them out to nurse" (1924, as cited in O'Doud, 2017). This statement reveals socially accepted infanticidal attitudes toward helpless and faultless children. As I describe further in Part Three, such attitudes have a psychologically murderous affect. Neglect, starvation, and the diseases that come with them were part of the baby farmer's trade. Whether deliberately, or due to poor conditions somewhat like the original foundling homes, unmothered babies in the Tuam mother-and-baby home died to protect secrets.

What do I mean by psychological neglect? Neglect refers to the deprivation of vital nourishment or care. In psychological terms it refers to a lack of being responded to in ways that foster a sense of existence and being of value. This lack of attunement is referred to as developmental trauma – the trauma that occurs, not when children are treated abusively or physically neglected, but when their parents fail to provide the attunement needed for psychological growth (van de Kolk, 2014). This has tremendous consequences throughout life in terms of physical and mental health, ability to relate to others, and ability to function well in life. Of course, psychological neglect may co-exist with actual neglect.

Grieving infants who have been separated from their mothers may fail to thrive due to this developmental trauma beginning so early in life (Bowlby, 1960, 1980). In a tremendous irony, it was in part John Bowlby's research on the terrible impact of maternal deprivation that led to a shift in the 1940s from institutionalising unwanted infants to a focus on adoption as in the best interests of the child (Else, 1991). Psychological theory of the time considered that an infant would attach well to any mother, ignoring the irreplaceable bond between biological mother and child (Verrier,

1993). To be deprived of what I term the 'right' mother, in the sense of the biological mother that 'fits' at the beginning of life when this bond is needed for survival, is a serious setback and a failure of the attunement that is vitally nourishing for the child. There is a psychological impact from having the 'wrong' (non-biological) mother.

Simpson (2014) discussed the consequences of being the wrong child, through an exploration of the experience for the child when the mother projects onto them that they are somehow wrong, not the ideal child she imagined. He stated that the child introjects this idea of being the wrong child and experiences a feeling of guilt for "going on living when you know your birth was undesired and you should have remained unborn" (McDougall,1992, p. 110, as cited in Simpson, 2014.

Simpson's (2014) clinical group suffered psychological experiences of being wrong, whereas the adopted person actually *is* the 'wrong' child. There may be a greater impact when this psychological trauma is also an actual traumatic reality (Verrier, 1993). Simpson went on to refer to the "wrong mother-child couple" (p. 187). This is the case with the adoptive-mother/adopted-child couple. I suggest here that the adopted child experiences the adoptive mother as the 'wrong mother', who is protested against and rejected whilst also needed for survival. The 'wrong mother', who cannot attune as precisely as the biological mother, reflects the experience for the child of being the wrong child, with the accompanying guilt of being unwanted and alive. The disconnection of the baby from its original matrix, its ground of being, is experienced as a lack of the vital input required for nourishment and growth. To experience being the 'wrong' child deprives the child of feeling allowed 'to be' in life.

The traumatised child survives by disconnecting from the body and needs help to reconnect somatically (Levine, 2010; van de Kolk, 2014). The denied aspects of psychological neglect and starvation are emotional hunger, bodily needs, longing and desperation. Many adopted people describe a terrifying black hole or cavern of emptiness inside them that they seem unable to fill.

Nothing pacifies this longing and emptiness, and one is compelled to find ever more desperate means to escape its ravaging. Addictive patterns arise in response to these hungers and longings that have been so invalidated by others and denied by the self (Brodzinsky, 1990; Lifton, 1994; Verrier, 2003; Wierzbicki, 1993).

Etymologically, the words 'mother', 'matter' and 'matrix' all come from the same Latin root, revealing a deep connection between mother, body, and the physicality and structure of embodied life as our nurturing and life-supporting ground of being. When this is disrupted it is difficult to feel incarnated into the realm of physical life (Estes, 1992, 1997). Disembodied people tend to overwork the body, denying its needs. Mind and will command the body rather than listening to, and collaborating with, the body. In this way, psychological neglect dehumanises the self, just as starving, drugged babies were seen by baby farmers as dehumanised objects, or 'its' – without needs or feelings. The result of this psychological starvation and neglect is self-punishment and breakdown of the body, which is forced beyond endurance and required to survive without what it needs.

Deprivation is a key word in the context of neglect. When deprived of something vital, we cannot thrive. This lack of nourishment, attunement, welcome, and right of existence is indicative of the Death Mother archetype, which I have discussed throughout this inquiry. Estes (1992) described a condition she called *hambre del alma* – starvation of the Soul. She described women suffering Soul starvation as so hungry they will take whatever is offered; even "poison on a stick" (Estes, p. 215). In vivid metaphors she described how the desperation of Soul starvation leads to wrong choices, addictions, abusive relationships, mind-numbing activities, and a lack of the good boundaries that engender self-preservation. The starved Soul is disconnected from her instincts and can no longer discern what is nourishing and what is poison. She does not know how to nourish or protect herself (Estes, 1992). Estes described this injury to instinct as a process of normalising the abnormal, which then becomes a cover-up of compliance and denial over the psychic anguish within. As we saw with the normalising of infanticide in Polly Dyer's life, adoption is also a process that tends to normalise the abnormal, denying the trauma for the infant separated from the mother; and therefore, misunderstanding and compounding the attachment traumas that occur in adopted families.

Having lived with trauma since birth, the adopted child experiences a lack of appetite for life and a difficulty connecting with desires. Not having been desired (wanted) makes desire problematic. Simultaneously, the adopted child may also experience an insatiable hunger to fill an unnameable emptiness, coupled with no means of satisfying their need for nurturance. This state is uncannily similar to nineteenth-century poet, Christina Rosetti's warning that people who eat goblin fruit develop an insatiable yearning for otherworldly food whilst starving because they are unable to take nourishment from mortal food. Rossetti (1924) explored the dangers of goblins to young maidens in her popular poem "Goblin Market". The poem focuses on the dangers of seduction (the purchase of goblin fruits that destroy life). It offers a warning to young girls not to succumb to seduction for their lives will be destroyed. One can imagine that the fruit of a goblin seduction might well be an unwanted goblin child.

Through the character, Changeling, in my second novel (Deed, 1995), I explored the theme of a goblin child who cannot be loved or accepted because they are the wrong child. This goblin child is with the 'wrong' mother and fails to thrive for lack of goblin food. 'Wrong' here indicates non-biological, which the child instinctively knows and grieves, rather than 'not-good-enough' which refers to the quality of the relationship between caregiver and child (Winnicott, 1965).

Evidently the nineteenth-century imagination was well versed in the idea of the goblin cuckoo in the nest. In terms of farmed babies, a healthy baby dwindling rapidly into an emaciated and thrush-infested baby may easily have appeared as if a goblin child had replaced the original.

Ascetism, Anorexia, and the Anchorite as Responses to Psychological Neglect

In my own experience of the effects and enactments of psychological neglect, in the early years after my breakdown I was unable to grasp hold of, or feel attached to, life. I identified with those ascetic saints and mystics who affirmed a path of denial of the body and an aversion to desires, appetites and attachments. I did not feel part of the world and withdrew, like Rapunzel in her tower, into the safe space of my mind. Feeling entombed in a kind of living death, I began to engage with images of the archetypal Anchorite (a live being, often a holy person, walled up in a cell in medieval times). I felt I was living the nun-like vows of psychological entombment and death to the world. Anchorites, along with nineteenth-century Gothic stories of hauntings by imprisoned beings who starved to death, gave me the words and myths for the parts of myself that had been shut up and left to die. This banishment to a slow isolated death is the essence of neglect.

There are strong links between ascetic mysticism and anorexia nervosa, particularly in medieval Christian female saints. For example, Bell's (1985) psychoanalytically informed discourse explored what is known of the family dynamics of those female Italian Christian saints who would be diagnosed with anorexia nervosa today. Many of them seemed to embody (or disembody) the restricted and powerless roles of women in medieval society, as well as the mother's tremendous power over her children and in the home. It was not uncommon, as in the case of St Catherine of Siena, for saints to die from starvation, exhaustion, and neglect of themselves, whilst offering vast energy for helping others. Estes (1992) described this phenomenon as the starved Soul who compulsively helps others and is incapable of nourishing herself. Denial of the feminine body, whilst embodying female values of nurturance, love and care to others, deprives vital nourishment for sustained life whilst offering a false experience of power (over the needs and perceived weaknesses of self).

It is worthy of note that St Catherine was the survivor of twins. Her sister, sent out to a wet nurse, died. Catherine probably experienced survivor guilt for the nurturance she received from the 'right' mother, which her sister was deprived of (Bell, 1985). This proximity to infant death, and the seeming randomness over who survives and who dies, concurs with currently known aetiologies of psychological infanticide (Kahr, 2007a, 2012).

The person with anorexia nervosa believes that the only power they have is the power of refusal and negation. The adopted child who denies life through negation of the needs of the body feels hated and rejected for their very existence and strives to take up as little room as possible, to exist as precariously as possible. The ultimate goal is death where they will become the perfect child they could not be in life. Again, we witness the dark presence of the Death Mother archetype.

I learned to survive my psychological pain through life-denying practices – denying food, warmth, sleep, pain – and resisting attachments with others. I strove to ascend beyond the body. I became afraid of food for its life-giving qualities and its relationship with growth, fecundity and fertility. After all, I was the result of appetites acted upon rather than denied. I was the goblin fruit of desires met. Not having appetite protected me from facing my own desires and fertility, my own potential to be sexually active, to be a mother, to conceive and grow a child. I wrote about my fears of fertility and desire in a poem based on Botticelli's painting, *Primavera*, which is an allegory of the evocation of Spring through the impregnation and fecundity of Flora by the west wind Zephyr:

Primavera: Variations on a theme *(excerpts).*

1.

...

The mother gathers herself dark and silent and perpetual.
The fruit are imaginary, they are not hers.

185

...

Seeing neither above nor below
I have sought to be intellectually virgin.
Beneath the blue, my legs
Are white and lovely and cold.
They do not touch the ground.
Flowers spring instantly under my feet.
The sky resplendent.
All this fertility astounds me. I am afraid of it.
I will not eat.

From certain angles I can see through my body.
I think I may be somebody else.
Your landscapes, your vineyards, your valleys.
Into the sweet arms of that quiet mother
Rocking me out on a west wind.

2.
...

I am sincere and uncorrupted.
I practice amnesia.
The clouds go gracefully overhead.
I am stitching the sun back in under my skin.
I am so pure it hurts.

...This man is eloquent. He matches me quote for quote.
Somewhere he has dropped his wings admitting the limits
of reason.
I remain virtuous and expelled.

3.
...The flowers multiply.

I have gone in and come out a stranger.
I return somebody else.

The moon shouts from my throat. She will not be quiet.
This is another story.

My halo is under me...
The elements seem to be sent by you.
By now, you will be sleeping.
And I?
I am deciduous, and already, it is only spring.
(Deed, 1994b)

We can explore this poem through the lens of the Greek Demeter-Persephone myth. The myth tells us that archetypally the mother and daughter are one, each contained within the other, therefore Demeter mourning her daughter is also a mourning of this lost innocent lightness (and paradoxical depth) within herself (Kerenyi, 1967). The separation of mother and daughter (internally as well as externally) causes depths of grief and depression so intense that life and growth may cease and the child may be forced to live in underworld darkness, unnourished and, therefore, psychologically neglected (Estes, 1992). This myth then reveals to us the depth and necessity of the mother-child bond, and the trauma to both mother and child when it is severed. Both are frozen in their development for some time. Persephone refuses to eat in the underworld, and Demeter refuses to let things grow on the earth. Persephone would be lost in eternal darkness if she did not keep connection with her earthy mother, Demeter.

Woodman (1980, 1982, 1985), described the sterility of the virginal state as that of remaining untouched by life. Transformation from this state of paralysis comes about through the metaphoric deflowering of the virginal – a ravishing by life – as in the myth of Hades's abduction of Persephone. Her innocence is lost as she begins to know and experience life and death, to let them in and let herself be transformed by them, and thus she matures into a real fertile (creative) life. Persephone returns from the underworld each year, bringing the new life of Spring (Woodman, 1985).

The united nature of Demeter-Persephone reflects the need to surrender into the underworld forces that open us into knowledge of the invisible world, the essences of things. This myth concerns the connection between the sacred and mundane, between surface and depth. Life must include a depth perspective of death within life. If we are not fully alive, if we are holding ourselves virginally closed to the depths of life, then the underworld forces of the unconscious rise up and force us to surrender (Berry, 1982).

Psychologically deprived children lose connection with their essence. Their recovery involves journeying to the underworld to reconnect with essence in themselves and in all things (Berry, 1982; Estes, 1992; Woodman, 1982, 1985). They need support to develop and make real their internal mother (Estes, 1997). Adopted children carry a pervasive trauma of shame about their existence. They may try to control themselves and their environment to cope with overwhelming fear of a life they feel they are not allowed to be part of. They may try to be perfect, to be allowed to maintain the little life and space they have allowed themselves. Many live precariously in the surface realm of adapted life, and it takes a great deal (a ravishing by Hades; a breakdown) to become acquainted with the depths and essences of self and life.

Berry (1982) described the Demeter depression that occurs after the loss of Persephone. Demeter withdraws from any sense of life and neglects herself fully, causing barrenness within herself and throughout the environment. Demeter can be considered here as the archetypal expression of the internal mother whose role is to help us nourish, cherish, comfort and protect ourselves. In the darkest depth of my breakdown, I became incapable of taking care of my basic needs. I neglected to shower, to eat, to wash dishes or clean. I no longer cared about life and was too incapacitated to try. From the inside, it all made a certain kind of sense; I had let go of the ropes that held me in life, and in any sense of humanness. I was both Persephone who had surrendered to dark forces beyond my control, and Demeter mourning and turning away from any connection to life.

During that time, when I visited the park, the homeless 'derros' who lived there accepted me, offering to share their bottles of alcohol. Facing the prospect of imminent homelessness, I imagined a home with them under the oak trees, a place I could be acceptable. Then a woman was murdered in one of the groves I used to frequent. I might not have wanted to live, but I did not wish to be murdered. This was one of those moments where reality intersected with my internal world: a rare glimpse of self-preservation. This suggests something of the fragile balance between control and helplessness in the adopted self.

After my recovery I continued a life of ascetic withdrawal. I was no longer physically anorexic, but I was still writing about psychological starvation:

a madonna's wrist bones are

shark fins
what you see on the surface
alerts you to the terrors beneath

marble triangles
blades
sharp enough to cut

lost words
I am drowning in

tender shadows
I sleep beneath on sultry afternoons

a madonna's wrist bones

refuse to let gravity
sink its teeth into them

are free from rational thought
(Deed, 2003a)

Anorexia nervosa and compulsive eating are symptoms of the Demeter-Persephone myth (Berry, 1982; Woodman 1982, 1985), which suggests they are symptoms of a psychological infanticide through separation from the external/internal mother. As aspects of the Great Mother goddess, both Demeter and Persephone tip into the Shadow of the Death Mother archetype when they are overwhelmed by the trauma of loss, and confronted with depths of life before they are psychologically mature enough to integrate them. As Berry (1982) has indicated, the healing comes from deepening, expanding and enriching the symptom. I did this by engaging in imaginal dialogues with Persephone, St Catherine, Hildegaard von Bingen, and Charlotte Brontë. They understood about starvation and neglect of the self, and together they helped me to understand the complicated depths of longing to be in life, and of feeling denied. Through them, I was gradually able to loosen the grip of invalidation and its consequent paralysis, and re-engage with life, step by painful step – though not without terror.

Looking back, I see now two aspects to the Anchorite. Those who were imprisoned and left to die represent the hidden plight of those whose requirements for life were ignored, and the crushing loss of hope and lack of right to survive. On the other hand, Hildegaard von Bingen was not walled up to die, but to live a potent life of meaning. In dialogues with Hildegaard, a saint of extraordinary creative vision, I explored how to survive beyond the entombment of psychological neglect by awakening creativity and imagination.

PART THREE

PSYCHOLOGICAL INFANTICIDE: A PERSONAL AND PROFESSIONAL SYNTHESIS

Chapter Nine
Eclipse: The Alchemy
of the Non-existent Self

Truly it is in the darkness that one finds the light,
so when we are in sorrow, then this light is
nearest of all to us.
Meister Eckhart (Smith, 1987)

This chapter describes my personal experience of psychological infanticide through closed stranger adoption using the metaphor of alchemy. I describe my sense of being a ghost self and amplify this image with a discussion of the alchemical black sun and the mystical *via negativa*. I unfold the mysterious nature of this experience as it revealed itself through my creative writing. Finally, I discuss the psychological effect of the closed stranger adoption process and its relationship with psychological infanticide.

Alchemy metaphorically describes psychological processes in vivid and poeticising ways that enable the richness of image and depth of experience to be brought forward. Alchemical imagery also resonates powerfully with the personal images through which I experienced psychological infanticide, indicating a correlation with universal images and themes recognisable in myth and history. Jungian, archetypal, and imaginal psychologies are steeped in rich alchemical images through which to explore and understand the psyche (Edinger, 1994; Hillman, 2014; Jung,

1953/1968; Romanyshyn, 1997; von Franz, 1996a). Such images and symbols are seen as universalised expressions of the psyche that exist throughout history and cultures.

In this, and the following two chapters, I demonstrate my commitment to burying and un-burying the dead: going down into the darkness and allowing myself to be touched/moved/shaped by what is found there – or by what finds me. For the dead are not inert and do not lie quietly in their beds. I endeavour to give voice to that which wishes to be heard: through dreams, symptoms, and my reflections in my journals and creative writing.

Through the fictions and reveries introduced in these three chapters, I was able to explore parts of my psyche and think more consciously about who and what in me had been killed off, or lived in terror of being killed off:

> *I begin my journey back down into the deep. One must never underestimate the land of the dead where you can lose your self in oblivion without the ability to think or act. Something, some part, must stay conscious and hold the thread, record the experience and return to the world sane and alive. The first time I went down into darkness I lost myself in a breakdown suffering the guilt of being alive, of having survived the death of my birth. Alone in the wilderness you are both lost and given up for dead. Given up for dead. Isn't that what happened to unwanted infants handed over to baby farmers? Isn't that the psychic landscape of adoption? Paradoxically, I anticipate that surviving being given up for dead can provide a powerful revelatory connection with Self, and a connection to a wellspring of deep inner life.* (Deed, journal, 2015)

The Ghost Self

In this section I explore the ghost self I felt myself to be, and how this situation might have come about. I also explore the link between non-existence and the need to biographise the self. Schulz (2005), in discussing the subjects that psychobiographers choose to write about, stated: "Our pursuit of their secrets may be a way of pursuing our own, a working through of conflicts and anxieties" (p. 113). Here I made this an explicit intention – to reveal my own working-through of my infanticidal attachment through identifying with an allegedly murderous mother figure (Minnie Dean) with just enough ambiguity about the truth to enable me to begin to explore and hold the tensions of my own internal conflict about mother and infant. Through autopsychobiography I pursue my own secrets, conflicts and anxieties through a weaving of personal reminiscence and universalised human experience, closely observing the themes and psychological theories of a select piece of my biography (Young, 2008a, 2008b).

Closed stranger adoption was built on dangerous secrets, which prevented adoptees from knowing their origins or their histories. For such a child, there is a serious handicap to engaging in life. "Cut off from blood roots that could ground her in the universe, she feels like a foreigner who needs a guidebook to show her the way that others know naturally" (Lifton, 1994, p. 23). I believe there is a link between these secrets of history and identity, and the need to write. The further I slipped into a sense of non-existence, the more I wrote about my inner life, as if I could write myself into life. The absence of a biography and the need to write felt connected. I recognised a need for stories that would tell 'me' to myself, much as a child is soothed by the evening ritual of bedtime stories.

Growing up knowing I was adopted, the idea of Mother was powerful and strange to me. However, it was not until I experienced my breakdown, aged 20, that I fully felt the impact of the idea of Mother in, and on, my life. In hindsight, I can realise the breakdown was precipitated by a deep loss of a significant relationship, in which we had discussed marriage and the idea of children. He wanted them. I did not. I considered the thought of having them, for the first time imagining in an embodied way what it might be like to be pregnant and to give birth to another life, another human being. The idea terrified me. This can be explained in terms of a pregnancy (the first in particular as a rite of passage from being a daughter to becoming a mother) tending to reactivate wounds from one's own infancy (Pines, 1993). Recognising our conflicting wishes, my partner saved me from myself by ending the relationship. I plunged, feeling alone, abandoned, rejected and unwanted, into the abyss.

In an attempt to save myself from falling apart completely, I began writing a journal, something I still do thirty years later. Writing was the container I found to hold the depths of grief and bewilderment, and to provide continuity for an increasing level of confusion and a sense of the discontinuity of my existence. It was at this moment in my life that I began to understand the way grief can dissolve the anchors that hold life in place. My need to write was an attempt to exist.

In the external world, I continued with daily life, attending law school, meeting friends, writing poetry, moving house. Internally, an increasing disconnection from life was occurring. I began to feel and act as if I was a ghost, not really able to exist unless someone was thinking me into existence. Charlotte Brontë (1853/1993), in her novel, *Villette*, acutely observed these terrors of non-existence, the ghost life of a woman without the right to live and express her true self, and the breakdown that can occur when a tenuous acknowledgment of existence is removed. In the novel, Lucy Snowe lives a buried life; her true passionate self living inwardly, while outwardly she can hardly bear her relations with others in her mundane and restricted life, teaching privileged schoolgirls in a private school. During the school break, when everyone else leaves, Lucy is left rattling alone around the school corridors, forlorn and abandoned, like a ghost. Eventually she breaks down under the pressure of psychic extinction (Gilbert & Gubar, 1979/2000; Showalter, 1978).

As I broke down, I developed an alarming terror of being killed. This terror became focused on the idea of being murdered by

Mother. As I became more terrified of being killed, I paradoxically became more suicidal. I heard the voice of an internal Mother urging me to die.

Although I was not able to articulate it at the time, the central dilemma that led to my hospitalisation was the belief that Mother was murderous, and in a twist of tortured logic, the only way to prevent myself from being murdered was to murder myself first. I refined this thinking as a need to murder the mother in myself (before she got me). This led me to attempt suicide. Lost in my internal terror, I could no longer distinguish between self and other, between internal and external reality.

I remember in the hospital feeling exquisitely vulnerable and afraid – not believing I existed – fearing that if I did allow myself to exist, I would be killed. I both longed for and needed a soothing mother at this time, but could not risk letting a maternal presence near me for fear of being destroyed. It was as if in order to survive I had to die; in order to be mothered I had to be dead. I expressed this later in a bio-fiction I wrote, in which I explored my motives for suicide:

> *The winged angel stands this way over all good children*
> *The only good child is a dead child*
> *So i must be good and dead*
> *Sings Violet*
> (Deed, 2006)

How does this thinking that you do not exist originate? What does it mean to feel you must be dead in order to be mothered? How does it alter the way you live and engage with life? These are some of the critical questions I engaged with, especially through my dialogues with Minnie Dean, which form a significant part of the next chapter. I intuitively felt my position was a result of several factors, including exposure to possible death wishes and/or dissociation in the womb, and the annihilating knowledge of my inability to survive without help after separation from mother at birth. The closed adoption legal process affirmed the nullification of the adopted child's existence through the severing of all connections with their origins, creating a new 'as if' identity, making them legally the child of the adopting parents (Else, 1991; Lifton, 1994). In writing my own bio-fictions (fictionalised biography or autobiographically influenced fictions) I was attempting to right (and write) the legal fiction that had been imposed on my identity. I was attempting to find the authentic truth of myself beneath the lie of my existence.

I felt I had no right to exist, that I was not really here. I had to earn a right to exist, or I must suicide. I was engulfed in a misery, depression and lack of engagement in life that I experienced as an eclipse of myself by a powerful darkness.

Eclipse: The Alchemical Black Sun

As discussed in Chapter Three, infanticidal attachments are evidenced by internal states of deadness or deadliness, terror of being killed, feeling one does not exist, frozen states, and murderousness or suicidality (Kahr, 2007a, 2007b, 2012). For me, psychological infanticide had a sense of eclipse, a darkness imposed from the outside, a sense of being snuffed out, or 'nipped in the bud'. This image is particularly poignant as it speaks to the destruction of an unlived potential: a bud not given the chance to flower. There is a conscious something that nips off the bud. Something dies before it opens out:

My mind loops and sings. My body has gone still. That state of suspended animation, like hibernation where the heartbeat slows and the body processes conserve for the winter, the dark season of dreams. And this is like the state of hypothermia, where a body falls into such cold water, beneath an icefloe say, that instead of drowning life is merely suspended in a state of apparent death, all the life processes preserved like peas by snap freezing, to be rekindled, trawled from the deep. (Deed, 2003b)

This is an experience of profound nothingness, the nothing of non-being, a merging into the great void, an implosion of self into the expanding black hole of the universe.

Eclipse is an image of *sol niger*: the black sun of the absolute absence of everything (Marlon, 2005). I am at the abyss of ceasing to exist and experiencing its inevitability. These states, which mystics and meditators over centuries have yearned for – the attainment of non-self, dissolution of the ego, merging with the oceanic oneness and the great void or Nothingness – can eventually release into a blissful letting go, a surrender to death or the state of non-being. James Hillman (2014) said of *sol niger*: "As negation of negation, the black sun ontologically eradicates the primordial dread of non-being, that unfulfillable abyss – or the abyss becomes the unbounded ground of possibility" (p. 94).

But before this happens, the small infant self instinctively feels terrified of being snuffed out and feels the enormity of the forces that will determine whether it lives or dies. Before mystic illumination can transpire, one must surrender to the darkness. The infant is helpless to act on its own behalf and does not have the resources to successfully negotiate this potential state of enlightenment. Instead, the infant, terrified and helpless, takes refuge in the primitive defence of dissociation and is consigned to living death.

I experienced this state as having crossed over into the underworld, the realm of shades. There was always the sense of living in an interior world, and that the real or living world was the wrong one. I felt stuck on the wrong side. I could not be fully alive, nor could I be fully dead. In this threshold place, there was a deep pull to get back to the side of death, to the relationship with death, which is where I felt more fully myself. Marion Woodman described this underworld as the 'trauma-world' (Sieff, 2017).

Sol niger, the absolute negation, is related to the phase in alchemy known as *nigredo*, in which the matter held in solution in the alchemical bath blackens, decays and disintegrates. It symbolises the destruction of the old form, which is necessary before new life, or new form can arise (Edinger, 1994; Marlon, 2005).

There are many familiar images of the *nigredo*. It is described in the dismemberment journeys of shamanic traditions (Halifax, 1979; Harner, 1980). It is known in mystical and Jungian psychology as the 'dark night of the Soul' (Jung, 1968) in which faith and hope break down. Doubt, despair and mental and physical torments assail the person (Edinger, 1994; Marlon, 2005; Moore, 1992, 2012). Jonah's sojourn in the belly of the whale is a *nigredo* journey, as is Christ's sense of abandonment by God the father during his crucifixion (Moore, 2012). The *nigredo* journey is characterised by suffering. The life force, or the ego, depending on your viewpoint, clings to life and resists surrendering to destruction of the present state. This is evident in the resistance to letting go of familiar habits or forms of self-definition. The ultimate *nigredo* experience is surrendering to our personal death (Edinger, 1994; Marlon, 2005).

Sol niger expresses a particularly engulfing form of *nigredo* in which the annihilating darkness is total. Marlon (2005) cited analyst Giles Clarke, who described his client Robert's 'black hole in the psyche' (p. 36) as like cosmic black holes that draw all matter into themselves. Robert had dreamed of a black hole that swallowed up the world. Afterward, there followed disturbing images that included abortions, miscarriages, stillborn babies, and monster or mutant births (Marlon, 2005). He developed severe migraines and sensory disturbances, became ill with cancer and subsequently died (Marlon, 2005). Marlon linked the black sun with "a chronic, psychic atrophy that can sometimes be literally fatal" (p. 36). The images reported in Robert's case show a strong parallel with the causes and effects of psychological infanticide, which so often are related to murderous wishes and/or near-death in the womb, as discussed in Chapter Three.

The similarity of Robert's images to my own suggests that the image of *sol niger* may relate to the annihilating experience of the unwanted unborn child or of a foetus in a womb that is precarious (for whatever reasons) and who feels the threat to its life. The womb, symbol of creativity and generation, is also an occult space (meaning both hidden and dark) that can be both the fruitful void from which life comes forth and the dark void that sucks life back into itself. I suggest the black sun is likely to be a common symbol for experiences of the Death Mother archetype.

In *sol niger*, the sun – usually a symbol of the daylight of consciousness, reason, clarity and the rational mind – becomes inverted into its negative – the Shadow of the sun, with its shadowy unconscious, in which mind is annihilated, and reason and clarity are destroyed. Marlon (2005) suggested *sol niger* is particularly relevant to the masculine consciousness overpowered by the feminine. However, the sun, which is often a masculine symbol in alchemical imagery, has an ancient history as a symbol of the Great Mother. So, extending Marlon's suggestion, the black sun symbolises the Death Mother, the darkest most negating aspect of the Great Mother. We can see in the black sun the qualities attributed to feminine consciousness. These can be described as non-rational, non-linear, intuitive, murky, embodied, and implicit (Baring & Cashford, 1991; Murdock, 1990). Within the womb of the Great Mother is the deepest darkness from which life emerges. This is what is suggested by the *caudis pavona* or peacock's tail that results from alchemical transformation of *sol niger*. When the Death Mother is constellated, the fruitful void becomes a lifeless vacuum of utter negation, unable to sustain life. Transformation comes through dying and dismemberment. I explore this feminine consciousness in greater detail in Chapter Eleven.

Neuroscience expresses these masculine and feminine opposites in terms of left and right brain thinking, with left brain engaged in linear, organised, verbal and language processes; and the right brain engaged in intuitive, embodied, holistic processes more akin to creative thinking and aligned with pre-verbal infant states of implicit memory held in body-mind (Siegal, 2009, 2010). These two sides of the brain are designed to work together in a harmonious balance of sensing and making sense of. Early relational trauma and culture bias that values one mode of thinking over the other create imbalances in this delicate integration (Siegal, 2009, 2010).

When taken over by the archetypal presence of the feminine, we are engulfed by feelings, sensations, intuited knowing, and a merging with unity consciousness. We lose the ability to think our way through challenges, or to separate ourselves enough, for an observing ego to hold a sense of separation from what is occurring. Williams (2012) supported the idea of this disconnection from an objective self, as occurring in both mystical and psychotic experiences, as a result of dis-integration of the thinking self. Both psychosis and mysticism therefore may have some link to our relationship with the archetypal Mother, influenced by our experiences with our personal mothers, beginning in the fruitful, or disallowing void, of the womb before birth.

Feminine consciousness is the common means of experiencing, before birth and in infancy before the development of language skills. During experiences when we lose touch with everyday reality (the archetypal masculine symbolised by the conscious light of the day), as in psychosis or mystical experiences, perhaps we are really in touch with a deeper, earlier form of the archetypal feminine (the hidden consciousness of the dark engulfing void) through which both creativity and destruction are expressed.

This idea has the potential to help us clearly understand the infanticidal nature of psychosis (as discussed in Chapter Three) and points to a means of healing this level of trauma. Transpersonal psychologies in particular are deeply aware of the relationship between psychosis and mystical experiences, and their methods offer maps for supporting people through the crisis of spiritual emergence/emergency (Grof, 1998; Lucas, 2011). One mystic path I related to, which takes up the sense of negation I have discussed in this section, is the *via negativa*.

Via Negativa

The *via negativa* is a term usually used to describe a religious path that embraces what cannot be seen or known, rather than the positivist approach of what *is*. It is a path of unknowing (Progroff, 1957; Smith, 1987). For the adopted person, all of life is lived through a lens of mystery and the unknown. As Lifton (1994) wrote, for the adopted child, "abandonment and mysteries are the origins that shape the child's life" (p. 20). This dark unknowing resonates with the alchemical image of the black sun. In this dark night of the Soul, something must break down completely before any kind of resurrection can occur (Edinger, 1994; Kristeva, 1989; Marlon, 2005; Moore, 2012). Francis Weller (2015) offered another perspective of the *via negativa* as the road through the depths leading to what he describes (citing mythologist Michael Meade) as "*dark wisdom*" (p. 8, author's italics). I lived my life through a *via negativa*, as if life in the world of day and light had been snuffed out. The true orientation of my life was towards death and non-existence.

In my ghostly life, I felt more present in the negatives or spaces between things rather than in concrete actualities: a life of absence more real than presence. As Hollis (2013) wrote: "All we can say of this phenomenon is that absences are still presences, and that death, divorce or distance do not end relationships" (p. 135). Although it was unspoken or even unthought by me, for much of the time, the absence of my original mother and the original self that belonged with that mother, were powerfully present absences. Hollis elaborated further in relation to these emotional absences:

> Nonetheless, these lacunae are filled in by all of us – through implication, speculation or necessity. In other words, what is not there is still there, and we are emotionally obliged to make do, jury rig a plausible fill-in for these messages, especially those who never knew their parents. (p. 136)

I suggest that absence-presence is the powerful haunting that begins when there is dissociation during pregnancy. As the mother dissociates from the *presence* of the child within her, so the child dissociates from the *absence* of the kind of maternal relationship that allows for a sense of existence – or perhaps even from the absence of themselves. Neither can bear to know about their experience. This disconnection from self and Soul attacks the capacity for meaningful existence, for integrated wholeness, and desire for life.

I experienced this disembodied existence as ghostlike, already killed off and haunting others with my absent-presence; much as the idea of Mother has haunted me with her present-absence. Lifton (1994) stated:

> The adopted child is always accompanied by the ghost of the child he might have been had he stayed with his birth mother and by the ghost of the fantasy child his adoptive parents might have had. He is also accompanied by the ghost of the birth mother, from whom he has never completely disconnected, and the ghost of the birth father, hidden behind her. (p. 11)

In this ghost life I inhabited an underworld, a secret life hidden behind extreme containment. My underworld was an interior world that in the case of trauma becomes a world of traumatic attachments and archetypal presences. Sieff (2017) described the activation of embodied and psychological survival systems in response to trauma as a shift of our reality into the parallel reality of a "trauma world" (p. 170). This world is characterised by fear, disconnection and shame. Sieff stated: "If a trauma-world is formed during childhood, it becomes our normality, whereupon we are unconscious of its impact on our lives" (p.170). How much more so when the trauma-world begins before birth?

My trauma-world was a ghost world where I 'lived' invisible, unseen, and dead. In the logic of this world, my so-called alive self was the ghost. This somehow explained why I was not myself but was somebody else. The 'real' self was the ghost. One of the effects of psychological infanticide is that it becomes difficult to maintain a sense of existence in the world, and to establish a presence and engagement in the external world. In particular, it becomes hard to leave the inner world and connect with other (real) people. I also felt no sense of any future. Life remained transient and precarious, as if I was on a day trip from the inner world of ghosts and must soon hand in my pass — or, closer to home, as if I was a psychiatric patient on approved leave and must behave well and return at the appointed time to avoid emergency measures being taken. The feeling of life being nipped in the bud led to great difficulty taking any action, or feeling that I could take a position on something or make a commitment. This sense of invalidation was reinforced by the idea that my identity itself was invalid. I experienced a pull towards oblivion or non-existence in many forms (including suicide, sedation, trance states, and illness states). I felt strongly that I was not being allowed to live; that my life and death were preordained by unknown others.

I also had the repeated experience, during frequent migraines that rendered me unconscious from pain, of dying and then slowly coming back to life. This Lazarus-like return from the dead echoed in Anna Kavan's (1945/1978) collection of short stories, *I am Lazarus*, in which she expressed her own journey with the energy of the Death Mother, though not using that term. Kavan's nightmare world of isolation and doom oscillates between deadness and her terrified anxious struggle for aliveness. Kavan's life and work influenced me significantly during my breakdown. It seemed my migraine states were a repetition of the painful struggle over whether to live or die.

As I gradually began to heal from my state of non-existence, I was more able to feel present, alive and welcome in the world. But when something triggered feelings of being killed off, I was plunged back into what I have come to know as the 'Land of Dis'. Dis is one of the names of the underworld. Kalsched's (2013) work on 'dis' words that express ways of feeling removed from the world of presence has been extremely resonant for me. In the Land of Dis, I reflected on the ways I have died to the world – through dis-appearing, dis-connecting, dis-associating, et cetera. This has led to deep reflection on what is actually meant and experienced by these terms. For example, when I dis-appear I appear in the land of the dead, when I dis-connect I connect with the dead, when I dissociate I am associating with the dead.

In dialogues with parts of myself whilst in the Land of Dis, I dis-covered (recovered from the land of the dead) a part of myself I called No-Voice, who expressed complete self-negation. This voice responded to all questions, suggestions, and options with a negative. This No-Voice represented the infant part of me that was completely negated, and whose only role has been to express this nullification. I refer here to the legal term *nullius filius* (child of nobody), which indicated the legal status and lack of rights of illegitimate children in the nineteenth century. Twentieth century adoption laws sought to address this by legally enforcing that adopted children were 'as if' born to the adoptive parents. The legalities of closed stranger adoption soon repeated and reinforced the sense of 'nobody' through legally severing any connection with original identity or history. As Else (1994) noted, this 'as if' identity has the effect of turning the child into a living fiction. Not just living a lie, but being a lie, damages innate self-worth and authenticity, creating despair and hopelessness.

Dialoguing with No-Voice I realised there was tremendous power being channelled into resistance to life, choice and action. It was a voice of terror attempting to control its fragile world and sense of self by limiting all possibility. Only the underworld was safe. If I was to become real I would be killed.

Through writing, I found a way to have imaginal dialogues with more parts of myself. Without understanding why at the time, I found it useful to discover more of myself and to understand the different perspectives within. Watkins (2000) described the integrative effect that can occur when dialogues between imaginal figures are able to relate with one another.

In a bio-fiction I explored key scenes in my personal myth through Violet, who I thought of as the dead poet. In the language of flowers, the violet signifies the death of a maiden. I wrote this poetic *Life* (as in the Victorian 'Lives' of well known people; Elisabeth Gaskell's (1891) *Life of Charlotte Brontë* being a pertinent example) in response to the fictional diary I was writing of another character, Lily, who became aware of Violet's suicide and wished to understand why she had killed herself. It was helpful to discover a part of myself who was curious, interested, and could 'see' other parts of me. Lily represented a part of me that was beginning to embrace life. She was curious, compassionate and interested in the hidden story of Violet's death. In embodying Lily, I was able to think and care about parts of me that lived death, and felt dead and buried.

Lily represented a growing capacity for integration and compassion. She demonstrated a motherly care and interest, enabling some hope for what had been dead to revive. Lily represented a nurturing rather than a murderous mother. Unfortunately, with the death of someone very dear to me, my connection with Lily disappeared. The murderous voice returned, and I became suicidal again. This time I found great help from a dream, in which I witnessed my suicide from three different perspectives: the suicide, the disinterested observer, and the one who feels the loss.

Loss holds an atmosphere of haunting and mystery as we engage with absence-presence. In the next section I go more deeply into the questions and mysteries that arose for me about adoption and its relationship with psychological infanticide.

The Mystery of Psychological Infanticide

In the two novels I wrote after my breakdown, I now see the themes of my internal world: longings and fears relating to Mother; dilemmas over what to do with unwanted children; how to survive being killed; and the question of loss of history and identity that does not just fragment the adopted child's sense of themselves but can nullify any sense of self. These two novels explored the key themes and critical questions of my personal myth.

Rereading the novel I wrote shortly after my breakdown (Deed, 1994a), the atmosphere of terror strikes me, as do the metaphors of killing off that are a hallmark of psychological infanticide. For years after recovery from my breakdown, I bargained with time. Not imagining an entitlement to life, I made Faustian-like pacts with an internal devil that if I agreed to suicide at say, thirty, then I might get to live through the preceding years. Making the pact enabled me not to attempt suicide. Surviving to the agreed age, the pact was renewed.

What does this have to do with psychological infanticide? Originally I did not think about the idea of murder in connection with being adopted. I understood the grief and loss, the sense of abandonment and the feeling of having died – all of which are accepted as psychological experiences of adopted children (Lifton, 2009; Verrier, 1993; Winnicott, 1965). My clue is in the precipitating dilemma of my breakdown: it was not simply the grief and loss over the end of a relationship that tipped me over the edge. It was the contemplation of the ideas of mother, pregnancy, birth and the impending sense of murder I experienced thinking about it. It seemed to me at the time that pregnancy or birth might kill me and that to have a child would be to invite the intentional death of either myself, or the infant. Here lies a glimpse of the murderous impulse that is indicative of infanticidal attachment. I note the language I use to begin the previous sentence is the traditional wording on a tombstone.

In the second novel (Deed, 1995) I explored the archetypal figures of Mother, Midwife and Child, represented in that narrative by a mother who is murdered yet remains a ghostly presence; an unseen midwife who is a healer, a witch, and a killer of children; a changeling figure, swapped at birth by fairies, whose life journey involves isolation for survival and the knowledge she must both let herself be killed and survive her death; and an amnesiac woman who is hospitalised when she does not know who she is and who is given the task of writing in order to piece together her memories, discover her identity and help restore her to a sense of wholeness.

In hindsight, they all represented parts of me. The novel demonstrates how I survived, and points a way towards healing. These characters can also be considered as archetypal presences activated in my internal world. As such, in the novel I explored the universal questions of feminism in a patriarchal system, and the dilemma of how best to deal with children who cannot be cared for.

These two novels demonstrate the profound healing potential of the imagination, in this case through the writing of fictionalised autobiography. Just as the inner world of my fiction revealed my experience, so my outer world reflected me back to myself. What we notice or perceive can tell us much about our internal dynamics, the way we relate to ourselves reflects how we were related to early in life. It is also the way we relate to others.

In an example of the parallels between external and internal life, in Oamaru, in 2000, I became a member of *The Vanished World*, a society that was formed to research and inform people about the pre-history of the local area. In my interior life I was already a life member of *The Vanished World*. My true home was with the extinct creatures of pre-history living through echoes in time in a parallel world. I felt a strong feeling of belonging and recognition as a member of *The Vanished World*. In the validation of my extinction I felt fully present and seen. No longer invisible. Perhaps even a valuable piece of pre-history. Pre-birth experience also needs to be acknowledged as a valuable pre-history of our individual lives.

To be extinct is to have died off, to no longer be able to sustain life in an inhospitable terrain, or to be killed off actively or passively by a phenomenon such as weather, disease or predators such as human beings. To be extinct is to no longer hold a place in this world. One becomes a vanished historical creature of legend or myth, its only evidence of existence possibly fossils, or imprints/impressions, a scattering of teeth here, a few pieces of hair there, a knuckle of vertebrae and an indent of body on soil. The evidence of the extinct being has to be gathered and imagined from scant evidence.

I try to think back to when and how I first felt killed off. I remember always having known I was adopted, and from a very young age I was aware of having been given another name by my birth parents. I tried to understand this complexity of identity. How could I just stop being that other person and become this one? How were they different? Why was the other one not acceptable so that she had to be sent away to another family and be called something else? Where was she inside me? What would happen if she came back and I was not wanted anymore?

The child who I was, who became extinct, showed herself in occasional glimpses, or pieces of history, but there are large unknowable gaps; she must be inferred as a living being from the occasional evidence that came to the surface, and in this imagining we can never fully know her truth. Always, the deepest most original part of myself can only be imagined; I cannot ever really know her as herself or as who she might have become. Is she, therefore, a mythological beast, made up of qualities and representations, and hints and hauntings rather than an actual once-living creature? Does she really belong in the realm of griffons and gargoyles, sphinxes, mermaids, yetis and freak shows? I wrote about this sense of myself as a kind of specimen or freak, resonant with the images of the case of Robert previously cited (Marlon, 2005) that included monster or mutant births and dead babies:

What is kept in a glass case? Museum exhibits, curiosities. Butterflies, insects, preserved animals. Books, jewels, artifacts. Bone chips, claws, chiselled stone blades. Shards, shells, fossils. Freaks of nature suspended in transparent liquids. Two-headed beasts. A forlorn mermaid. An homunculus in his glass jar. The rare, the strange and the valuable. Things of nominated beauty and fragility. A woman who is misunderstood. A dead woman. La morte. A mortified woman. A woman in a glass case is an observable absence, preserved under glass for as long as it takes. How long will you keep staring like that? Into her observable life. (Deed, 2006)

The glass case is reminiscent of the glass coffin in fairy tales that keeps the feminine unconscious and dead to life until she is revived by a heroic act. The glass case may also represent the *alembic*, the glass vessel in which liquids are transformed in the alchemical process. As discussed earlier, this vessel could also represent the womb. Each of these images requires that life be touched and nurtured toward being, or it petrifies into an object without life.

The dissociation, invalidation and nullification experienced by the adopted child create the shameful fear that there is something terribly wrong with the original self. The dehumanising nature of the adoptive process gives rise to the sense of not being a person but an object to be observed as monstrous *other* by the scrutinising stare of the person on the other side of the glass. The experience of being made extinct and the feeling of being non-existent combine with a feeling of entrapment between worlds or in the wrong incarnation.

My sense that I was wished dead, or non-being, is what makes this experience a psychological infanticide rather than simply a psychological death. As if an external force wanted me not to exist and I picked up and internalised this message.

Adoption: A Tale of Psychological Murder, Ghosts, and Hauntings

Destruction of original identity and connection to personal history murders something of the original self. Shengold (1989, 1999) defined Soul murder as an attack on the identity or self of the child. This Soul murder leads directly to haunting as the child internalises the persecuting ghosts for whom she or he was not allowed to live as his or her own precious self, and the shame that goes with it.

By internalising this psychological murder, I learned to deaden this original self, to hope she would stay hidden, to keep her shut up in some internal dungeon out of sight and knowledge as a protective measure against further harm. Perhaps I was repeating the ways society and the adoption process had decided this other one needed to be silenced in order for me to be accepted into a new family. They attempted to murder my original presence by legally depriving me of connections with myself – my birthright of knowing who I was, and of belonging with a familial group and place. Perhaps they imagined that if I ran out of breadcrumbs to show the way, as with Hansel and Gretel abandoned in the woods, I would just give up and not remember that something had been taken from me. They were nearly right. This was the logic of closed stranger adoption.

In my imaginal experience, I work with the emotional or psychic truth as felt in the body or sensed through image in order to understand what is both known and not known until it is brought into consciousness. Of course, I cannot establish the actual truth of psychological infanticide. I cannot point out the literal body of the dead child I experience within. I can reveal the evidence of her psychological murder through dreams, symptoms and other glancing knowings from the implicit memory of what I call the 'dark interior'. In this quest, I encounter ghosts, glimpses, hauntings, and theories impossible to prove.

This mysteriousness is an uncanny parallel to the story of the adopted child whose internal world is filled with ghosts and hauntings, with absent-presences and present-absences, and with murdered selves and glimpsed internal others (Lifton, 1994, 2009). To be fully alive and authentic in one's self, one must face into the ways one has been sacrificed and has sacrificed one's self.

Marion Woodman (2005) defined the destructive and traumatic Death Mother archetype, which drains vitality and paralyses the ability to engage in life (Harris & Harris, 2015; Sieff, 2017; Woodman & Sieff, 2015). "Ultimately the Death Mother carries the wish that we, or some part of us, did not exist" (Sieff, 2017, p. 5). When there seems no right to existence even before birth, where else is one going to turn than back toward the loving, blissful and annihilating arms of Mother Death? There is no sense of going forward into life.

Chapter Ten
Minnie Dean and a Poetics of Engagement

Then turn to the dead, listen to their lament
and accept them with love.
C.G. Jung (Hillman & Shamdasani, 2013)

Figure 7. Minnie Dean. Marriage portrait. 1872, Public Domain

Exploring the profound grief that results from damage to the Soul, I wrote in my journal: *"The invisible-visible needs to no longer be a duality. We need to find the visibility in the invisible and the invisibility in the visible."* In other words, we need to find the illumination in our darkness and the shadow in our consciousness. These words came in response to writing about Minnie Dean, and they revealed the process I was instinctively working through.

In my adult life, I have felt haunted by Minnie Dean, and I feel I have haunted her through my intense imaginal engagement with her. This was a haunting in which I could re-turn and work through, past trauma by engaging with a representative imaginal figure rather than re-enacting my psychological infanticide as I had previously done during my breakdown. Watkins (2000) has described the integrative creativity of a collaborative dialogue between internal voices. Here the main dialogue is with Minnie. However, there were other dialogues in this exchange, with Charlotte Brontë, Saint Colette, Hildegaard von Bingen, a Victorian baby who died in infancy, Emily Dickenson, Thomas de Quincey, Samuel Taylor Coleridge, and various historic ghosts.

Introducing Minnie

I first met Minnie Dean, so to speak, in an episode of Ken Catran's (1985) television series, *Hanlon,* which explored the legal career of barrister, Alf Hanlon, who defended Minnie Dean against charges of child murder. The episode centred on the legal complexities and sensationalism of Minnie's case. She was found guilty, sentenced to death, and hanged. Even at the time of her trial there was controversy over whether Minnie was guilty of murder – or manslaughter, which did not carry a sentence of death. More than a century later, the question of Minnie's intent and, therefore, the degree of her guilt are still debated.

I was young when I watched the episode. The legal details passed over my head. What struck home was the realisation that this woman had killed babies. Legend had it she had killed them by piercing their fontanelles with a hatpin. The dead babies had been carried in a large hatbox before Minnie was able to get them to her home and bury them in her garden.

This is where my personal myth and history first began to entwine. As an adopted child, my original story, my identity and links with my original family had been legally erased, and I lived with my adoptive family *as if* I were their own child. This narrative already sounded to me like a fairy tale. Inside me there was a Dead Baby, a baby who had not been allowed to live, and with whom I had a strange relationship.

Seeing the episode about Minnie, the idea of dead babies became horrifyingly real to me, along with the realisation that some mothers who took in babies killed them, whether intentionally or otherwise.

My adoptive mother had a large hatbox sitting on top of a tall wardrobe in her bedroom. As a small child, I was fascinated with what might be inside it. Curious and terrified, like the bride in Bluebeard's castle, I felt irresistibly drawn to look inside the hatbox. What would I do if I found someone dead in there? What if there was nothing? I worried that this would not be a relief; it might simply mean my mother was clever and had hidden the evidence somewhere else.

As an adult I returned to Minnie's story when I read Lynley Hood's (1994) biography, *Minnie Dean: Her Life & Crimes*. I was drawn into the question of Minnie's intentions. Did she intend to murder the children or did their deaths happen unintentionally? But underneath this I was worried about the established fact of two dead infants. The reality of nineteenth-century history resonated with my personal history; in a different time, I could have been one of those dead children.

Suddenly I had an historical context for the myth I had been living. I learned about baby farming and felt haunted by Minnie and her story, much as during childhood I was haunted by Eastman's (1960) children's story, *Are you my Mother?* In this story a baby bird leaves the nest and goes on a search for its mother, asking anyone along the way, "Are you my mother?" It is only soothed when the mother bird is found, and they go back to a happy nest. In contrast, wherever I looked there was never the 'right' mother who would take me home and tuck me into the 'right' nest. I worried for that baby bird that might be tricked by a wolf or fox pretending to be the right mother so it could eat the baby bird. My infanticidal fears were already activated.

Oamaru: A Victorian Interlude

Moving to Oamaru, in the South Island of New Zealand, in my mid-30s, also moved me into a role in an historic Victorian precinct there which was like a live piece of history, with people in Victorian clothes, working in traditional Victorian occupations in the nineteenth-century limestone buildings. Life and fiction had interwoven. I was already living a Victorian kind of existence, constricted and entombed within myself. Contemplating Minnie, my interior and exterior lives merged in an increasing engagement with the consciousness and bodily experience of a Victorian woman, embodying outer restraint and a hidden, passionate inner life:

> *[Working]In the bookshop on a Sunday afternoon, in my black bustled skirt and silk blouse, my black lace shawl and my jet beads, I think about stillness. How I sit motionless, like a statue, barely blinking, my mind travelling in all directions. I feel trapped and deal with it by becoming still. I become adept at listening to my body, its tempos and compositions. Sometimes I wonder if I will remember how to speak.* (Deed, 2003b)

Living a Victorian life brought me closer to my imagining of Minnie's life, and physically she was closer. There is something intimate about wearing authentic clothing from another century. I was fortunate to wear some historic items borrowed from the

North Otago Museum, and to experience the feeling of being a body inside such clothes. This embodied intuition is an attunement to the language and memories of the body through its symbols, symptoms and sensations. Cobb (1992) went further in his essay on Persephone, introducing the concept of far memory; the art of recalling memory from before one's current lifetime. Indeed, I felt I remembered a Victorian life, mediated through the dark lens of the Queen of the Underworld. I felt, as I moved my body in the ways required by Victorian garments, that it somehow remembered this way of being from another century. Attuned to this poetics of the body, I experienced intuitions and knowings about Victorian women through wearing Victorian clothes and spending time amongst the extensive collection of Victorian garments held in the museum. I contemplated the complexity and presence of loss and grief in Victorian society. My connection with Victorian history reflected my haunted, imprisoned and restricted self back to me:

Alone in the silent upper floor of the museum is like taking tea with ghosts, I feel surrounded by women of all walks of life, at all times of the day and night. Waking, preparing or receiving breakfast, walking the main street, hauling water from the well, sitting down to dinner with guests, waltzing dizzily round a hot and brilliantly lit ballroom, stirring the air with an ostrich plume fan.

For myself, if I read correctly, I would not at present be attending dances. I would be wearing deepest black. I would be demure; eyes downcast, keeping it all hidden, a slinking shadow granted respect for my silence.

I resolve to be true to the language of the body. I wear governess black and jet beads. The introspective role – that of the invisible woman, suits me well. Charlotte and I are quite happy to sit in a corner together, our faces seemingly turned to the wall, noticing everything in our hunger. (Deed, 2003b)

In Oamaru, the trains I walked past every day reminded me of Minnie's love of train travel. During Victorian Heritage celebrations, a steam train took people through the precinct dressed in their Victorian costumes (see Figure 2). I could ride the train imagining I was Minnie, looking out of the window, a hatbox and a bunch of flowers wrapped in paper on the seat beside me. I imagined that last journey. Minnie knowing she had two dead infants in her hatbox. Keeping her composure. Stifling the frantic panic inside. These reveries arose out of my fiction-writing process of imagining myself as a character. It was much later, studying psychotherapy, that I came to know Jung's active imagination process (Hannah, 1981; Johnson, 1986). According to Bachelard (1971/2005) reverie is an essential synthesising activity of the imagination, which aids poets and therapists in receiving an impression of their subjects.

Figure 8. Photo of the researcher as Minnie Dean. 1999.

Minnie had often travelled to Oamaru to pick up a baby, and Eva Hornsby, the second infant who died on that last journey with the hatbox, was from Oamaru. Daily I walked past the hotel where

Minnie stayed when in town. I stayed in it myself after I had left Oamaru and returned as a guest poet at a writers' festival. Almost directly across the road is the *Annie Flanagan* hotel, named after a nineteenth-century New Zealand mother convicted of the infanticide of her daughter's illegitimate child (Hood, 1994). All of this was turning in my mind, along with the internal journeys involving dead babies and disowning mothers. In haunting Minnie's psyche, I was exploring the Murderer, Rescuer, Victim and Witness within myself.

When I lived in Oamaru, my street had a cemetery, with many graves revealing nineteenth-century glimpses of the regularity of infant, and mother, mortality. Being a childbearing woman was a life and death business. I began another imaginal dialogue, this time with a deceased nineteenth-century infant named Susan. I see now that this was a way of engaging an imaginal relationship with the Dead Baby inside myself. I worked this imaginal relationship in poems:

Songs for a drowned woman 4

...
I sit on a worn headstone
listening to the ghost
of a child

this small quiet I can take with me
turn in my hands
beneath the yew
another song to be sung
(Deed, 2006)

I also recorded in my journal a moment of numinous awe as the spirit of the Dead Baby appeared to come alive in response to my reverent attention:

The yews are dark and dense. They seem to suck up life from the ground. I edge round a yew draped in ivy to visit Susan, who died in 1880 aged eleven weeks. Susan was my first friend here. There's half her headstone sprawled on the ground, a slab with the facts of her brief life, and an ornamental fragment, a gigantic knuckle or the vertebra of a small whale. Beneath the shade of the yew there's the lower half of her monument, a bare piece of stone where I sit shaded in summer while we talk.

Today, after the damp weather, Susan's name and history is highlighted in luminous green. Water has collected in the grooves of her inscription and cushiony moss fills each letter, raised, in emerald velvet. I keep this secret image neatly in my thoughts, to be unwrapped in quiet moments, a polished treasure, curious and personal to me. (Deed, 2003b)

Jung realised that "until we come to terms with the dead we simply cannot live and [that] our life is dependent on finding answers to their unanswered questions" (Hillman & Shamdasi, 2013, p. 1). I was learning this for myself as I connected with the dead in order to more fully understand myself. I was also grappling with the history of women, feminism, and the unanswered, and perhaps unanswerable, question of the (predominantly) female problem of unwanted children.

Yearning for the Child Killer

During my time in Oamaru, both the Dead Baby and the Murderous Mother were being given vital and vitalising attention in my psyche. Reflection, and journals kept over a long period of time, revealed to me the persistence of grief and a sense of annihilation surrounding my birth date. Over many years I had become desperately depressed for several months before my birthday. I felt as if the bottom had fallen out of the world, and I no longer existed in it, or had any right to exist. I became suicidal, at times actively wanting to suicide; yet later, I was clinging to life as if some external menace was trying to kill me. If I could hang on until a month or so after my birthday I would return to life and wellbeing. Over time, with psychotherapy, and through my engagement with Minnie, I no longer become suicidal or depressed, but there is always a lingering darkness waiting to engulf me at this time of year. I intuitively re-experience a feeling of dread from before I was born, which could not be verbalised and I could not consciously remember.

In this time of darkness, I yearned for a figure I called the Child Killer, personified by Minnie. Realising that I attempted to soothe myself by reaching out to a killer helped me to recognise the internal dynamic between Unwanted Child and Infanticidal Mother:

Wanting the solace of the child killer, wanting to destroy, all this self-hate seemingly up out of nowhere. No life. This folder of writing opening the lid of a grave and letting out? Life? Hope? Despair? Eyes full of tears. Wanting to be killed. Wondering if I am the killer. Listening to Bach's Magnificat and going straight back to my cemetery and a solitary world crowded with music. I'm feeling the same despair of that time and since, a lonely grieving heart...
When I thought about drawing the vault [my inner underground prison] I realised how womb-like it is, and how strong is the pull to get back there. And then thinking about being willed dead in the womb, that numbing of feeling of life – that attraction to laudanum and to dear Minnie – trying to resolve the situation of the child killer, whether for criminal intent or not the outcomes were the same, the pain is the same. Trying this time to either completely die or completely survive. (Deed, journal, 2007)

As I engaged with the presence of Minnie, in order to think about my own history and psychology, she came to symbolise for me the concepts of mother I needed to understand inside myself. At times it felt terribly risky to invite her inside my head, and I intentionally kept her outside of me; she was thought about but not part of my inner landscape. At other times she was very much present inside my mind as part of myself; the aspects of me that were complex and conflicted about relationships between mother and child, and that involved and included potential murderousness, abandonment, dissociation, and neglect. Dialogues with Minnie enabled me to recognise and work through these aspects of myself. At first she only appeared in dreams. The following dream reflected the transformational power of engaging in a personified and embodied process:

I am creating an effigy of Minnie using strands of her own hair, which has been saved for me. It is brown and fine. I use it carefully, sparingly, with reverence. There is something reminiscent of witches creating effigies to do magic on people; the power of personal material – hair, nails, teeth – that allows magic to be worked on that person. (Deed, dream journal, 2016)

In Oamaru, this seemingly magical process began in a poetic dialogue with the nineteenth century that reflected my own restricted and distorted relationship to the feminine. These reveries are presented here as they illuminate the central questions I had about the Dead Baby inside myself, my sense of having been killed off, and about my relationship with murderousness and the feminine.

Jung described active imagination as a means of working with inner figures of the psyche through imagining them as real beings and allowing them to reveal themselves through dialogue, painting, movement, **and so forth** (Hannah, 1981). Jung's (2009) own imaginal process, now published as the *Red Book*, was kept hidden for decades out of fear it would be misconstrued as proof of mental instability. Likewise, I feel vulnerable exposing my personal and imaginal processes; yet, I also feel it is essential that survivors of psychological death speak out, describe the terrain, the traps, and the possible means of surviving a sojourn in the underworld. I intend that my journey may inspire hope for resurrection for both patients (those who must patiently work through their terrifying inner underworld) and the clinicians who accompany them and must understand and embrace their role as guide for the living self to enter the land of the dead and be 'animated' by them (Hillman & Shamdasani, 2013; Jung, 2009).

The ambiguity and complexity of Minnie enabled me to work with her as an imaginal figure through which I was able to explore many aspects of the Death Mother archetype. She is capable of appearing as benign child minder, adoptive mother, chaotic, disorganised mother, psychotic mother, and child murderer. Minnie was able to hold or contain this process with me. It is essential to clarify that the Minnie I write about is imaginal, not a literal Minnie, just as the infanticide I'm exploring is psychological rather than literal. I do not presume to know the truth about the real Minnie Dean's story.

When I first met Minnie, I related to her literally. She was either the 'good' mother or the 'bad' mother, and I had difficulty reconciling elements of both. I grappled with the pieces of her story that did not fit with whichever pole I was aligned with at the time. Minnie was both elusive and willing to be searched for, and able to hold roles of both 'bad' and 'good' mother as I worked through integrating these two in my internal world. In a sense, as during her own lifetime, Minnie was willing to take on this otherwise abandoned baby (myself). At times she was the longed-for Rescuer, at other times the Murderous Mother, sometimes idealistically naïve, sometimes sinister. She became mediator of my own dark recesses, holding the balance alongside the perfect idealised mother of the Madonna, who paradoxically, in my world, could only love a perfect child, who could only be a dead child. This Madonna revealed herself in my poems to be talented in the art of dissociation:

A recipe for flight
take a madonna
who doesn't wish to remember
who wishes to forget
what her body is waiting
to tell her

she sleeps for centuries
her breath carelessly unravelling

she dreams a landscape
a meadow of purple wildflowers
butterflies dancing
in the field of her vision

though she doesn't see
she remembers

here is where she takes off
hovers
in a place without meaning
devoid of context
in the astronomical air
(Deed, 2003a)

In Oamaru, I was also compulsively collecting images of the Madonna (Figure 3), imagining my way into the Divine Mother who would perfectly love and care for me. She appeared remote, contained and unreachable. Collecting Madonna images was also a way of working with the split Mother archetype.

Figure 9. Photo. Icon by Donna Demente, 1999.

Both Madonna and Minnie represented, at different times 'good' and 'bad' aspects of mother:

In a café in Thames St I'm pierced with the dangerous allure of [artist Donna Demente's] icons on the whitewashed wall. I can barely breathe with desire. A particular madonna speaks to me with heavy-lidded sensuality, her cruelty betrayed in her narrow smile. She affects a pious look, but this madonna has thorns if you don't know how to approach her. I know to interpret this language in layers, this looking glass world where nothing is as it appeared on the surface, all the fragmented complexities of a Byzantine mosaic held in such initial simplicity.

For some time I have been collecting madonnas in my mind, a whole repertoire of madonna-ness that is the internal language that helped me interpret myself to myself. Here was an outward expression, a dialogue rather than a soliloquy. (Deed, 2003b)

The Language of Flowers

After my breakdown in my early 20s, I existed in my imaginal world in which I tried to be allowed to live and to gather together all the ghosts. I had moved psychologically from a delusional but very real internal battle with the Murderous Mother during my breakdown through to the identification of different parts of myself with which I could work through all the parts of the story. This process has taken long years of careful engagement, eventually culminating in deciding to trust Minnie as my guide as I descended again into the underworld themes of my breakdown in order to understand and heal my murdered self. This re-search into my historical self deepened, focused and eventually synthesised and integrated my self inquiry.

I began to write letters to Minnie in an attempt to make imaginal contact. Rather than write to an aspect of myself, I aligned myself more with Romanyshyn's (1997) concept of transference dialogues with a personification of the work, as discussed in his methodology of alchemical hermeneutics. Both methods aim to activate hidden materials, whether they are considered subconscious parts of the self, intuitive or tacit knowings, or a connection with archetypal personifications in the collective unconscious (Moustakas, 1990; Romanyshyn, 1997). Because Minnie was from an era in which writing letters was the medium of communication, and because she had prided herself on her education and writing ability, I decided to invite the dialogue in the form of letters handwritten with fountain pen and ink.

In my initial letter I felt aware of Minnie's evasiveness. At other times when I had tried to engage her in a dialogue she had not been forthcoming. There was a stubborn silence (I almost wrote here, a pregnant silence). I felt a need to entice Minnie through a friendly and respectful tone, being clear about my intentions, and hoping to draw her out through safe conversations about domesticities and her garden, which she loved. Mention of the garden could also potentially be seen as provocative, given that several babies' skeletons were unearthed there. Writing to Minnie directly was intended to invite hidden aspects of my engagement with Minnie, and to invite her to guide and direct me toward what needed to be explored. Minnie was willing to have a voice through my pen, and the letters triggered themes and dream visitations by Minnie, leading me intuitively through symbol and image. I had instinctively chosen a domestic and feminine means of drawing out a conversation between Minnie and myself, positioning us talking, as if over a cup of tea, about women's things and the domestic life of a nineteenth-century mother. As themes emerged, I became aware of a distinct feminist thread of ideas alluded to between thoughts of flowers and teapots. I also noticed the developing warmth and compassion with which I corresponded with Minnie, and which mirrored my own developing self-compassion for this Minnie-like part of myself.

Dear Minnie,

This is the first of a series of letters I hope to write to you. I've been wanting an opportunity to use this pen and I think you may appreciate it. I'm sitting here with a cup of nettle tea - it's lunchtime - and wondering what we will have to say to each other and how our dialogue will unfold. I do hope you will respond. It's so hard to fit in something like writing letters in between all that has to be done in a day, and I only have to look after myself, and my cat. Yet I know you write letters - good ones. I've read the letters you wrote advertising for children to care for. And I've read your personal statement - one long letter to the world from gaol. Your life and psychology and modus operandi have always been of interest to me. Since I first met you in the late 1990's - almost exactly 100 years since your death - I've wanted to know you better, to understand you, to make sense of your life through the glimpses (and false trails) you left for us. I want to get it right. I want to do write (sic) by you - of course I meant right but I do also mean to write. I will deeply appreciate any input you are able and willing to offer toward this process as I would very much like it to be a co-creation, an offering we can both feel comfortable with. And I do intend for it to be a healing fiction, not just for me in my adoption journey, but for you, for Dorothy and Eva, and all the other little ones unkept by their mothers. And for the souls of those who did what needed to be done because somebody had to. Well Minnie, I'm near the end of my first page to you. I hope this finds you well and in good spirits. The heavy rain is fining up now and I'm about to cook a spinach and feta frittata. I have a garden here that needs planning and planting. I know you love gardens - what might you suggest?

I look forward to hearing from you.
Respectfully, Bron

From Minnie:
A garden is a delightful thing. A plot is a place to grow things and bury them. It is also a cunning plan and the structure of a story. Many things to grow from a few seeds or cuttings.

That night I dreamt:

My friend and I are in the middle of a place that looks like a town square. There are car parks, children playing and a grassy area. All around us are people and it soon becomes clear we are all part of a rehearsal of a Shakespeare play. The director directs scenes around us and we play our parts. It could be Hamlet or Macbeth but I think it's a play I don't know. There is a murder in it. The set is established in the wild grass – a tombstone with a life-size monument and image of a woman on it, next to a translucent blue pool. Something else I can't quite see is in the woods nearby. As the actors quote their lines I'm astounded by the rich complexity of Shakespeare's imagery: as it is spoken I see a visual image. One line is a metaphor of something like grains of sand, which I recognise as quantum physics and I visualise as a brightly coloured kaleidoscope of shifting patterns. The other I can't recall. They are both eternal images. Archetypes. The rehearsal finishes and we are up the hill talking about the play. From here the tombstone is very visible in the long grass, as if erected overnight, as if someone was buried here in the night. It looks extremely real. (Deed, dream journal, 2016)

The dream references plots: Shakespeare's plots and the burial plot, an archetypal endless re-patterning of plots. This writing has a plot also, something in which things are brought together into a retelling of a universal and mythic story — a burial plot I am unearthing the contents of. I hold two roles here. I am the undertaker who facilitates the process of safely interring the dead through ritual and procedure. In doing so she holds together the threads, the relationships of living and dead and facilitates a process of mourning, relinquishment and revivification through story. She is a figure who lays to rest what is no longer of living presence. I am also the resurrectionist: the stalker in the night, stealthy in the dark, clutching my shovel and sack, digging around unearthing corpses with which to dissect, discover and reconstitute a human life. The undertaker safely buries what is no longer living, leaves only a marker above ground: a clue for stories to be unearthed if one is willing to dig deep.

Thank you Minnie. That's helpful and appreciated. I hope we can talk again soon and cultivate our plot and what shall grow in it.
Ps. You and I are both keepers of family secrets. You have kept secrets - been secretive. I have been a secret, still am a secret, and live a secret life as well as my visible one. I think in future I shall use my other name when I write to you.

Respectfully, Violet

Sgarci (2002) described the secret as an independent archetypal form that evokes mystery and holds tensions between concealment and revelation. She suggested the archetype of secret works to protect the fragile psyche, especially within dynamics of wounding and healing. The secret has a powerful archetypal presence in the history of adoption.

Dear Minnie,
It's been longer than I intended since I last wrote. I found our last exchange very stimulating and thought-provoking. It stirred a lot of associations and images. I dreamed about plots in all their complexity and then, a day or two later, I lost the plot so to speak. Do you know this feeling Minnie when dark chaos descends and you just can't hold onto your thoughts and everything seems to be disintegrating all around you? I simply couldn't get my disorganised thinking together. I did manage

to do a lot of writing however. When I imagine you having to deal with journeying with 2 dead infants on a train, knowing you are under police surveillance, I can well suppose you know what I'm describing. However, I don't want to assume & would rather hear your own responses on these matters. Since then the work has been a bit derailed with visits etc. I started thinking about a beautiful floral teapot I saw and thinking you might like it very much. A delicate ladylike teapot in crimson, pinks, reds & gold. Spring flowers. Elegant. I wondered about your teapot; you sitting at your table pouring the tea into cups, a steady stream of thick strong brew. One hand on the handle, one over the lid so it'll stay snug. Somehow I see you holding the handle with a green cloth - why? And is the strainer in the cup or are you holding it rather than the lid? I'm guessing your teapot is warm dark brown, maybe with a crocheted cozy to keep the tea warm, and that you like your tea strong, sweet, hot. I would love to hear from you - these domestic details; the brief moments between babies, noise, busyness, where you can sit and think and dream while you sip tea.

How is your garden Minnie now that spring is unfolding? Do you have little bulbs coming up through the frozen clods? Have you picked the early narcissi and daffodils for some winter colour in the house? Are you waiting for the fragrance of freesias and crocuses so full of their creamy yellow joy for life? And what are you planning to plant in your summer garden? Is it a luxury to have a flower garden or does it seem a necessity for you - to be able to plunge hands in the earth, bedding down cuttings and seeds, coming up fragrance and flowers. Of course there will be a kitchen garden too - vegetables and some herbs for medicinal use. Do you know about gardens, having grown up in a city piled and paved, crowded and stifled? Where did you learn about gardens & the simple grace of a posy of flowers on the scrubbed kitchen table. I see/sense you also like to stand at the window and look at the flowers in the path out front, the small piece of beauty you have made. Such a pleasure to have flowers -do you have favourites?

Well that's all for now Minnie. I shall think of you as I sit enjoying my fragrant tea, and as I enjoy the flowers I love to have in my room - at the moment the last of the winter cyclamen, some small yellow daisies, and pots of multi-coloured violas - pale blues, mauves and black; and a spray of green orchids that have lasted weeks, now nearly done. There is life all around - and yet the flowers too wither. I look forward to hearing from you.

Respectfully, Violet

Dear Violet,
Flowers indeed. I do love them, their dear fragrant heads nodding. Though I don't much like the mess they make on my clean table as they drop. You seem to have quite a picture of me in your mind's eye, quite a vivid imagination as my mother used to say — mind that, for curiosity killed the cat. Which always gets me thinking of silence. Cat got your tongue? I'm not one for giving away secrets. I am what I am and don't wish to explain myself, except as I wanted to leave a record in the gaol because they had got me so wrong & twisted my words. I may have had no choice but to meet my maker but I worked to make things right for my children — for all the children. Pity that they should suffer further because of me. If you read carefully there you shall find me. That's all I'm saying about it. It was kind of you to think of me and the floral teapot. I dare say, decadent though it seems, I should be very partial to a floral teapot and feel myself such a lady for pouring tea from such a one. I'm not one for grandiosities but

something pretty lifts the spirits, and Lord knows spirits need lifting in this forsaken life and you take it where you can, whether its the drink, or flowers, or gossiping about other people's business, or idle dreaming. I should say mostly my means were simple, planting a few things here & there where I might have planted vegetables & fed us all, scraping by as we were. A luxury those flowers. But not harmful to anyone. Only perhaps my dreaming, my idle wishing to get beyond where I found myself in life. They say the devil makes work of idle hands. My hands were never idle but perhaps the devil made use of my daydreams, for never would I have dreamed such a predicament as I found myself in — 2 dead babies and then a death sentence to follow. We all go down to the earth before long. Some, such as these babies, before their time. Me, I'd had my lot, and most of it was hard. Which is not to say I found it easy having life taken when it is not spent.

Sincerely, Minnie.

On that last journey with two dead babies in her hatbox, Minnie was carrying a posy of cuttings for her garden from the hotel she had stayed at. When she left the hatbox by the track to pick up later, she told Esther Wallis (one of the older children who served as household help in the busy cottage) it was heavy because it was full of bulbs to plant. When police searched her garden they dug up, amongst the recent cuttings, two dead infants and the skeletal remains of several children.

In these first letters, Minnie is reticent, referring me to the official document she had written whilst in gaol awaiting execution. This is her version of her life, setting her record straight. In it she admits unintentionally causing the death of the infant Dorothy through opium poisoning, and she claims her innocence with regard to any other child deaths. She expresses love and concern for the children she cared for. Yet, there are some significant gaps in her story and several children unaccounted for, as well as questions regarding the suspicious death of the second infant, Eva Hornsby.

Dear Minnie,

I'm sitting on my balcony in the sun, my little ginger cat snoozing beside me; looking out over rolling green hills, an endless blue sky & the still blue-green shimmer of the estuary tide. Birds are calling & there's a sharp chill in the wind that reminds me we're still close to winter. Downstairs where there's less light it's quite cold. I don't have the heater on. I wonder how much light you have at the Larches, how much warmth from the sun & how much from endless stoking of the fire or woodstove. They're like friendly & sometimes temperamental beasts, woodstoves - you have to learn how to tend & feed them. What pastures or landscapes do you look out on Minnie? I know you have your flower garden, & I believe some vegetables. Do you have fruit trees? A cow? A cat to catch the mice? Are there rabbits eating up the green around you? Are there birds that you hear daily, seasonally? Do you get the chance in your full household & life to look up at the sky & feel the vastness of things? I have a sense of you now trapped - financially, in the house, in this poverty, in this need to keep taking in children to try to cover the loss. No charity accepted here yet it gets harder & harder to make ends meet. And your husband? He does what you ask or tell him to do but he doesn't take initiative. Isn't the powerful clearheaded man you thought he was. You see his weakness now, and you accept him for himself because God and the two of you chose this path but sometimes you wish for a bit of backbone, mettle, that you could lean into & trust. But this is me imagining, Minnie. I would much rather hear from you what your life is like & how you came to be & do the things that have unfolded. Some people seem to

*meet unfortunate circumstances throughout their lives.
How do you see it, Minnie? I look forward to hearing
from you.*

Respectfully, Violet

There is a painting by New Zealand artist, Kathryn Madill, that vividly illuminates the lives of nineteenth-century New Zealand women. I saw Madill's (2001) exhibition, *Through the Looking Glass,* while I was in Oamaru and was haunted by its commentary and images. I visited the exhibition daily and later saw it in Auckland, where I took notes from which I wrote a series of poems. The painting, *Those Victorian Days,* is long and narrow with lines of horizon in blue, silver, green. There is a woman in Victorian dress on either side, one holding a pitcher. On one outer edge are the folds of a red curtain. Words sprawled across the horizon say, "Yes always someone dies, someone weeps, in tune with the laurels, dripping, and the tap dripping, and the spout dripping into the water-butt, and the dim gas flickering." The life of a Victorian woman is not romanticised.

Madill's art was destined to haunt me. Her images suggest deep loneliness and have an opium-like dream quality. The Victorian theme is coupled with images of graves in solitary landscapes, of corpses tucked inside snug fitting coffins, of women bearing a coffin and shovelling the earth into a grave. The implication being that death, like birth, is women's business.

*Dear Minnie,
I've been thinking about the practicalities of running
a baby care business, taking in other people's unwanted
infants & what that was like for you on a daily basis.
Were you passionate about children or was this the best
option you could find for financial survival? Perhaps
there's an element of both because you seem to genuinely*

care for your charges, the ones in your care - mostly. There are a few unaccountable gaps, Minnie, in which the mind wanders over dark possibilities & which you haven't enlightened us on. Survival as a desperate mother. Did it sometimes come down to you or the child? I know that's common for mothers - whose needs to put first? I chose not to have children knowing I couldn't devote myself fully to them in the way I thought a mother should. I don't regret that but I sometimes wonder what it might have been like to be a mother. You know. Again there are the mysteries. What were the circumstances of their births (& conceptions)? And what are the echoes preceding and reverberating on from Ellen's death along with your two tiny grandchildren? I can imagine how devastating & life changing this might be. I'm sorry Minnie, I didn't leave you an opportunity last week to reply fully. My hope is to redress that this week. I leave you now to respond.

Respectfully, Violet

I am referring to Minnie's own children. When she arrived in New Zealand to stay with her aunt, known as Granny Kelly, Minnie had one child, Ellen, and was pregnant with another. Minnie claimed she was the widow of a doctor. Despite rigorous research, Hood (1994) was never able to establish any proof of a marriage, nor could she discover anything about Minnie's life during the gap of several years between leaving Scotland and appearing in New Zealand. Was Minnie actually a mother of illegitimate children herself? If so, how had she managed to keep and care for Ellen when so many were not able to? Perhaps it was only the home offered by Granny Kelly that saved Minnie and her children from the destitute lives of other "fallen" women. Is this where Minnie's compulsion and compassion for unwanted babies began? As I wondered about the possibilities of Minnie's life, the separation between her and myself began to blur. In my dream:

> *I am at my friend's house though she is not there. I am Minnie Dean, wearing black Victorian garments. I'm worried about being Minnie and want to leave. I wait for an opportunity to slip away. The others aren't nice to me. Then I am in a courtroom listening to a bi-lingual testimony. A Māori woman is being translated to the court, and then a Māori man. I can tell the man doesn't trust the translator. I don't know what they're saying or how the testimony relates to me. I reflect on how stories change shape as they are translated and interpreted. I feel a sense of gloom, no hope. Back at my friend's I try to leave but my shoes are caked in mud. I have been spending a lot of time in the garden. Later I am outside on the branch of a tree. I feel safer here but still want to get away across the expanse of garden.* (Deed, dream journal, 2016).

As I started to ask more questions in the letters, my dreams engaged with Shadowy parts that offer testimony but are afraid of misinterpretation and are unsure how they will be received.

Dear Violet,

Pretty name. I am partial to violets though they have a dark meaning in the language of flowers. Mourning and graves. Especially of young women dead before their time. My Ellen was one who needs respecting with violets. Those perfumy flowers shall always remind me of her. Such loss, as you say, devastating. But I've had so many losses in my life — one must go on as God wills, meet what is offered with stoicism & fortitude. There was something wrong with Ellen that she couldn't do this. Did I do something wrong, that she suffered so much & took her own life and her children's lives? If I had been there could I have saved her — or the children? If I had loved her better, been a better mother could it have been prevented? Or was she sick in her soul? I don't believe she was evil, a sinner, as people would have it of a suicide. I'm an upright Christian, a believer, but I know my Ellen: she was not bad. Yet such a sinful act, wilfully taking the life of a child — two children. A mother's guilt. How did I survive her rather than she me? How could I not have taken her little ones to care for if only I had known she was so sick and needed care. How did she not love me enough, or trust my love, for her to tell me, and ask my help. I lost my mother early. Sisters too. Perhaps death cast a shadow on my soul too early and now there is something black and dead there, something/some grief I cannot get to. You cover it over and get on, for such is life & many suffer it. But you carry it with you & something gets hard, sealed over like a scar. Was I hard with Ellen in case I lost her too? Did I hold my mother love back? Did she feel motherless like me, helpless to know how to change her life? I have felt those dark wings of despair & desperation. But, plunging my hands in warm earth I also know life, the beauty and fleetingness of flowers. You have opened up a dark place in me Violet, with your questions & your passion for flowers & your kindness & concern for my Ellen, my grandchildren, myself. I am not a monster, though sometimes I judge myself harshly for what I fear I have caused in others' lives. I never meant to cause harm to any soul. Believe me.

Sincerely, Minnie

In the Victorian language of flowers, violets signify the death of a maiden. The Victorians were partial to communicating in the language of flowers. Just as there was a complicated code for mourning dress, there was a code for flowers. Violets were usually laid on the graves of young women or girls. Jung (1968) in his work on alchemy, referred to a 'violet darkness' that symbolises the darkness in the psyche that is worked on in the alchemical process. Through dreams and reveries on the lives of Victorian women, aided by Madill's wonderful art, the violet darkness revealed itself and its workings.

In this exchange of letters, Minnie was thoughtful about the death of her daughter, Ellen, another 'dead maiden'. Ellen drowned herself and her two children in a well. It was shortly after Ellen and her children died that Minnie began collecting babies through the business of baby farming. Madill's (1999) artwork '*The Well*', provided a haunting image for reverie:

> *The well in the ground like a grave and the virginal figure, a ghost in white. Flat landscape and dark, broody, ominous clouds. The shape sometimes warm and comforting, like the depression/hollow left by an egg. The well of loneliness. Bowed head, as if in prayer.*
> (Deed, journal, undated)

In my reverie, I associated water and death with pre-birth – the egg. Death is experienced as comforting but also hollow, a depression.

Dear Minnie,
Your last letter moved me immensely. To connect with the tremendous ongoing legacy of loss through women's lives and the spectre always of death in childbirth. Birth and death always closely linked. I'm sorry for your feelings of guilt at thinking you could have done more for Ellen. I took note - paid attention - that you acknowledged you felt motherless & wondered if Ellen felt that too. I know the feeling of losing a mother, the sadness and terrible emptiness & longing to be loved properly with a mother's love from one's own mother. Were you trying to offer all those unmothered infants some reparative love? As you may have discovered, Minnie - or not - you cannot replace a mother just as you cannot replace a child. Both parties instinctively know the replacement is the wrong person; not the right

fit. Sometimes circumstances make this a necessity if a child - or a mother - is to survive - but it brings its wounds & its dissatisfactions. I would be very interested to hear more from you, Minnie, as to your reasons for taking in babies, your uppermost reasons, and the reasons not so clearly known about but hidden more deeply within. The secret reasons we sometimes don't even admit to ourselves. I've done nothing yet with the garden, it's still too cold to plant & I've been reluctant to start preparing. My indoor flowers continue well and I have a fresh spray of delicate mauve orchids, and a white flowering geranium. I look forward to your reply.

Respectfully, Violet

Dear Violet,

There's something about growing up without your mother. I remember her, clear as day, how much I loved & wanted to please her. How helpless & afraid I felt to watch her in her dying bed. How brave she was & how despicably helpless I was. If my love could have saved her it would have. But all my love for her did nothing, nor all my prayers. I wondered then — perhaps I was a heathen, unloving girl & that was why my mother died. But she loved me I know so I must hope I was worthy of that love. I bend my head in shame that it has come to such an end. How could I have wronged my mother so poorly. I have been thinking on what you said about replacement. You are right. No one could ever replace my mother & I hated the stepmother who came into my life. I wanted to be loved but she wasn't my mother and I had to keep pushing her away. Perhaps that was how I began to wish for a baby of my own to love & who could love me. When I had my own dear Ellen I learned it was not all roses a mother's love & you can't erase the dark marks of loss that blot all the good feelings. I did love her dearly, & do still, yet I also found it hard to show her my love. I had been a mother all my life in practical ways but I had *not been mothered, neither was my mother there for me when I needed her in the distress I felt after Ellen's birth. I needed a doctor to care for my sickness & so I created one. I can see what you are thinking — that I began taking on the babies, to replace my lost dear Ellen & her little ones, to replace the lost mother/child bond in my own heart, to make up for the lost mothers of all those infants who would feel the deathly emptiness through life otherwise. The great chasm where there should have been mother. I didn't set out to have Ellen then & in such circumstances. But you could say I did have my heart set on having a child – & I brought the same heartfelt determination into having those other babies too — if no one wanted them I would want them with all my willpower — which is considerable. To make up for all the pain of feeling unwanted by a mother who chose to suffer & die, to be with my dead sisters rather than stay with me.*

Sincerely, Minnie

Mothers and death are intimately linked in this exchange of letters. The effect is a devastation of self-trust and the wound of feeling unwanted that is a significant theme in the trauma of the adopted child. The compulsion to rescue others from this fate is also explicit. This compulsion can become murderous and was discussed in detail in Chapter Five. Psychotically depressed mothers at risk of killing their infants may express thoughts of wanting to kill themselves, and to kill their child, rather than risk handing it over to someone who might harm it (Stanton, Simpson, & Woulds, 2000).

Dear Minnie,
It's October. All the blossoms are coming out on the trees and the birds are stirring with new energy and life. I'm thinking still of gardens but there's also such a lot to be done to keep things going here - this project, business, finances etc. I wonder, Minnie, how did you plan and/

or think about your business? Did you discuss with your husband or present him with a fait accompli? It seems from what I've read he kept himself out of your business, hands off, yet he shared that life with all the children in the house & he supported you at the trial & at the end of your life. Such complex characters you both appear to me, so very far away in time yet so very near in terms of emotional experience. I have no judgment Minnie. I do sometimes wonder if you did kill a child - intentionally or accidentally -actually we know, you admitted, Dorothy Carter died from too much opium administered in your care. But I don't judge, I simply put myself in your position & in the context of your time - so many unwanted babies or mothers without support, so much shame & secrecy - vulnerability of single women - & I can see how the answers are not simple. And I don't think you were a cruel woman, unlike some in this business. You have a heart about you - a sentimental, stoic, hidden, hurt heart. I suspect you identified with those women who had no place for their babies. There but for the grace of God and Grandma Kelly might you have walked, widowed or not. Making ends meet makes the difference. So you end up responsible for caring for many little children, not having had any of your own with Charles. You knew about mothering from your own two, and you knew I think the precariousness of a widow (or other) parenting alone. Minnie! Did you love children? Were you sad not to be bringing up your own family with Charles? Were you substituting with other babies? Perhaps you were more of an adoptive mother than I have realised before.

I look forward to hearing from you.
Violet

That night I dream:

> *I visit a museum, watching a young woman who I think of as a French maid who is sewing up the gauze on an exhibited frock. She wears a white lace wedding dress and her dark black hair hangs down her back. I finger a detail of the frock. An opium plant is woven into the fabric and as I touch, a bud or seedpod rolls off onto the floor. I feel embarrassed at having 'nipped the bud'. The woman takes it and carefully sews it into an invisible pocket inside the dress. She continues to stitch the opium flower onto the dress, muttering in French. She is very annoyed with me. As I move closer she begins to growl at me like a wild animal. I step back, say* merci beaucoup *and* grazie, *and walk on.* (Deed, dream journal, 2016)

Here the themes of my life begin to synthesise: history, opium (dissociation), shame, being nipped in the bud, wild anger, and the tensions between exhibition and invisibility that come from secrets.

Dear Violet,

Thank you for your thoughts. I have been so unjustly accused and attacked it has been hard for me to ever trust again. I am naturally suspicious of compliments and my heart has hardened with pain & fear since I became troubled by busybodies & police. I wondered at first if you were one of them, the busybodies, putting their noses into all my cupboards, my gardens, my travels, my secret life. Yet you have consistently offered me glimpses of flowers & kindness, thoughtful & respectful questions. I cannot say I fully trust, only the foolish would do so in my position. But I begin to believe that you do not wish to believe the worst. You at least are willing to hear me out. Again, I direct you to my statement, you will find me there, and answers to your questions. I cannot say I always told the utter truth, but I told it as I believed it in myself, it is my story & I told it as my own. No stickybeaks, stickyfingers. You also appear to have a heart, and a graciousness. How lovely of you to consider my choice of flowers & to ponder whether my life was hard. In Scotland we grew up hard & learned early how to fend. I grew up nursing other people's babies. They are a familiar part of my life. I loved them & sometimes they were a nuisance, but a woman is not a proper woman if she is not a mother. I was sorrowful Charles and I didn't conceive and saw a welcome opportunity when Margaret's mother was dying. I loved that child as I loved my own. She thrived with me and was saved from something worse. With the others I hoped the same. That all would know the love of a mother & the security of a home. Of course some of them were bad from the start & rejected all I could offer them. They disrupted the others. I could not keep them under such circumstances. One plucks out the rotten apples before they rot the whole barrel. Those who stayed loved me back & we were happy enough with our mean lot. Yes — I know about poppies. I have sometimes grown them but it is easier to buy the syrup prepared from the chemist. We did that in Scotland. Laudanum for this, that & the other. The panacea for all the dark dirty dangerous disgusting & terrifying things that happen all around a child who must be soothed. I wouldn't be without it. Quiet children are good children. I do not like to see them disturbed. Some children fight it, others respond very quickly. It can be hard to know how much to give, and perhaps in my anxiety not to disturb others I'm a little generous in the dose. I have learned my lesson in a frightful way with little Dorothy. If I had not needed my wits about me then I would have taken a large dose myself. Less harmful than the drink they say, of which I do not touch a drop, being a respectable widow & married woman with mouths to feed. Like little fledglings in the nest they are — all bundled up snug & tight in our tiny rooms, chirping & calling for their mother, food, warmth, petting, sleep. Sometimes Mother is tired out & wishes them all to be quiet just to get some rest & peace. The laudanum is handy then & no harm was ever done by it until Dorothy.

Sincerely, Minnie

In Oamaru, I began to reflect deeply about opium as a metaphor for dissociation and denial. The themes I discovered in my reveries on opium included suspended animation and paralysis, a sense of an insect dying in the cocoon rather than transforming into a butterfly, a sense of dying in the womb before being able to birth.

Dear Minnie,

It's taken me a whole month to reply to you. Life has been full & I haven't been in a good frame of mind. Not an excuse because I have thought of you. I feel since September it's been harder to connect with you and the work. I really value your guidance, relationship and input into this re-search & I reach out to you here for your support and creative input. You bring fresh insight & ideas & you make me think more deeply about the issues. I'm feeling a little stuck in the work, a little nervous about going back into it as I've got so disconnected from the momentum of it & afraid I won't be able to get it done as time slips away. Can you remind me of its relevance? I don't want my connection with you to slip away. As I write this I begin to hear an attachment pattern - a moving towards that becomes a fear of loss and a pulling away. I wonder how many of your little ones were like that, Minnie? Either clinging desperately or pushing away all the love and connection you had to offer. Was that frustrating, Minnie? Claustrophobic? Attachment theory is a significant part of this work. As I write I'm also thinking of meeting up with my birth parents yesterday & how this is going so easily & well after years of fear, disappointment, longing, grief, rejection & withdrawal - on both sides. There is something about this research - re-search that is healing the wound of lost mother-child, of search for mother. The anxiety, insecurity & bitterness of grief has drained out for me.

The joy flows in. What a gift from working with your energy & your story alongside my energy & story. Thank you Minnie.

Respectfully, Violet

As I got deeper into the conversation with Minnie, themes of connection and disconnection appeared. I entered a difficult time, finding it hard to stay connected with myself. My thinking felt disconnected, and I was overwhelmed with fear and anxiety. I felt isolated and alone, bereft of any support and afraid to reach out. Recognising a disorganised attachment pattern helped me to understanding what was happening and to reconnect.

Dear Violet,

I've been wondering where you were & thinking you had changed your mind & given up on me. I too have lost so much — my mother, sisters, my daughter & grandchildren, my hope for more children of my own, my trust in a husband to provide well for us, and finally my reputation & my life. I learned early the attachment dance you describe — the pushing for anything I can get for action from those who should take it, and the withdrawal with silence & evasiveness when questioned or threatened. I realise now that made things worse for me. But it was all I know about protecting myself through the strife & bitterness of life. I built a wall around myself & determined to recreate myself beyond the miseries & disappointments of childhood: the guilt of being the one who survived, who only wanted to make my mother happy & could not save her. I felt her love & that sustained me enough to have some heart for others in this world. Yet if I'm honest it was a selfish kind of love, rescuing babies, believing I loved them, yet mostly rescuing myself from the oblivion & fear I detected there at the heart of things. Truth is such a complex & fragile thing. I still believe I was doing good, that I was coming from a place of kindness & care about the plight & problem of these orphaned children. If I didn't take them who would? Someone less kind perhaps, more neglectful of their welfare, or outright cruel. I know the precariousness of the motherless child. How I have wished for my mother at times when I've been alone with some difficult task in my life. Granny Kelly was a big help — warm heart, tough heart — but no substitute for my mother. I loved her. I wanted to be loved like that. I wanted to be needed & important otherwise I felt I was nothing. Insignificance is frightening in such a big world. Thank you for writing.

Sincerely, Minnie

Dear Minnie,

This is my 8th letter to you. It has been hard keeping the energy & intensity of the work since I went back to work in September. I would appreciate anything you can offer in terms of direction. Especially as I begin to plan the actual thesis & the writing of a biography of your story. You will be aware of my research proposal, which is nearly ready for review & presentation. Is there anything I've left out, haven't covered? Or anything you're not happy with, it would be helpful to have your comments & advice before I hand it in next week. That brings it slowly into focus: I have today & tomorrow, then a meeting on Thurs, then Sunday, Monday, Tues the following week in which to make revisions. That's a tight turnaround but I think I can make it if I get myself together. So Minnie, a little more direct than usual:

Have I described accurately & appropriately baby farming in the contexts of adoption and infanticide?

Have I made the links between them so readers can follow?

Do you have any comment on the nature of psychological infanticide?

How do I ground the archetypal approach & contain & integrate those energies so they are safely channelled? What other suggestions need to be made?

Once we get this completed Minnie I hope we can return to a deeper conversation on the nature of these things & how to honour the writing of your life & how helpful you've been in helping me with my life. Thank you.

Respectfully, Violet

Dear Violet,

Thank you for your kind words. I hope indeed I may be helpful & am glad to hear I have been able to be so in your life. I do not forget the time you sat with me in my cell & held my hand when I was so afraid. You comforted me as I sat facing my own death. You helped me find my courage. Now I hope you find yours on this psychological journey via the PhD pathway. I would have liked the opportunity to study — to set my mind to something. Honour that privilege & don't waste it. Use it to help others with their suffering — as I did in my own way. Yes, it had some selfish motives & intentions too — the meeting of needs, as does your story. We are all attempting on some level to heal our own wounds. I lost your attention there for a moment. You went off into your own wounded place. It's important to stay focused, keep tracking what happens around you so you know how to stay safe.

So to your questions:

You need to link more clearly the process of actual infanticide through baby farming & then to adoption so the reader has a clear understanding of — what you mean & how it has occurred. The progression from killing to abandonment to the handing over to us baby farmers who hold a particular tension that mothers refused to hold for themselves any longer & then to the denials of adoption. I know it for myself, the dangerous belief that displaced children simply need a mother who is a replaceable figure. I would never replace my own mother in my life or memories.

How could an infant relinquish that first relationship? Of course a baby farmer's intentions are varied & complex, and possibly not focused on mothering. There's a strong dark thread here with feminism & the need for women's control over their own bodies & fertility. More on this another time.

Sincerely, Minnie

Ps. The structure of the hero's journey may be a useful one as you begin to write about your struggles & mine. Write from that place & see what you discover: it may be a good way of grounding & channelling the energies — as you asked about. Scly. M.

It is apparent from these letters and dreams that my relationship with Minnie, and the Minnie-like part of myself was changing. In my last letter I invited a more collaborative approach, and a desire to represent Minnie in ways we negotiated together rather than making unilateral decisions. There was a warmth and feeling of connection in these last letters. Having asked Minnie for guidance I dreamt:

> *Minnie's biographer has given me permission to search a space above her house with which Minnie has some connection. It is like a hidden vault, disused, cramped, forgotten, the wood blackened and charred as if there has been a fire here. It can only be reached by going up a ladder and I need a flashlight to see in the darkness. Again, I am respectful in this space of mystery, not sure what I will find or even what is meant to be here amongst the stored junk that is being moved out. I am concerned because we don't yet know what might be sacred or hold a subtle clue. I go up the ladder to look around and then go back a second time. My friend's father has left me a note asking me to keep any books or movies called*

'Hatching'. He has written a long list of titles all with this word in them. (Deed, dream journal, 2016)

Something, perhaps many things, are hatching out of this dark space. New life hatches. Also plots are hatched – created out of imagination. Both types of hatching unfold through time. Hatching seems to be the antidote to that opium state of suspended animation. I am curious about the space where Minnie is 'housed' in my dream, up a ladder and also inside a vault, which is more typically situated underground. Bachelard (1964) wrote of the polarities between vertical spaces, suggesting the roof represents rationality and conscious construction where the cellar (or vault) reflects the "irrationality of the depths" (p. 18). My dream invites both the conscious construct of research and the digging into hidden depths of history and memory.

Writing letters provided a playful and serious means of discovering themes and intentions of my inquiry process itself (Romanyshyn, 1997).

In the process of writing to Minnie, I became more compassionately aware of the greater circumstances that led to the situation of child-murder. I felt attuned to the feminism inherent in the deep questions of the issue of unwanted children. Minnie developed in her complexity as a person and took on a new role in my psyche as guide and advisor rather than longed-for and feared attachment figure. Through our growing collaboration, trust and care was emerging. It is also noticeable that Minnie had, in our final letter exchange, become more integrated in serving the greater purpose of my inquiry. I experienced this blending of her and myself as similar to the attunement of a mother following the signals and needs of her child.

Postscript

I wake in the night and sense the presence of Minnie Dean close by. In the spirit of our dialogues I invite her to communicate with me through dream:

> *There is a serial killer about. There is a feeling of menace and also mystery. Then I see an infant being held out by a dark figure. She is being held out in space and she is not held safe. The scene turns and I witness her face, my infant self, looking terrified. I find it hard to look at her because it is so distressing. I reflect on the serial killer and begin to realise I am the murderer. Then I prepare to do some baking.* (Deed, dream journal, 2016)

Cooking is a metaphor for the alchemical process of transformation that can occur in psychotherapy and depth investigation. Raw ingredients are mixed together and placed under intense heat, causing their transformation into a new synthesis of form. In this chapter I faced into my early terror of being killed and the serial ways I had killed off the small, weak, vulnerable, and unwanted shadow parts of my Soul. In the next chapter I take the alchemical process further, into the phase of *solutio*.

Chapter Eleven
Solutio: The Alchemy of Drowning and the 'Trauma-world'

Let not the waterflood overflow me,
Neither let the deep swallow me up,
And let not the pit shut her mouth upon me.
Psalm 69:15 King James Bible (KJV 1900)

In this chapter I explore the alchemical phase of *solutio* as a psychological process. I begin with reveries on the drowning theme from my personal experience. I explain the term *solutio* as an alchemical process and as a metaphor for the process of depth psychotherapy. I explore, through the relationship between water and the feminine, the idea of the great round that links birth, death, and rebirth in a continuous cycle. Within this context I consider the trauma world of the unwanted child in the womb. Finally I consider the Breton myth of the drowned city of Ys and the Melusine as a figure of the archetypal feminine.

My descent into the realm of grief as I engaged with my psychological infanticide was elementally associated with water. I thought of myself as the drowned woman. I was not drowning. I had already drowned. Living in Oamaru, I imagined the place as a drowned city, an inverted underwater world. I was eventually to discover that this *Kingdom by the Sea* (Frame, 1961) was indeed a natural valley bowl that was completely under water in prehistoric times. The surrounding area was named the Valley of the Whales because of the many fossilised whale remains found there. This sunken city was a grave for Leviathan, that creature of the psychological deep in which mind and matter are plumbed and bridged (Melville, 1967; Slattery, 2015). Intuitively, in my reveries I had connected with this place as a watery tomb for subterranean beings. This image connects the watery world of the unborn child and the underworld Land of Dis.

In a series of poems centred on this image of the drowned woman I articulated the feeling of inverted life that also recollected the *via negativa* of eclipse:

Songs for a drowned woman 5

I can find that yew song
that days of rain & green & mist song
the haunted valley song
the mountain drew closer song

I have it all in me here
in my body
all the traces
pulsing beneath the skin
...

& the angel steps out
& closes her granite eyes

for an instant a negative
black lilies embracing a white sky
black monument to time
black wings in snow

she steps out of the frame
as if picking up her medieval skirts
to walk over glass

as if kicking her tango shoes off
in a corner
as if dancing on bare sand
in a cave at the edge of the world.
(Deed, 2003c)

Feeling my way now into my actual experience of the drowned woman sunk in a drowned city, I find I lose definition, tangibility and in particular, *words* to describe it. I enter an amorphous, aqueous, amphibious territory without defined boundaries or solidity. I am no longer a self, a discrete person with a body that has a definite form that separates inner from outer, self from other. I am in a state of merging into the void, of dissolving.

It is a swirling, dark, murky, intangible dissolution. This is sometimes a terrible feeling, a sense of ebbing away, dissolving into nothing, and it is accompanied by the terror of an awareness that is aware of its own disintegration. A transformative process is occurring, and I am helpless within it. I know in my body, without words, that I will not survive without help from another, and that the one who should sustain me and keep me alive does not wish it. This is a wordless terror that creates death anxiety perhaps before the beginning of life. As we discovered in Chapter Three, the unwanted foetus experiences the mother's rejecting feelings towards it. This earliest relationship with the mother has effects throughout life (Grof, 1988, 1998; Irving, 1989; Verny and Kelly, 2001; Ward, 2006). It seems likely that the experience I describe above is a womb experience. It is also recognisable as an experience of the alchemical stage of *solutio*.

Solutio

Solutio is the stage of alchemy in which the *prima materia* (original material) undergoes a process of transformation through dissolution (Edinger, 1994; Hillman, 2014; Jung, 1969/1983). This is also part of the process of depth psychology, an internal working through of images, as I do in this inquiry by following my dreams, images, body sensations, and their associations.

Solutio is the phase of medieval alchemy that relates to water, and to immersion in a vessel of fluid: the alchemical bath. Jung (1969/1983) named the alchemical vessel as representative of the womb and the process of growth and transformation that occurs there. This phase is reminiscent of transformation that occurs in the chrysalis when a caterpillar disintegrates out of its old form and re-integrates as a new form of life. The cocooned caterpillar emerging as butterfly is frequently a metaphor for the transformational aspects of death: in order for new life to emerge, the old form must die. I explored this metaphor in greater detail in Part Two, in the essay on opium.

Edinger (1994) wrote extensively on alchemical symbolism in psychotherapy. He described *solutio* as the process of dissolving rigidities and fixed ideas of the personality. He referred to the immersion of the *prima materia* into the mercurial bath as "a descent into the unconscious, which is the maternal womb from which the ego is born" (Edinger, p. 48). Additionally, Jung (1969/1983) referred to the waters of the unconscious rising up to meet consciousness (the alchemical King and Queen) as they descend into the alchemical bath. Some alchemical texts describe this as a very pleasant process. Others describe it as a painful dismemberment (Bachelard, 1983).

Edinger (1994) elaborated that an immature ego will regress into a blissful *solutio* experience, whereas a mature ego will feel anxiety at being threatened with dissolution. He suggested that a blissful *solutio* is the most dangerous. As I understand it, this passive love of death is a regression in which the Great Mother takes the little child back into herself, and the child both longs for, and passively surrenders to, this reunion. We see in this nostalgic romanticism and longing for death a link between the experience of dissolving into nothing and an infant (immature) ego, and a connection made between mother and death by the infant ego who surrenders to self-dissolution in a desire to be re-absorbed by the mother. Bachelard (1983) used the term Ophelia complex to describe this passive seduction by feminine death.

Jung (1969/1983) explained that the womb is its own contained world, and is capable of both killing and revitalising. He commented: "The immersion in the 'sea' signifies ... 'dissolution' in the physical sense of the word and at the same time, according to Dorn, the solution of a problem" (Jung, 1969/1983, p.79).

These ideas resonate with my own experience. The original infant had no place, identity, or meaning in the world and longed to withdraw into a soothing union with Mother Death. I wish to emphasise that this is only one face of the Great Mother. The soothing vision that I named Mother Death is also the annihilating Death Mother that destroys the ability to be in life (Harris & Harris, 2015; Sieff, 2017; Woodman, 2005; Woodman & Sieff, 2015). Harris and Harris (2015) described the Death Mother as follows:

> The Death Mother is the foundation of a destructive complex that is both personal and cultural, and it is a special form of the negative mother. With certain complexes, we cut off some of our particular gifts and are unable to live out some of our potentials. But the Death Mother causes us to cut off the essence of life within us. (p. 11)

As Harris and Harris (2015) stated, our complexes begin in our deepest experiences, which may be seen as centred round a crisis. Erik Erikson's (1958) theory of the development of identity throughout the life cycle builds on recognisable stages that we all go through. Human development, according to Erikson, begins in infancy with the developmental crisis of 'trust versus mistrust', and goes through certain crises, or stages of initiation that we are continually developing throughout life. At each new stage we progress and integrate the previous stages in the process of becoming whole persons. Lifton (1994) claimed that the adopted child frequently remains stuck in the life cycle as a result of a lack of access to history and family necessary to develop identity cohesion. Without accomplishing these developmental tasks, the adopted person experiences identity confusion: "an inability to know who you are, what you want to become, and what you want to do in life" (Erikson, 1958, as cited in Lifton, 1994, p. 66). I propose that this identity confusion occurs even earlier and is not simply a result of a lack of connection to family and history but a result of psychological infanticide before birth.

I propose, as a contribution to Erikson's theory, that the initial crisis of human development occurs before birth and is centred round the developmental stage of the foetus and the crisis of 'life versus death'. It is in the womb that archetypal patterns are constellated and begin to be activated. Before we are able to face into the challenges of trust, autonomy, self-worth, identity etc., we must first negotiate whether to embrace or deny life. At each further developmental stage or crisis of initiation, this initial engagement with 'life versus death' is revisited.

Developmentally, the first half of life invites us to fully open and engage with living and creating. If we have already had difficulty negotiating the stage of life versus death we will have difficulty engaging with life, relationships and making choices. Life will seem imposed on us rather than something we participate in creating. We will lack vitality and joy and may suffer endless negativity, passivity, and despair. We may wish to end our lives prematurely rather than learn how to live.

As we begin to decline in the middle years, we age and face into the end of our lives, reviewing what it means to be alive, adjusting to illness and degeneration, gathering wisdom, and making peace with our death. If we have had difficulty with the stage of life versus death, the end of life will feel terrifying and inflicted upon us. We will be faced with the emptiness and lack of meaning of our lives, and we will be afraid to let go into death even while hating and rejecting life.

The return at the end of life to the initial stage of development in the womb is a completion of our beginning and the crisis of life versus death. The myth of eternal return (Eliade, 1954; Grof, 1988) describes this transformational birth, life, death, rebirth cycle of continuous creation and destruction. All stages of our lives invite us to develop our relationship with living and dying.

In the situation of psychological infanticide occurring before birth, I propose that the spaciousness within which the unborn child negotiates 'life' as its first developmental initiation is collapsed through the death wishes and dissociation it experiences. This collapsing of the sense of 'being' into a sense of imposed 'non-being' is a state of living death, which the unborn child feels no choice but to submit to. The state of being neither fully dead nor fully alive is the place in the life cycle that the person who experiences psychological infanticide remains stuck in, unless they are able to negotiate it successfully during other developmental phases through life. When stuck at this stage of the life cycle, it is highly likely that each successive stage will be experienced as a life and death crisis.

Returning to the *solutio* phase, we can now consider it as an expression of the lack of engagement with life that comes with not negotiating the initial crisis of life versus death before birth. The danger of the *solutio* phase is being overwhelmed and paralysed by the feminine unconscious, which equates to becoming stuck in the parallel universe of the 'trauma world' (Sieff, 2017; Woodman & Sieff, 2015). The potential of this phase is to come to new possibilities as a result of dismembering, or dissolving, the defence structures that enabled survival of the original trauma at the cost of development of the original self (Jung, 1969/1983; Kalsched, 1996). When this happens, the person is able to emerge transformed into new patterns of relating – internally and externally.

What happens to this infantile longing for the womb if the actual experience in the womb was not bliss, but was in fact infanticidal? Perhaps then, the soothing that is longed for is the return to an opium-like state of dissociation, of not knowing, not feeling, not existing. Perhaps even a return to some experience before conception, before there was a womb-experience that was not nurturing or welcoming. What then of the relationship between love and death identified in the *solutio* phase and the Ophelia complex? Could there be a longing for merging with the cosmic love that might exist (as the mystics point to) beyond death? Is it possible in the case of negative womb experiences that there is a regressive pull to a psychotic symbolisation of non-existence and non-being that is not 'pregnant with possibility' – the way a foetus in a loving womb might experience it? My earlier chapter on eclipse suggests this might be so.

What is the relationship between Mother, Love, and Death for the unwanted child? As discussed in Chapter Three, when Mother, Love, and Death get merged in a situation of helpless terror an infanticidal attachment is formed. Kalsched (1996) described the patterns of dissociative self-soothing fantasy that occur when the infant psyche splits in response to trauma. The traumatised child is entranced by archetypal presences in the psyche that aim to protect the child from further harm but also limit growth into the world. The self is held in a state of suspended animation. These concepts were introduced in Chapter Three and elaborated in the chapters in Part Two. In order for healing to occur these archetypal presences must be worked with in order for the whole psychic system to feel safe enough for the imprisoned original self to come out (Kalsched, 1996).

Jung (1969/1983) clarified that the outcome of the alchemical work of dissolution of the royal couple in the bath is "to bring the work to its final consummation and bind the opposites by love, 'for love is stronger than death'" (p. 34). In other words, healing from trauma requires integration of the psyche and the development of loving rather than annihilating internal carers.

The dissolution of the old form in *solutio* proceeds into the *negrido* or black phase commonly described as depression. *Solutio* often becomes a *mortificatio* in which what is dissolved is experienced as an annihilation of self (Edinger, 1994; Hillman, 2014; Jung, 1969/1983; Marlon, 2005). I explored this *mortificatio* in the image of *sol niger* in Chapter Nine. The experience of psychological infanticide can leave one stuck in *mortificatio* in a terrible state of living death.

There is another level of *solutio*, known as the greater *solutio*. The ego is dissolved in an experience of the numinous in a transpersonal process that has been likened to the great flood myths, in which anything that is not worth saving is destroyed (Edinger, 1994). This crisis of breakdown or breakthrough is now termed in transpersonal language as spiritual emergency versus spiritual emergence (Lucas, 2011). Bachelard (1983) described this greater *solutio* as the cosmic water complex in which the feminine moon is drowned in the great floods. This is a personal crisis, often termed a night sea journey or dark night of the Soul (Jung 1969/ 1983; Moore, 1992, 2012). The potential and power of the drowning experience, therefore, is the reorganisation of the self once anything no longer of service has been destroyed. It is the return from the dead into a higher state of being that brings with it the knowledge that we survive death.

I associate the drowning theme with Minnie, her daughter, and infanticide. After several months of debility that appear to have been, at the very least, a serious depression, Minnie's oldest daughter, Ellen, drowned herself and her two children in a well. I turned this piece of information over and over in my mind, trying to imagine what it was like to be the desperate Ellen who could find no other options, and what it was like for Minnie to lose her daughter and two grandchildren to such a death. I expressed my reverie in a poem written from Ellen's perspective:

Ellen's Song

It's myself I look for
in the blank of this
cold eye

rippling its skin
beneath the sky
I long for it all to be still
call my children close
one under each wing

folded tight in this pupa
we shall sleep through the winter

my son leans into me
hid in my skirts against
the prying faces of strangers

the baby floats
feet pale petals
almond blossom drenched in dew
wax pearls dropped
from a moving candle

their bleached faces
wait for the alchemy of change
belief laced with memory
of warm entombment
not this tight seal of damp
the inside of an eye

there was nothing better on this day
frost on the clods
a day trudged through dark while the sun mocks
blinded with dark fumbled through
threaded needles, smoking fires, boiling coppers
vegetable patch laid fallow like an open grave
the frozen wash hung stiff from its noose.

(Deed, 2003a)

I related to Ellen's despair and the hopelessness that led to her suicide and the filicide of her children. During my phase in the drowned city, symbolised by Oamaru, I felt overwhelmed, but the self who has survived is transformed and strengthened, more deeply connected to both creativity and being of service to others. As noted in the next section of this chapter, I went from the watery grave of *solutio* and the black torments of *nigredo* and *mortificatio* through a greening phase. Jung (1968) mentioned that in Kundalini yoga, the 'green womb' is the name for Shiva manifesting from a latent condition. He also noted that the *viriditas*, or greenness, follows the *nigredo* in exceptional cases, though without elaborating what these might be (Jung, 1968). I felt great kinship when I later discovered Robert Romanyshyn's (1999) reveries of greening of the Soul in his memoir of loss and grief.

Womb and Tomb

I turn now to the relationships between water, woman, fluidity, womb, and death. There is a common expression 'from the womb to the tomb' intended to express the trajectory of a life. Yet, there is a deep relationship between the womb and the tomb, between pre-birth and post-death, expressed through themes of disintegration and dissolution. Archetypally, this is an aspect of the myth of the eternal return, or the great round, in which things are born, live, die and disintegrate, eventually to rebirth in new forms. This archetypal process of transformation requires both creativity and destruction. In order for new forms to evolve, old forms must break down (Eliade, 1954; Grof, 1994). I have come to think of these dis-integrative and dissolving experiences as opium-like and dissociative. The pull is strong for the psychologically killed infant to return to the nothingness before it existed. To be submerged is the living state of the foetus, which breathes as if underwater in the amniotic fluid in which it is suspended:

I'm listening to whale songs. I sink instantly into another world. The sounds vibrate directly into the base of my heart and solar plexus. It's a direct hit, a direct line. A communication that speaks to the heart with deep power, deeper than the beating of drums. Where drums connect with the rhythm of a heart beating, whale songs take me deeper into the ancient depth conversations at the heart of this planet/world. As I listen my body responds and my heart thrills and opens and pulsates with this sound that is womb-like – the sounds heard by an unborn child through the walls of the uterus – the sounds of the watery world, the ocean of cradling the unborn child swims or floats in. I'm reminded of Wordsworth's lines about being connected to a depth of feeling too great for tears – plumbing the depths – whale song connects at a soul place from a time when the soul is in limbo, suspended in watery currents, breathing water, a sunk soul preparing to enter air and light and connect with the earth. It also makes me think of my belief that whales hold the songlines or maps for the planet, that their songs continue to dream the world into being and through their singing they keep the world dreamed into existence – lullabies to hold the idea of the world safe and cradled. Whale songs as cradle and cradling of the world. The sounds themselves are eerie, utterly strange for a human ear, as if heard from such a vast lost place, beyond time, beyond light. Some vast lost place. That's where I started. With feeling lost, a sense of some part of myself drowning, lost and losing, sinking into the waves and needing a hand to reach out. No one is there... who is this lost one who seems to belong to water? (Deed, journal, 2015)

Bachelard (1983) explored psychological themes of water relating to both womb and tomb. He termed the Ophelia complex as a particularly feminine desire for death – the seductive element of death – in which Ophelia surrenders passively to a death that is

264

like a return to the watery world of the womb. Water is considered a feminine element, related to feeling, a fluid and amorphous realm that Bachelard likened to the realm of dreams, which links it to the unconscious realm. The state of drowning, of being overcome by the watery element, is to be haunted and saturated by states of feeling, reverie, dreaminess and images, which seem more real than ordinary life. This vivid dream-like state is one of suspended animation or inaction, similar to nineteenth-century descriptions of the seductive inertia of overpowering reverie in opium states (Alvarez, 2001; de Quincey 1821/1971; Hayter, 1968; Holmes, 1989, 1999).

Ophelia is also mad. Hamlet works out his grievances and confusion through the masculine logic and rhetoric of the mind. Ophelia, immersed in the overwhelming atmosphere of the feminine, her full self submerged by patriarchal culture, drifts to her death, claimed by her reveries. Ophelia has much to be mad about, but she has no place to put her mad-ness but in madness. As Bachelard (1983) stated: "Her short life in itself is the life of a dead woman" (p. 81).

While living the experience of a drowned woman in a sunk or drowned city, I had not consciously thought about Ophelia. Yet, I had drowned in the overwhelming isolation of my sorrows, a lifetime of grief and despair reactivated by the recent death of a loved one. Ophelia-like, I had nothing to anchor me, and I became sunk in states of dream and reverie and a longing to return to the bliss of nothingness.

Several years later, after I had left Oamaru, I began walking a new landscape. It was now, as the drowned woman in me began to surface, like Aphrodite from the sea, that the image of Ophelia and the haunting reverie of her watery death became clearer:

Here I walk in the heat amidst the bronze smell of the baking bracken, its medieval shapes, the cabbage trees in blossom this year, an intoxicating scent. I walk past the pond where Ophelia drowns daily. I come just after, when she has vanished and the water gone still and mysterious again. (Deed, 2003b)

I began to work with my reveries of Ophelia and, over time, the image transformed into a pilgrimage to a dead king. This transformation from the feminine to the masculine was unclear to me at the time, but I simply accepted that the reveries and images had their own intentions that I was not yet able to fathom. However, I was no longer drowned but able to reflect on drowning:

> *This year, Ophelia's watery grave having lost its magic and turned into a shallow stagnant weed-choked puddle on the side of the road, I find a new pilgrimage. Along the sandy track along the side of the river, I make a pilgrimage to the island of the dead king. Walking towards the sand dunes, the shallow riverbed ridged and rippling, golden dark, I see, as if with new understanding, a small elongated island of grasses, a clump of water buttercups two thirds along as if held between sleeping arms. For me it's become the grave of the sunken king, a submerged ancient bogman, an El Greco long-limbed warrior, a chivalrous sleeping king, resting beneath this shallow mound, folded arms across his breast clutching his clump of buttercups. The sound of shallow water calls me. I need to go there daily, to sit and ponder at the grave of the king, another underground life. Always the sound of water and the greenness of life calling me, a secret meridian or wellspring to tap into. (Deed, 2003b)*

Later, I discovered that, alchemically, the drowned king represents the dissolution of ego in psychological transformation (Edinger, 1994; Jung, 1969/1983). In this transformation of an image, Ophelia's compelling, seductive, and mad death transformed as I become disenchanted with the womb it represents. Ophelia's pond transformed into a new place of reverence for a figure associated through death with greenness and life, the mystery of a life fully lived and honoured. As in the alchemical stories, the old king dies in order for new life and a new order to come

266

through (Edinger, 1994). He has earned his restful death, unlike the tragedy of lost Ophelia gone before the expression of her life came to fulfilment. Where Ophelia's life was nipped in the bud, foreshortened, the sunken king has lived a life of meaning, and his grave makes homage to that life. This greenness of life, *viriditas*, is a revivifying energy, signifying a metaphorical transformation of the psyche. Romanyshn (1999) described this 'greening of the soul' as the transformation of the Soul through grief towards new life.

In Oamaru I felt entombed in stone, submerged in water, deprived of light, warmth and air. I hungered for greenness, which I experienced as a deep mystery, as for example when baby Susan's grave lit up with velvet emerald green moss after a vivifying downpour of rain.

Eventually, through my long process of transformation from psychological death to renewed engagement with life, I ceased dressing entirely in black as I had done for years. I began to wear vivid green, feeling nourished by my resonance with the green of the surrounding landscape. I absorbed Emily Dickenson's (1959) phrase 'a Resonance of Emerald' (p. 193) as if on a cellular level, experiencing a kind of photosynthesis, a transmuting of light through the energy of green into what felt like a new way of breathing, new inspiration. For a time, I felt I was breathing both water and light, perhaps going through some amphibious process of moving from water into air just as a baby does at birth.

Looking further into the depths of the Ophelia complex, I discovered I had also written from a watery perspective about surfacing from a suicide attempt and returning to some level of consciousness in the intensive care room:

Violet drifts to the surface, limbs marble, pale in the watery light. She lies suspended in tender currents, weed shadow, dappling light, shadow songs. There is nothing to do but float on the sweetness, breathe water, try to stay with this body immersed in glitter and light. Her legs seem fused into a languorous serpentine curve, her hair weed tendrils swaying about her head.

Once there were green lawns full of daisies and summer promise. The green of a lawn is always only green. Green as it is. Sea colour is something else entirely. Green can suck you in, take your breath away, roll you under, drown you and take the flesh from your bones. Green can pull you under.

Take note, things always depend on their translation.
(Deed, 2006)

Here it is apparent there is another side to the resonance of green, and a connection made between green, water, and death. Water is needed for things to grow, for the greening of life; yet, the opposite of nurturance is death, and this is the dark face of the Mother archetype.

Melusine and the Archetypal Feminine

There are also mythological aspects to the drowned city. Both Bachelard (1983) and Mindell (2000) linked the psychology of water with reveries of flow, waves, and the figure of Melusine who is representative of the archetypal feminine unconscious. In Celtic myth, the city of Ys is a drowned city located in Brittany that forms an inverted parallel city with Paris. In the story, the King's daughter, Danaut, is taken under the waves where she becomes a Melusine or mermaid. This mythic tale was taken up in Byatt's (1990) neo-Victorian novel *Possession,* which weaves the dual stories of Brittany's city of Ys and the passions of two poets that result in an illegitimate child. The poets are hunting, and haunted by, the symbol of the Melusine: she in myth, he in her embodiment of the myth. We can see Byatt's novel as an exploration of the relationship between passion and Soul, between the archetypal masculine and the feminine.

The mythic drowned city of Ys has a parallel life to that of Paris, the city representing the realm of day and earth. This parallel is reminiscent of the idea of the inner world of trauma (Kalsched,

1996) or the 'trauma-world' that exists alongside the everyday world but is lived by different rules (Sieff, 2017; Woodman & Sieff, 2015).

We can also consider this mythic underwater world as the realm of the archetypal feminine and be open to exploring the ways we relate to this underwater, feminine world. Harris and Harris (2015) discussed the qualities of the feminine and how to approach them:

> In order to bring the feminine into our world, we must begin in a personal way...But in order to value the feminine and have it reborn within us, we must take the time to reconnect with the wholeness of who we are. We have to take the time to listen to our dreams, to write them down, and to reflect on our lives. Honouring the feminine means having the patience and taking the time... to ponder these things in our hearts. We must recognise that there are things going on within us that need to be perceived, accepted, felt, said, lived, grieved, and raged over. We need to give these things our attention, concern and understanding. (p. 40)

The drowned city represents the fluid, wet, merged, and murky world of the womb, the feminine body, the feminine mind, and the feminine aspect of Soul (Baring & Cashford, 1991; Murdock, 1990). Early religion was centred on a Great Mother goddess who was a goddess of the sea (Baring & Cashford, 1991; Murdock, 1990). This dreamlike, dissolved feminine world is also a pre-verbal world in which a pre-thinking embodied being merges with the mother. It is the bliss state of connection within mother, and its opposite is the terrifying state of disconnection, when the destructive face of this mother is revealed. This dark side of the goddess is expressed in the myth of Medusa who represents the archetypal Death Mother. I introduced the myth of Medusa in Chapter Three in the context of infanticidal trauma. Medusa has a connection with the ocean, as does Aphrodite.

In trauma, the drowned city is a world of dissociation, the disengaged, de-realised and depersonalised experiencing in which one is no longer really there but drifting somewhere away or apart and not fully present to the experience of things. Bachelard (1983), taking the Ophelia complex further, described it as the cosmic complex of moon and floods, as representing the "irresistible upward surge of the imagination" (p. 87). Medusa and Melusine hold different relationships with water that I explore here through my reverie and fiction. Both are aspects of the traumatised Sacred Feminine.

Melusine in the drowned city legend is an allusion to the original Great Mother of the Sea, an awesome and terrifying cosmic figure. Melusine is able to go between both earth and sea, and she represents feminine ways and the liminal spaces between fixed ideas.

My *solutio* experience in Oamaru was something like the being in the mythic underwater cities of Ys or Atlantis, and I felt like a drowned woman; but, also, at times like Melusine, breathing water as well as air. In the previous excerpt relating my surfacing from near-death, I described my legs having fused into a serpentine curve. Was this an echo of the feminine unconscious I was immersed in? Instinctively, during my time in the drowned city, I wrote glimpses of the Melusine figure of the feminine consciousness, which I recognised was wounded in me, and which I was trying to find my way towards – or back to:

> *a madonna may have a serpent's tail*
> *she lies in state*
> *the compartments of her open coffin*
> medulla oblongata cerebellum
> temporal lobe
> *the interior vision of her mind*
> *junk & precious objects in*
> *the dusty half light*
> *secretly growing themselves*
> (Deed, 2003a)

This reverie imagined into the death of the Mother goddess, the archetypal mother and her ways, killed off by the rational and logical thought valued by our masculinised culture. The poem also describes the fragmenting and disconnected experience of dissociation. Perhaps Melusine is also an expression of an altered state of the feminine consciousness in which she sinks back into herself when she is not mirrored by the culture.

Arnold Mindell (2000) considered this question in his exploration of the edge between physics and psychology. He described Melusine as the elusive aspect of ourselves whose qualities – imaginality, fluidity, and eternality – vanish when doubted by the linear and rational thinking and ideas valued in current Western culture. Similar to Bachelard, he imagined Melusine as metaphoric of the watery and dreamlike state of the feminine aspect of consciousness. He suggested Melusine is dreamlike, dreaming, and familiar with altered states of consciousness. Mindell suggested that, similar to the Death Mother archetype, whose feminine wound leads to paralysis and disconnection from the essence of life, we feel lifeless and depressed when the Melusine aspect of ourselves is doubted, ignored, or dismissed. Melusine is, therefore, perhaps another face of the Death Mother, who disappears under the sea with her children when she is not taken seriously. According to Mindell, she symbolises the non-consensus reality of nature marginalised by the consensus reality observer. Similarly, the researcher's position influences the research, and the imposition of an adoption identity disturbs the natural identity processes of the original being.

If we value only the rational and logical (often seen as masculine qualities) we marginalise other ways of knowing that are considered more feminine – such as intuition, implicit or tacit knowing. This leads to uncertainty as we leave out or banish significant aspects of our ways of knowing or interpreting our experiences. This addresses the value and relevance I place on the telling of a personal, imaginal, intuitive experience that can provide means of knowing that may be missed by more rational methods.

Through my breakdown, I was initially overwhelmed by the imaginal realm in a flood of unconscious material that led to the feeling of having drowned. As I began to embrace my imaginal and intuitive knowledge it seemed I was able, like Melusine, to come up for air and go between water and earth. Writing has also been a process in which this imaginal self could live.

Melusine, according to Mindell, is also indicative of processes that we are not normally aware of. By becoming more conscious of these underlying processes and reflecting on them we become more attuned to our deeper more intimate intentions and desires. We must woo Melusine, or she vanishes where we cannot follow her. Earlier I quoted Harris and Harris (2015) on ways to reconnect with the archetypal feminine on her own terms, emphasising receptivity, patience and reflection.

For me, Melusine, like Leviathan, embodies the bridge between consciousness (air) and the unconscious (water) — between conscious thought and hidden, or implicit, ways of knowing. Known for her beautiful voice, perhaps she too maps and cradles the world into existence through song.

In my search into the inner drowned world of marginalised feminine being, I intuitively described the face of the Great Mother that was purified by the patriarchal Christian tradition – the Madonna – as having a serpent's tail. She has a side to her other than the purity of the Virgin. In Chapter Four I also described her as misunderstood, forlorn, observed by an infanticidal objectification that imprisons, exploits and devalues her, turning her into a freak to be gawked at.

I am also instinctively describing, in what I have termed the feminine wound, the traumatised Soul of the archetypal feminine that results in the destructive aspect of the archetype presenting in our culture and world situation. *Anima mundi* or the World Soul is traditionally feminine, and many psychologists suggest that our world situation is a result of the oppression of the archetypal feminine. We must, they claim, heal our relationship with the Sacred Feminine in order to heal the Soul of the world (Sardello, 2008).

Chapter Twelve
Conversations in the Dark

*We can never move beyond the bonds of the past
until we can say, and suffer through, "I am not what
happened to me; I am what I choose to become."*
James Hollis (2013)

The alchemical process completing itself, readying to begin its cycle again, this chapter begins with a visual synthesis of the themes of my personal myth in an art collage I made whilst I was still in the grip of the Death Mother complex. The integration of dark and light is evident in a poem at the end of the chapter, written after the alchemical transformation was complete.

Whilst reflecting on the relationship between my personal trauma and psychological infanticide as an archetypal experience, I created a collaged triptych altarpiece, with the architectural geometry of a cathedral on the outside panels that fold over the central panel in the manner of a personal icon (see Fig.4).

Figure 10. Photo. Tryptich. Collage made by the author, 2015

Within, on the central panel, is Duccio's Madonna, her halo embellished with tiny beings; a skeleton woman disembowelled by a cross; a crypt of stone crosses; a woman holding a heart at the foot of a flight of stairs leading to the crypt. At the bottom of the panel are opium flowers and seedpods, and Leonardo da Vinci's sketch of a foetus curled within a dissected womb. On the left panel stands Minnie Dean in front of a backdrop of Piranesi's imaginary prisons. On the right panel are Leonardo da Vinci's sketches of foetuses, and a cemetery angel.

This representation of related images revealed, in one vision, all I had been piecing together of my psychological infanticide over years of writing. Placed here at the conclusion, it speaks for itself.

My self-inquiry into my personal myth deepened over years of journaling – paying attention to dreams, symptoms, images, reveries, synchronicities, and a re-view of my creative writing written over three decades. The themes of the psychological infanticide and the Death Mother archetype amplified as I read fiction, biography, poetry, social history, mythology, and psychology related to my experience. I visited historic sites – such as the Melbourne Gaol where several baby farmers were hanged – to get a feel for the experience of those whose stories are our history and therefore part of our personal stories.

It is through looking back that I could see how the story develops over time, and that the transformational process has its own innate intelligence. Through allowing the space for the story to work itself, and being willing to re-search (look back) and re-vision (see through new perspectives looking back from a different place) the conditions for transformation were provided. Romanyshyn (1997, 2004) described this method of re-turn and re-search as Jung's psychological method, based on the myth of Orpheus who went down into the underworld in search of his dead wife, hoping to return her to life.

Allowing my writing to speak for its self, rather than analysing and interpreting my text, gave the experience of psychological infanticide its own voice. The result was a thematic synthesis of psychological infanticide that could be validated as archetypal patterns, or universalised experiences.

As a result, I experienced a shift from living enclosed within a personal myth of archetypal intensity to being more fully integrated in my human presence and an experience of the humanity of the world only subtly shaded by archetypal echoes.

I began this journey with a numinous connection to a Dead Baby in a dream. Following this Dead Baby led me into an Orphic underworld of desperate mothers, an unsupportive patriarchal system, the sentimentalising of the concept of Mother, and the painful history of the mass exploitation and murder of infants. My self-inquiry into the experience of psychological infanticide under the closed stranger adoption system, and my exploration of its historical links with the nineteenth-century practice of baby farming, led to a number of interconnected themes and ultimately to an exploration of the Death Mother archetype.

My inquiry revealed themes of internal deadness, non-existence, being killed or obliterated, being a ghost, being haunted by internalised figures, terror of being killed, and an opium-like state of suspended animation or paralysis that I identified as a dissociative trauma state. I also identified intensely conflicted relationships with the idea of Mother and what Mother represents – security, comfort, tenderness, nurturance, nourishment and support. I identified strong themes related to the relationship between mother and unborn child, which, when traumatic, lead to extreme dissociation by both mother and child as a means of psychic survival.

I no longer feel trapped in a ghost world with the dead. Nor do I feel at the mercy of a murderous internal mother. Exploring the ways Minnie Dean's story reflected something of my own helped me shift my perception, and broaden and deepen my insight, as she enabled me to reflect on the collective story of women in trouble without support, and as she helped me to reflect on the murdered, murderous, and ghostly aspects of myself. The Death Mother archetype reveals the wounded Sacred Feminine in our patriarchal and masculine-valued Western culture, and the call to repair the wound for the sake of life itself.

My inquiry was initially a response to the cry of the abandoned and neglected parts of myself and to my awareness that I was not alone in this abandonment and neglect. Eventually I experienced a profound sense of wholeness, unity, and healing as little parts of me that felt abandoned, murdered, neglected, and exiled were attended to with compassionate care. Equally abandoned and rejected nurturing parts were able to grow and become the caring holding supports I needed. I also had to face into, and accept with compassion, the internalised murderous parts of me who had lived only in darkness.

This healing extends into the world as I work compassionately with the Wounded Innocents, Orphans, Feral Children, and Murderous Mothers in the adults I see as a psychotherapist, and as these words find their way into the world to be of service to others. This is reflected in a dream that suggests deep healing of the feminine wound between mother and child:

> *I visit two simple old folk who are my original parents.*
> *Everything in their home, and they themselves are simple,*
> *homely, as if they are from another time, or outside time.*
> *In the house there is the palpable absent-presence of*
> *their 'lost' daughter. The old man hands me two pieces of*
> *jewellery that belonged to her. I have the sense suddenly*
> *I am on the right path in my life. Then I am sitting with*
> *the old woman. She's behind me, telling me her stories*
> *and I lean back against her. She wraps her arms around*
> *me and holds me close. I can feel her voice resonating*
> *deep inside my body. It is the original voice from before I*
> *was born and I experience such a sense of belonging and*
> *being at home. I rest in this homecoming. I tell her how*
> *I might cry as I tell her about this feeling of belonging.*
> *She responds and we are held in a deep warm embrace.*
> (Sherwood, dream journal, 2017)

Ultimately facing into the Death Mother archetype resulted in my reconnection to the Sacred Feminine, reflected in a healing vision of the Great Mother:

> *I have a sense of inner/outer falling away. There*
> *are patterns of colour (violet, blue) and an intensely*
> *luminous light forming deep in my inner eye. I sense an*
> *orb of luminous blue light around me, enfolding me as a*
> *little baby sinking into sleep. In this orb I feel the divine*
> *consciousness of the Great Mother. I feel connected to*
> *the Earth, deeply held by this mother and I feel her blue*
> *mantle of protective love spread over me, leaving a space*
> *for the auric blue orb field. I feel even younger, glimpse*
> *or sense myself as a cosmic embryo forming inside this*
> *blue egg of fluid/light. I realise there is a silver cord*

attached to me and coiling down into the earth. I feel even more warmly held and nourished by this deep connection to the Great Mother, mother Earth. Deeply loved. My consciousness expands and contracts, moving towards and away from actual sleep. I am content here in this breathing space of unfolding potential, nourished by the divine love of all creation. (Sherwood, journal, 2017)

My engagement through reverie, writing, imaginal dialogues, dreams, art, and through a synchronous transposition into a nineteenth-century context (during my time in Oamaru), pointed to some means of healing and transformation – and some cautions. Imaginal engagement with dark archetypal forces may be dangerous if archetypal material overwhelms one's grip on conscious reality. In researching psychological infanticide, I experienced terrifying physical symptoms, episodes of psychic disintegration and internal chaos, periods of extreme vulnerability and anxiety, and a brief return of suicidal despair. It is necessary to caution anyone undertaking a personal journey through psychological infanticide not to do so alone. This level of engagement needs to be well grounded and supported by a psychotherapist or other guide who understands the life-death nature of the journey.

However, I also offer hope for the possibility of healing and growth in people who live the effects of psychological infanticide. Self-expression using creative writing and journaling methods is one means of healing through an imaginal engagement with images, dreams, symptoms, and dialogues with personified figures. In particular, the method of fictionalised writing of self-experience offered freedom to explore psychological truths without necessarily being conscious of them at the time of writing. Writing fictionalised autobiography, for which I used the term bio-fiction, also has the capacity to offer different perspectives of an experience, and is a useful means to develop a complex understanding of the themes, and in developing compassion for all concerned. It enables the development of a witnessing stance that focuses on a universal issue rather than a personal story. My inquiry moved beyond a personal literal narrative toward a witnessing consciousness and the development of compassion, self-compassion, and forgiveness.

The process of imaginal engagement with archetypal themes and figures enabled me to engage in a relationship with an archetypal Murderous Mother in transformational ways. I found that the themes of psychological infanticide through closed stranger adoption did correlate with the themes identified by Brett Kahr's (1993, 2001, 2007a, 2007b, 2012) infanticidal attachment theory, and were corroborated by B. J. Lifton's (1994) theoretical perspective of closed stranger adoption. I found strong common themes between the methods of baby farmers and the infanticidal experience of adopted people. Myths, legends, and stories, and the themes illuminated in the works and lives of published writers who had histories related to psychological infanticide, supported and affirmed that the themes of my initial inquiry were indicative of a universal experience. They also added richness, depth, complexity and authenticity to my self-inquiry.

Psychological infanticide as an experience of closed stranger adoption remains an extremely controversial and difficult experience to speak out about, as many people wish to remain in denial about the infant's experience of adoption. There is an understandable societal protectiveness against perceived blame of mothers and a focus on the painful grief experienced by birth mothers, which serves to silence the adopted child. I have anticipated that, unless aware of the power of this denial, clinicians working with adult adoptees will be drawn into a psychological re-enactment of this denial, which may result in further reinforcement of the original psychological infanticide.

Through the revelation of a personal journey I hope to have contributed rich creative compassionate knowledge which may guide clinicians in the healing of clients living psychological infanticide. It offers real support for the assistance of deeply troubled people who are too often given up on by mental health systems ill-equipped to work with such profound trauma.

The Death Mother archetype, expressed in the question of what to do with unwanted children, and the experience of infanticide, are psychological themes that will continue to appear in the human psyche and will need to be grappled with.

The insider knowledge of my personal story contributed original insights into what may be happening inside the minds and bodies of people who experience psychological infanticide, and people who were adopted under the closed stranger adoption system. Practitioners would do well to become aware of the imaginal dimension and archetypal themes within the 'every day' stories of trauma. This level of attunement opens the practitioner to the fuller dimension of trauma, offering deeper empathy, compassion and hope to patients.

Psychological work with people who have experienced psychological infanticide needs to extend into the realm of the unborn child (depending on causation). I emphasised profound dissociation pre-birth as a pervading factor in the distress of psychological infanticide related to closed stranger adoption.

My intention is to have alerted clinicians to the perilous nature of the journey through psychological infanticide, and to the need for a consistent, warm, open and nurturing approach – the antidote to the Death Mother archetype and the model for the growth of a life-supporting internal mother.

The heroic journey is never fully completed. The endpoint marks the beginning of a new phase of life's journey on the next level of development. Consequently, there is more to learn about the nature of infanticidal attachment, adoption, and the wound of the sacrificed child. Kahr (1993) stated:

Sadly, few psychotherapists have fully appreciated the importance of these discoveries, and few have yet fully recognised that contemporary death threats towards youngsters can be understood as the modern day variant

of the ritual murder of babies which spattered the pages
of history with oceans of blood. (p. 269)

Psychotherapy, particularly in the areas of trauma theory and
attachment theory, has come some way toward recognising the
early trauma evident in people suffering serious mental health
diagnoses. Yet, there is also strong denial of our own helplessness
and, despite the evidence that adoptees are vastly over-represented
in mental health statistics, I feel understanding of the inner world
of adopted children is still denied. It remains too hard to think
about what to do with children who are unwanted or cannot be
cared for, and too hard to think about the experience of the child
who is born in an already traumatised state.

I believe it will be healing for wounded people to find ways
to express their personal experiences and for society to be open
to hearing it. In this way, personal healing and healing of the
feminine wound in the world unfold together. Further research
into humane and strengthening ways to accompany infanticidally-
attached people on their heroic journey will be valuable.

Transformative writing is a powerful means of entering the
psychic underworld, surviving, and returning with a healing elixir
that restores life. Our historical past is tremendously valuable in
finding links and building bridges of recognition and compassion
that can help us with our personal past.

I have held a space for the greater mystery of the Sacred
Feminine to hold and heal aspects of the feminine wound, inviting
a wider recognition of the need for nurturing life-giving energies
to be valued and restored in our relationships between each other
and on this planet – this Mother Earth who holds us all in her
embrace.

Finally, this poem appeared fully formed in my consciousness
as I completed this work, as if the figures of my imaginal realm
wished to express their own experience and integration:

Conversations in the dark

Darkness is our first home
Our first memory
Our first resting place.
We return to it in the night
Homage to our original landscape.

Darkness is not empty.
It surrounded us in the beginning
And we were life, fruit, seed
Following the hidden path
Toward ourselves.

Darkness reveals what we hide
From ourselves in the daylight.
It has invisible eyes attuned to
The obscured, the outcast, the imprisoned,
The discounted, the forgotten.
Demons, lusts, terrors rise up
To haunt us.

Darkness is our own foul treachery,
Our horror, our blindness
That leads to fury
When we fight the great formlessness
That longs to give us solace.
It is a torture pit of broken minds
And limbs and animals
Snarling, vicious
Afraid.

Darkness is our nightmare of history.
What was done we perpetuate while we forget;
We reject while we remember

Saying
I am not this.

But I am.
I am this too,
And this, and this.

Darkness is the embrace
The deepest compassion
The greatest mother
Of our needs and hurts.
In our terror we threaten
To annihilate her and then wait
For her to eclipse us.

She is the resting place
Nurturer of dreams
Keeper of the mystery
Weaver of all that longs to
Know itself and therefore grows,
Lives, is recognised
And dies into her love.
Darkness is the abyss
Of our true freedom.

Stepping into the secret
Dark of ourselves
We embrace the lost kingdom.
We restore the banished ones to their light,
Singing praise for the return
Of the holy within the body.

Tenderly we hold hands with those
Lost and found in the dark,
Hands with eyes that see truth, and therefore,

The way.

Hands that in holding truth
With love
Build stone by stone
A cathedral of living light
In the wellspring of the heart
That pours its river of love
Unceasingly
Through the dark valleys,
A secret song, not hidden,
Though sometimes not seen.

The well nourishes us
In the sanctity of freeing
The chained ones
We banished and forgot.
They have laboured in deep mines
Weaving the wound into rivers of stone,
Of gold, and finally,
Through a myriad of chasms, into
Liquid rivers of diamond.

Pure living light that
Sings in the darkness
The joy of knowing
I am here
I am here with myself
I am here with myself and
The blessed angel
Who waits for me to turn inward.

Violet Sherwood, 2017

References

Allen, J. A. (1990). *Sex & secrets: Crimes involving Australian women since 1880.* Melbourne, Australia: Oxford University Press.

Alvarez, A. (2001). Drugs and inspiration. *Social Research, 68*(3), 779-793.

Bachelard, G. (1971). *The poetics of reverie* (D. Russell, Trans.). New York, NY: Orion Press.

Bachelard, G. (1983). *Water and dreams: An essay on the imagination of matter* (E. R. Farrell, Trans.). Dallas, TX: The Dallas Institute of Humanities and Culture.

Bachelard, G. (1998/2005). *On poetic imagination and reverie* (C. Gaudin, Trans.). Putnam, CT: Spring Publications.

Barbash, F. (2017). Irish excavation confirms mass grave of babies-toddlers at former home for unwed mothers. Retrieved December 23, 2018, from www.washingtonpost.com/news/morning-mix/wp/2017/03/04/irish-excavation-confirms-mass-grave-of-babies-toddlers-at-former-home-for-unwed-mothers/?noredirect=on&utm_term=.5542dc763241

Baring, A., & Cashford, J. (1991). *The myth of the goddess: Evolution of an image.* London, England: Arkana.

Barker, J. (2010). *The Brontës.* London, England: Little Brown Book Group.

Bell, R. M. (1985). *Holy anorexia.* London, England: University of Chicago Press.

Benton, M. (2005). Literary biomythography. *Auto/Biography, 13*, 206-226.

Berry, P. (1982). *Echo's subtle body: Contributions to archetypal psychology.* Dallas, TX: Spring Publications.

Bettelheim, B. (1976). *The uses of enchantment: The meaning and importance of fairy tales.* London, England: Thames & Hudson.

Bettelheim, B. (1979). Schizophrenia as a reaction to extreme situations. In B. Bettelheim (Ed.), *Surviving and other essays* (pp.112-124). New York, NY: Alfred Knopf.

Bloch, D. (1979). *"So the witch won't eat me": Fantasy and the child's fear of infanticide.* London, England: Burnett Books Ltd.

Bollas, C. (1987). *The shadow of the object: Psychoanalysis of the unthought known.* London, England: Free Association Books.

Bolton, G. (2010). Explorative and expressive writing for personal and professional development. Unpublished PhD by publication. Uk: University of East Anglia. Estes, 1990 p. 48; p. 71

Bolton, G., & Rowland, S. (2014). *Inspirational writing for academic publication.* London, England: SAGE Publications.

Bowlby, J. (1960). Grief and mourning in infancy and early childhood. *Psychoanalytic Study of the Child, 15,* 9-52.

Bowlby, J. (1980). *Attachment and loss* (Vol. 3). New York, NY: Basic Books.

Braunias, S. (2013, November). Minnie Dean retrial "likely". *Metro.* Auckland, New Zealand.

Brenner, I. (2001). *Dissociation of trauma: Theory, practice and technique.* Madison, CT: International Universities Press.

Brenner, I. (2014). *Dark matters: Exploring the realm of psychic devastation.* London, England: Karnac.

Bright, B. (2010). *Facing Medusa: Alchemical transformation through the power of surrender.* [Unpublished doctoral thesis]. Pacifica Graduate Institute, California, United States of America.

Brodzinsky, D. M. (1990). A stress and coping model of adoption adjustment. In D. M. Brodzinsky & M. D. Schecter (Eds.), *The psychology of adoption* (pp. 3-24). London, England: Oxford University Press.

Brontë, A. (1848). *The tenant of wildfell hall*. London, England: Penguin Classics.

Brontë, C. (1993). Jane Eyre. In *Complete novels of Charlotte & Emily Brontë* (pp. 9-330). London, England: Harper Classics. (Original work published 1847)

Brontë, C. (1993). Villette. In *Complete novels of Charlotte & Emily Brontë* (pp.731-1072). London, England: HarperCollins Classics. (Original work published 1853)

Brown, R. J. (2010). *Infanticide: A case study*. Retrieved June 2015, from www.richardjohnbr.blogspot.co.nz/2010/10/infanticide-case-study.html

Byatt, A. (1990). *Possession: A romance*. London, England: Vintage.

Campbell, J. (1968). *The hero with a thousand faces*. New York, NY: Bollingen Series.

Cannon, M. (1994). *The woman as murderer: Five who paid with their lives*. Melbourne, Australia: Today's Australia Publishing Company.

Cara, E. (2007). Psychobiography in search of a home. *British Journal of Occupational Therapy, 70*(3), 115-121. Retrieved from http://www.ingentaconnect.comezyproxy.aut.ac.nz

Carlile, M. (2016). *The death talker: What we need to know to help us talk about death*. London, England: New Holland Publisher.

Catran, K. (1985). In defence of Minnie Dean. In *Hanlon*. Wellington New Zealand. Retrieved September 29, 2015 from NZ On Air. OCLC 268791231.

Clarke, N. (2006). The shocking truth about baby factories. Retrieved January 13, 2019, from https://www.dailymail.co.uk/femail/article.../The-shocking-truth-baby-factories.html

Cobb, N. (1992). *Archetypal imagination: Glimpses of the gods in life and art*. Hudson, NY: Lindisfarne Press.

Coleridge, S. T. (1956). *Biographia literaria: Or biographical sketches of my literary life and opinions*. London, England: J. M. Dent & Sons. (Original work published 1817)

Coleridge, S. T. (1957). *Poems*. London, England: Oxford University Press.

Collins, W. (1860). *The woman in white*. London, England: Gordon Classic Library.

Cossins, A. (2014). *The baby farmers: A chilling tale of missing babies, shameful secrets and murder in 19th century Australia*. Sydney, Australia: Allen & Unwin.

Crotty, M. (1998). *The foundations of social research: Meaning and perspective in the research process*. St Leonards, Australia: Allen & Unwin.

Dalley, B. (1999). Criminal conversations: Infanticide, gender and sexuality in 19th century New Zealand. In C. Daley & D. Montgomerie (Eds.), *The gendered Kiwi* (pp. 64-85). Auckland, New Zealand: Auckland University Press.

Damasio, A. R. (2000). *The feeling of what happens: Body and emotion in the making of consciousness*. New York, NY: Houghton Mifflen Harcourt.

Dean, M. (1895). *Her last statement*. [Unpublished]. Filed in National Archives, Wellington, New Zealand. Ref J1 1895/643.

De Bazin, S. (2012). *The day she cradled me*. Auckland, New Zealand: Random House.

Deed, B. (1994a). *Fragments of sky*. [Unpublished manuscript].

Deed, B. (1994b). Primavera. *Takahe 20*, 40-41. Christchurch, New Zealand: The Takahe Publishing Collective.

Deed, B. (1995). *Hysterie*. [Unpublished manuscript].

Deed, B. (2003a). *Singing the madonna blues*. [Unpublished manuscript].

Deed, B. (2003b). *The drowned city*. [Unpublished manuscript].

Deed, B. (2003c). Songs for a drowned woman. In A. Paterson (Ed) *Poetry NZ 26*. Auckland New Zealand: Brick Row Press.

Deed, B. (2006). *The book of light*. [Unpublished manuscript].

Deed, B. (2010). *Putting poetry back into the mind: How can therapeutic writing benefit clients of psychodynamic psychotherapy?* [Unpublished master's dissertation]. AUT University, Auckland, New Zealand.

de Mause, L. (1974). The evolution of childhood. In L. de Mause (Ed.), *The history of childhood – the untold story of child abuse* (pp. 1-73). New York, NY: Peter Bedrick Books.

DeMeo, J. (2006). *Saharasia – The 4000BCE origins of child abuse, sex-repression, warfare and social violence in the deserts of the old world*. Portland, OR: Natural Energy Works.

de Quincey, T. (1971). *Confessions of an English opium eater.* London, England: Penguin. (Original work published 1821)

Derrida, J. (1993). *Specters of Marx: The state of the debt, the work of mourning and the new international*. London, UK: Routledge.

Dickens, C. (1997). *Oliver Twist: Or the parish boy's progress*. Hertfordshire, UK: Wordsworth Editions. (Original work published 1837)

Dickenson, E. (1959). *Selected poems and letters of Emily Dickenson*. New York, NY: Doubleday Books.

Donohue, E. (2014). *Frog music*. London, England: PanMacMillan.

Douglass, B. G., & Moustakas, C. (1985). Heuristic inquiry: The internal search to know. *Journal of Humanistic Psychology, 25*, 39-55. doi:10.1177/0022167885253004

Eastman, P. D. (1960). *Are you my mother?* London, England: Random House.

Edinger, E. (1994). *Anatomy of the psyche: Alchemical symbolism in psychotherapy*. LaSalle, IL: Open Court.

Eliade, M. (1954). *The myth of the eternal return: Or cosmos and history* (W. R. Trask, Trans.). New York, NY: Princeton University Press.

Else, A. (1991). *A question of adoption: Closed stranger adoption in New Zealand, 1944-1974.* Wellington, New Zealand: Bridget Williams Books.

Erikson, E. (1958). *Identity and the life cycle.* New York, NY: Norton.

Estes, C. P. (1992). *Women who run with the wolves: Contacting the power of the wild woman.* London, England: Rider.

Estes, C. P. (1997). *Warming the stone-child: Myths and stories about abandonment and the unmothered child.* Audiobook. Sounds True.

Farrell, M. (2011). *To have and to hold.* [Unpublished paper presented at Forum]. AUT University, Auckland, New Zealand.

Feder, L. (1974). Adoption trauma: Oedipus myth/clinical reality. *International Journal of Psychoanalysis, 55,* 491-493.

Fischer, J. (2017). *Healing the fragmented selves of trauma survivors: Overcoming internal self-alienation.* New York, NY: Routledge.

Frame, J. (1961). *Owls do cry.* London, England: Penguin.

Francus, M. (2012). *Monstrous motherhood: Eighteenth-century culture and the ideology of domesticity.* Baltimore, MA: John Hopkins University Press.

Frankiel, R. V. (1985). The stolen child: A fantasy, a wish, a source of countertransference. *International Review of Psychoanalysis, 12,* 417-430.

Frank, K. (1990). *Emily Brontë: A chainless soul.* London, England: Penguin Books.

Fraser, R. (1988). *Charlotte Brontë.* London, England: Metheun.

Freud, S. (2005). *Civilisation and its discontents.* London, England: Norton. (Original work published 1930)

Frick, W. B. (1990). The symbolic growth experience: A chronicle of heuristic inquiry and a quest for synthesis. *Journal of Humanistic Psychology, 30,* 64. doi:10.1177/002216789030100

Gaskell, E. (1891). *The life of Charlotte Brontë, author of 'Jane Eyre', 'Shirley', 'Villette', 'The professor'.* London, England: Smith, Elder & Co.

Geller, J. (2005). The lobotomist: A maverick medical genius and his tragic quest to rid the world of mental illness. The pest maiden. A story of lobotomy. In *Psychiatry Online.* Retrieved February 2, 2019, from https://doi-org.ezproxy.aut.ac.nz/10.1176/appi.ps.56.10.1318

Gendlin, E. (1969). Focusing. *Psychotherapy, 6*(1), 4-15.

Gilbert, S., & Gubar, S. (2000). *The madwoman in the attic: The woman writer and the 19th-century literary imagination* (2nd ed.). London, England: Vale University Press. (Original work published 1979)

Goodchild, V. (2001). *Eros and chaos: The sacred mysteries and dark shadows of love.* Newburyport, MA: Nicolas-Hays.

Goodchild, V. (2012). *Songlines of the soul: Pathways to a new vision for a new century.* Newburyport, MA: Nicolas-Hays.

Gordon, L. (1995). *Charlotte Brontë: A passionate life.* London, England: Vintage.

Grbich, C. (1999). *Qualitative research in health: An introduction.* London, England: Sage Publications.

Grierson, J. (2017). *Mass grave of babies and children found at Tuam orphanage in Ireland.* Retrieved December 23, 2018, from www.theguardian.com/world/2017/mar/03/mass-grave-of-babies-and-children-found-at-tuam-orphanage-in-ireland

Griffith, K. (n.d.). *Adoption New Zealand.* Retrieved November 1, 2015, from http://adoptionnz.com/

Grille, R. (2005). *Parenting for a peaceful world* (rev. ed.). Richmond, England: The Children's Project

Grof, S. (1988). *The adventure of self-discovery: Dimensions of consciousness and new perspectives in psychotherapy and inner exploration*. Albany, NY: State University of New York Press.

Grof, S. (1998). *The cosmic game: Explorations of the frontiers of human consciousness*. New York, NY: State University of New York Press.

Haertl, K. (2014). Writing and the development of the self-heuristic-inquiry: A unique way of exploring the power of the written word. *Journal of Poetry Therapy: The Interdisciplinary Journal of Practice, Theory, Research and Education, 27*(2), 55-68. doi:10.1080/08893675.2014.895488

Halifax, J. (1979). *Shamanic voices: A survey of visionary narratives*. New York, NY: E.P. Dutton.

Hannah, B. (1981). *Encounters with the soul: Active imagination as developed by C.G. Jung*. London, England: Chiron Publications.

Harner, M. (1980). *The way of the shaman*. New York, NY: HarperCollins.

Harris, B., & Harris, M. (2015). *Into the heart of the feminine: Facing the death mother archetype to reclaim love, strength and vitality*. Asheville, NCA: Daphne Publications.

Hayter, A. (1968). *Opium and the romantic imagination*. London, England: Faber & Faber.

Henderson, H., & Hamblin, D. (1995). Minnie Dean. In *Have your own way*. Produced by HH Music, Still Working for the Man Music Inc.

Herman, J. (1992). *Trauma and recovery: The aftermath of violence – From domestic violence to political terror*. New York, NY: Basic Books.

Higginbotham, A. (1989). "Sin of the age": Infanticide and illegitimacy in Victorian London. In Eastern Connecticut State University (Ed.), *Victorian Studies* (pp. 319-339). Connecticut, IN: Indiana University Press.

Hiles, B. (1991). Paradigms lost – paradigms regained. Paper presented to the 18th International Human Science Research

Conference, Sheffield, UK< July 26-29, 1999. www.psy. dmu.ac.uk.

Hiles, B. (2001). Heuristic inquiry and transpersonal research. Paper presented to CCPE, London. Retrieved September 15, 2015, from www.psy.dmu.ac.uk.

Hiles, B. (2002). Narrative and heuristic approaches to transpersonal research and practice. Paper presented to CCPE, London. Retrieved September 15, 2015, from http://www. dmu.ac.uk/about-dmu/academic-staff/health-and-life-sciences/david-hiles/david-hiles.aspx

Hillman, J. (1994). *Healing fiction*. Putnam, CT: Spring Publications.

Hillman, J. (2014). *Alchemical psychology: Uniform edition of the writings of James Hillman* (Vol. 5). Putnam, CT: Spring Publications.

Hillman, J., & Shamdasani, S. (2013). *Lament of the dead: Psychology after Jung's Red Book*. New York, NY: Norton & Company.

Hogg, R. (2013). A Māori worldview. In S. Shaw, W. L. White, & B. Deed (Eds.), *Health, wellbeing and environment in Aotearoa New Zealand* (pp. 35-52). Melbourne, Australia: Oxford University Press.

Holmes, R. (1985). *Footsteps: Adventures of a romantic biographer*. London, England: Flamingo.

Holmes, R. (1989). *Coleridge: Early visions*. London, England: Flamingo.

Holmes, R. (1993). *Dr. Johnson & Mr. Savage*. London, England: Vintage Books.

Holmes, R. (1999). *Coleridge: Darker reflections*. London, England: Flamingo.

Hollis, J. (2000). *The archetypal imagination*. Houston, TX: Texas A&M University Press.

Hollis, J. (2013). *Hauntings: Dispelling the ghosts who run our lives*. Asheville, NC: Chiron Publications.

Holub, M. (1996). *Supposed to fly: A sequence from Pilsen, Czechoslavakia*. Trans. E. Osers. Bloodaxe Books.

Hood, L. (1994). *Minnie Dean: Her life & crimes*. Auckland, New Zealand: Penguin.

Hopper, J. W. (2015). Harnessing the seeking, satisfaction and embodiment circuitries in contemplative approaches to trauma. In V. M. Follete, J. Briere, D. Rozelle, J. W. Hopper, & D. I. Rome (Eds.), *Mindfulness-oriented interventions for trauma* (pp. 185-209). New York, NY: Guildford Press.

Hunt, C. (2000). *Therapeutic dimensions of autobiography in creative writing*. London, England, Jessica Kingsley Publishers.

Hunt, C., & Sampson, F. (Eds.). (1998). *The self on the page: Theory and practice of creative writing in personal development*. London, England: Jessica Kingsley Publishers.

Hunt, C., & Sampson, F. (2006). *Writing self and reflexivity*. Hampshire, England: Palgrave MacMillan.

Irving, M. (1989). Natalism as pre-and peri-natal metaphor. *Pre and Peri-Natal Psychology Journal, 4*(2), 83-109.

Johnson, R. A. (1983). *We: Understanding the psychology of romantic love*. New York, NY: Harper San Francisco.

Johnson, R. A. (1986). *Inner work: Using dreams and active imagination for personal growth*. New York, NY: Harper Collins.

Johnson, R. A. (1991). *Owning your own shadow: Understanding the dark side of the psyche*. New York, NY: Harper Collins.

Jones, C. A. (2013). *Heal your self with writing*. Studio City, CA: Divine Arts.

Jung, C. G. (1967). *Symbols of transformation* (R. F. C. Hull, Trans.). In H. Read (Ed.), *The collected works of C.G. Jung* (2nd ed., Vol. 5). Princeton, NJ: Princeton University Press. (Original work published 1952)

Jung, C. G. (1968). Psychology and alchemy (2nd ed.), (R. F. C. Hull, Trans.). In H. Read (Ed.), *The collected works of C.G. Jung* (2nd ed., Vol. 12). Princeton, NJ: Princeton University Press. (Original work published 1953).

Jung, C. G. (1983). *The psychology of the transference*. London, England: Ark Publications. (Original work published 1969)

Jung, C. G. (1989). *Memories, dreams, reflections*. New York, NY: Random House.

Jung, C. G. (2009). *The red book: Liber novus*. (S. Shamdasani, Ed.). New York, NY: Norton & Co.

Kalsched, D. (1996). *The inner world of trauma: Archetypal defences of the personal spirit*. New York, NY: Routledge.

Kalsched, D. (2013). *Trauma and the soul: A psycho-spiritual approach to human development and its interruption*. New York, NY: Routledge.

Kahr, B. (1993). Ancient infanticide and modern schizophrenia: The clinical uses of psychohistorical research. *Journal of Psychohistory, 20*(3), 267-274.

Kahr, B. (2001). The legacy of infanticide. *Journal of Psychohistory, 29,* 40-44.

Kahr, B. (2007a). The infanticidal attachment. *Attachment: New Directions in Psychotherapy and Relational Psychoanalysis, 1,* 117-132. Retrieved from http://www.karnacbooks.metapress.com

Kahr, B. (2007b). The infanticidal attachment in schizophrenia and dissociative identity disorder. *Attachment: New Directions in Psychotherapy and Relational Psychoanalysis, 1,* 305-309. Retrieved from http://www.karnacbooks.metapress.com

Kahr, B. (2012). The infanticidal origins of psychosis. In J. Yellin & K. White (Eds.), *Shattered states: Disorganised attachment and its* (pp. 7-126). London, England: Karnac Books.

Karpman, S. (1968). Fairy tales and script drama analysis. *Transactional Analysis Bulletin, 7*(26), 39-43.

Kavan, A. (1978). *I am Lazarus*. London, England: Peter Owen. (Original work published 1945)

Kavan, A. (1986). *Ice*. London, England: Peter Owen. (Original work published 1967)

Keats, J. (2011). *Keats's poetry and prose.* (J. N. Cox, Ed.). New York, NY: Norton & Co.

Keleman. S. (1999). *Myth and the body: A colloquy with Joseph Campbell.* Berkeley, CA: CentreP.

Kelly, F. (2011). A tale of Minnie Dean: The Wilton baby-farmer. *Neo-Victorian Studies, 4*(1), 44-54.

Kelly, F. (2017). *The idea of the PhD: The doctorate in the twenty-first-century imagination.* London, England: Routledge.

Kerenyi, C. (1967). *Eleusis: Archetypal image of mother and daughter* (R. Manheim, Trans.). Princeton, NJ: Princton University Press.

Kirschner, D. (1992). Understanding adoptees who kill. *International Journal of Offender Therapy and Comparative Criminology, 36*(4), 323-333. doi:10.1177/0306624x92

Kristeva, J. (1989). *Black sun: Depression and melancholy* (L. S. Roudiez, Trans.). New York, NY: Columbia University Press.

Laing, R. D. (1960). *The divided self: A study of sanity and madness.* London, England: Tavistock Publications.

Leonard, L. S. (2001a). *Witness to the fire: Creativity and the veil of addiction.* Boston, NY: Shambala.

Leonard, L. S. (2001b). *On the way to the wedding.* Boston, NY: Shambala

Levine, P. A. (2010). *In an unspoken voice: How the body releases trauma and restores goodness.* Berkeley, CA: North Atlantic Books.

Lifton, B. J. (1994). *Journey of the adopted self: A quest for wholeness.* New York, NY: Basic Books.

Lifton, B. J. (2009). Ghosts in the adopted family. *Psychoanalytic Inquiry, 30*(1), 71-79. Retrieved from https://citeseerx.ist.psu.edu/index;jsessionid=B8F52728EE3FF8AC-129D4A3397C1D603

Liotti, G. (2012). Disorganised attachment and the therapeutic relationship with people in shattered states. In J. Yellin & K. White (Eds.), *Shattered states: Disorganised attachment and its repair* (pp. 127-156). London, England: Karnac Books.

Lloyd, D. (2001). This long underwater. In *Down at the end of the garden*. Produced by Cloudboy. Dunedin, New Zealand: Loop and Arclife.

Lopate, P., & Teachers & Writers Collaborative. (1995). *The art of the personal essay: An anthology from the classical era to the present*. New York, NY: Anchor Books, Doubleday.

Lorde, A. (1982). *Zami: Another spelling of my name*. Freedom, CA: The Crossing Press.

Lucas, C. (2011). *In case of spiritual emergency: Moving successfully through your awakening*. Scotland, England: Findhorn Press.

Luigjuray, D. (2003). *The formation of a soulful therapist*. Retrieved August 24, 2015, from Proquest Int.

Madill, K. (2001). *Through the looking glass*. Art exhibition. Forrester Gallery, Oamaru, New Zealand.

Mahler, M., Pine, F., & Bergman, A. (1975). *The psychological birth of the human infant*. New York, NY: Basic Books.

Marlon, S. (2005). *The black sun: The alchemy and art of darkness*. Houston, Texas: Texas A&M University Press.

Masson, J. M. (1996). *The wild child: The unsolved mystery of Kaspar Hauser*. New York, NY: Simon & Schuster.

Mate, G. (2003). *When the body says no: Exploring the stress-disease connection*. Hoboken, NJ: John Wiley & Sons.

Mate, G. (2010). *In the realm of hungry ghosts: Close encounters with addiction*. Berkeley, CA: North Atlantic Books.

Matousek, M. (2017). *Writing to awaken: A journey of truth, transformation and self-discovery*. Oakland, CA: Reveal Press.

Melville, H. (1967). *Moby Dick*. New York: US: W.W. Norton & Co Inc.

Merchant, N. (1998). Ophelia. In *Ophelia*. Produced by Elektra Entertainment, New York, NY: Warner music.

Merleau-Ponty, M. (1968). *The visible and the invisible*. Evanston, England: Northwestern University Press.

Merleau-Ponty, M. (1992). *The phenomenology of perception*. London, England: Routledge.

Merleau-Ponty, M. (2002). The world of perception. London, England: Routledge.

Miller, A. (1981). *Prisoners of childhood: The drama of the gifted child and the search for the true self* (R. Ward, Trans.). New York, NY: Basic Books.

Miller, A. (1983). *For your own good: Hidden cruelty in child-rearing and the roots of violence*. New York, NY: The Noonday Press.

Miller A. (1998) *Thou shalt not be aware. Society's betrayal of the child*. New York, NY: Farrar, Strauss & Giroux.

Miller, A. (2004). *The body never lies: The lingering effects of hurtful parenting*. New York, NY: Norton & Company.

Miller, L. (2002). *The Brontë myth*. London, England: Vintage.

Mindell, A. (2000) *Quantum mind: The edge between physics and psychology*. Portland, OR: Lao Tse Press.

Mogenson, G. (1992). *Greeting the angels: An imaginal view of the mourning process*. Amityville, NY: Bawood Publishing Company.

Montaigne de, M. (1958). *Essays* (J. M. Cohen, Trans.). London, England: Penguin Books.

Moore, T. (1992). *Care of the soul: An inspirational programme to add depth and meaning to your everyday life*. London, England: Piatkus.

Moore, T. (2012). *Dark nights of the soul: A guide to finding your way through life's ordeals*. London, England: Piatkus.

Moustakas, C. (1990). *Heuristic research: Design, methodology and applications*. London, England: Sage Publications.

Moustakas, C. (1996). *Loneliness*. London, England: Jason Aronson.

Murdock, M. (1990). *The heroine's journey: Woman's quest for wholeness*. Boston, NY: Shambala.

Nevins, J. (2018). *Three identical strangers:The bizarre tale of triplets separated at birth.*
  28 June 2018. Retrieved from theguardian.com on 24/1/19.

Newton, M. (2002). *Savage girls and wild boys: A history of feral children.* New York, NY: Picador.

O'Donohue, J. (1992). *Anam Cara: Spiritual wisdom from the Celtic world.* London, England: Bantam Books.

O'Doud, N. (2017, August). *Tuam babies: It would be kinder to strangle these illegitimate children at birth.* Retrieved December 23, 2018, from www.irishcentral.com/news/tuam-babies-it-would-be-kinder-to-strangle-these-illegitimate-children-at-birth

Ovid, (1965). *Metamorphoses: The Arthur Golding translation (1567)* (J. F. Nims, Ed.). New York, NY: MacMillan.

Pearson, C. (1986). *The hero within: Six archetypes we live by.* Broadway, NY: HarperElixir.

Pearson, C. (1991). *Awakening the heroes within: Twelve archetypes to help us find ourselves and transform our world.* Broadway, NY: HarperElixir.

Pennebaker, J. W. (2000). Telling stories: The health benefits of narrative. *Literature and Medicine, 19*(1), 3-18.

Pennebaker, J. W. (1997). Writing about emotional experiences as a therapeutic process. *Psychological Science 8* (3),162-166. Washington DC, WA: American Psychological Association.

Pines, D. (1993). *A woman's unconscious use of her body.* London, England: Virago Press.

Pinzon, L.A. (1996). *Witnesses to a sacrifice: The use of metaphor as a mode of survival in surviving siblings of schizophrenics.* Unpublished PhD thesis. Ann Arbor, US: UMI Company 9701077. Bloch, 1978 p. 58

Polanyi, M. (1958). *Personal knowledge: Towards a post-critical philosophy.* New York, NY: Routledge.

Polanyi, M. (1966). *The tacit dimension.* Chicago, IL: University of Chicago Press.

Polanyi, M. (1969). *Knowing and being: Essays by Michael Polyani* (M. Grene, Ed.). New York, NY: Routledge.

Pozorksi, A. L. (2003). *Figures of infanticide: Traumatic modernity and the inaudible cry.* [Unpublished doctoral thesis]. Emory University, Atlanta, GA, United States of America. UMI Number: 3080351. Retrieved June 2015, from Proquest International.

Progroff, I. (Trans.). (1957). *The cloud of unknowing.* New York, NY: Dell.

Rattigan, C. (2012). *What else could I do: Single mothers and infanticide, Ireland 1900-1950.* Dublin, Ireland: Irish Academic Press.

Rattle, A., & Vale, A. (2011). *The woman who murdered babies for money: The story of Amelia Dyer.* London, England: Andre Deutch.

Reich, W. (1974). *Listen little man.* New York, NY: Farrar, Strauss & Giroux.

Reiner, A. (2012). *Bion and being: Passion and the creative mind.* London, England: Karnac Books.

Roe, N. (2013). *John Keats: A new life.* New Haven, CT: Yale University Press.

Romanyshyn, R. (1997). *The wounded researcher: Research with soul in mind.* New Orleans, LA: Spring Journal Books.

Romanyshyn, R. (1999). *The soul in grief: Love, death and transformation.* Berkeley, CA: Frog Ltd.

Romanyshyn, R. (2002). *Ways of the heart: Essays toward an imaginal psychology.* Pittsburgh, PA. Trivium Publications.

Romanyshyn, R. (2004). "Anyway why did it have to be the death of the poet?" The Orphic roots of Jung's psychology. *Orpheus:A Journal of Archetype and Culture, 71*(Spring), pp. 55-87. Retrieved from www.robertromanyshyn.jigsy.com/articles

Romanyshyn, R. (2007). *The wounded researcher: Research with soul in mind.* New Orleans, Louis: Spring Journal Books.

Rose, L. (1986). *Massacre of the innocents: Infanticide in Great Britain 1800-1939*. London, England: Routledge.

Rosetti, C. (1924). *The poetical works of Christina Georgina Rosetti: The globe edition*. London, England: MacMillan & Co.

Rothschild, B. (2000). *The body remembers: The psychophysiology of trauma and trauma treatment*. New York, NY: Norton & Company.

Rymer, R. (1993). *Genie: A scientific tragedy*. NY, US: HarperCollins.

Sachs, A. (2007). Infanticidal attachment: symbolic and concrete. *Attachment: New Directions in Psychotherapy and Relational Psychoanalysis, 1*, 297-304. Retrieved from http://www.karnacbooks.metapress.com

Sachs, A. (2013). Intergenerational transmission of massive trauma: The holocaust. In J. Yellin & O. B. Epstein (Eds.), *Terror within and without: Attachment and disintegration: Clinical work on the edge* (pp. 21-38). London, UK: Karnac.

Saint Colette. (n.d.). The testament of St. Colette: The pure vision into sanctity. *Boston Catholic Journal online*. Retrieved February 6, 2019, from https://www.boston-catholic-journal/ the-poor-clare-testament-of-st-colette.htm

Sardello, R. (2008). *Love and the soul: Creating a future for earth*. Berkeley, CA: Goldenstone Press.

Sarmet, Y. A. G. (2016). Medea's children and the parental-alienation syndrome. *Psicologia USP, 27*(3), 482-491. Retrieved from http://dx.doi.org/10.1590/0103-656420140113

Schultz, W.T. (Ed.). (2005). *Handbook of psychobiography*. New York, NY: Oxford University Press.

Sela-Smith, S. (2013). Heuristic self-search inquiry – January 2003-Updated September 2013.

Shaw, D. (2014). *Traumatic narcissism: Relational systems of subjugation*. New York, NY: Routledge.

Shawyer, J. (1979). *Death by adoption*. Auckland, New Zealand: Cicada Books.

Shengold, L. (1989). *Soul murder: The effects of childhood abuse and deprivation.* New York, NY: Ballantyne Books.

Shengold, L. (1999). *Soul murder revisited: Thoughts about therapy, hate, love and memory.* New Haven, NJ: Yale University Press.

Shengold, L. (2000). *Is there life without mother? Psychoanalysis, biography, creativity.* New York, NY: Routledge.

Shengold, L. (2013). *If you can't trust your mother, who can you trust?: Soul murder, psychoanalysis, and creativity.* London, England: Karnac.

Sherwood, V. (2017). *Conversations in the dark.* [Unpublished poem].

Showalter, E. (1978). *A literature of their own: British women novelists from Brontë to Lessing.* London, England: Virago.

Sgarci, J. A. (2002). *In the labyrinth of secret: A meditation on the nature of secret.* [Unpublished doctoral thesis]. Pacifica Graduate Institute, California, United States of America.

Sieff, D. F. (2017). Trauma-worlds and the wisdom of Marion Woodman. *Psychological Perspectives, 60*(2), 170-185.

Siegal, D. (2009). *Mindsight. Change your brain and your life.* Victoria, AU: Scribe Books.

Siegal, D. (2010). *The mindful therapist: A clinician's guide to mindsight and neural integration.* New York, NY: Norton & Co.

Simpson, D. (2014). Some consequences of being the wrong child: Effects of the intergenerational transmission of an ideal-ego. *British Journal of Psychotherapy, 30*, 181-196.

Sinason, V. (2013). When murder moves inside. In Sachs, A. & Galton, G. (Eds.) *Forensic aspects of dissociative identity disorder* (pp. 156-166). London, England: Karnac.

Slattery, D. (2000). *The wounded body: Remembering the markings of flesh.* Albany, NY: State of New York Press.

Slattery, D. (2012). *Riting myth mythic writing: Plotting your personal story.* Carmel, CA: Fisher King Press.

Slattery, D. P. (2015). *Bridge work: Essays on mythology, literature and psychology*. Carpinteria, CA: Mandorla Books.

Smith, C. (1987). *The way of paradox: Spiritual life as taught by Meister Eckhart*. London, England: Darton, Longman and Todd.

Sophocles, (1947). *The Theban plays* (E. F. Watling, Trans.). London, England: Penguin.

Spinelli, M. (2010). Denial of pregnancy: A psychodynamic paradigm. *Journal of American Academy of Psychoanalysis, 38*, 117-131.

Stanton, J., Simpson, A., & Woulds, T. (2000). A qualitative study of filicide in mentally ill mothers. *Child Abuse and Neglect, 24*(11), 1451-1460.

Stern, D. (1985). *The interpersonal world of the infant*. New York, NY: Basic Books.

Stevens, A. (1982). *Archetype: A natural history of the self*. London, England: Routledge.

Stewart, S. (1993). *On longing: Narratives of the miniature, the gigantic, the souvenir, the collection*. Durham, NC: Duke University Press.

Stone, L. (1977). *The family, sex and marriage in England 1500-1800*. London, England: Penguin.

Styles, J. (2010). *Threads of feeling: The London Foundling hospital's textile tokens, 1740-1770*. London, England: The Foundling Museum.

Styron, W. (1979). *Sophie's choice*. New York, NY: Random House.

Swain, S. (2005). Toward a social geography of baby farming. *History of the Family, 10*, 151-159.

Thomas, R. (2014). Personal communication.

van den Berg, J. H. (1971). *A different existence*. Pittsburgh, PA: Duquesne University Press.

van der Kolk, B. (2014). *The body keeps the score: Mind, brain and body in transformation of trauma*. London, England: Penguin.

van Manen, M. (1990). *Researching lived experience: Human science for an action sensitive pedagogy.* Ontario, Canada: The University of Western Ontario.

Verny, T., & Kelly, J. (1991). *The secret life of the unborn child.* New York, NY: Delta.

Verrier, N. N. (1993). *The primal wound: Understanding the adopted child.* Baltimore, MD: Gateway Press.

Verrier, N. N. (2003). *Coming home to self: Healing the primal wound.* London, UK: BAAF (British Association for adoption & fostering).

Viorst, J. (1986). *Necessary losses.* New York, NY: Ballantine Books.

von Franz, M-L. (1996a). *Psychology and alchemy: An introduction to the symbolism and the psychology.* Toronto, Canada: Inner City Books.

von Franz, M-L. (1996b). *The interpretation of fairy tales* (rev. ed.). Boston, NY: Shambala.

Walker, C. (2014, June 25). *The art of the essay.* Retrieved December 23, 2018, from www.theopennotebook.com/2013/06/25/the-art-of-the-essay/

Ward, S. (2006). Anger related to pre-conception, conception, and the pre- and perinatal period. *Journal of Prenatal & Perinatal Psychology & Health, 21*(1), 57-74.

Watkins, M. (2000). *Invisible guests: The development of imaginal dialogues.* Putnam, CT: Spring Publications.

Weller, F. (2015). *The wild edge of sorrow: Rituals of renewal and the sacred work of grief.* Berkeley, CA: North Atlantic Books.

Williams, M. (2013, August 8). *Ballad of Minnie Dean.* Melbourne, Australia: BalconyTV.

Williams, P. (2012). *Rethinking madness: Towards a paradigm shift in our understanding and treatment of psychosis.* San Francisco, CA: Sky's Edge.

Winnicott, D. (1965). *The family and individual development.* London, England: Routledge.

Winnicott, D. (1974). Fear of breakdown. *International Review of Psychoanalysis, 1,* 103-107.

Wierzbicki, M. (1993). Psychological adjustment of adoptees: A meta-analysis. *Journal of Clinical Child Psychology, 22,* 447-454. Retrieved from https://psycnet.apa.org/home

Wolfreys, J. (2002). *Victorian hauntings: Spectrality, Gothic, the Uncanny and Literature.* New York, NY: Palgrave.

Woodman, M. (1980). *The owl was a baker's daughter: Obesity, anorexia and the repressed feminine.* Toronto, Canada: Inner City Books.

Woodman, M. (1982). *Addiction to perfection: The still unravished bride.* Toronto, Canada: Inner City Books

Woodman, M. (1985). *The pregnant virgin: A process of psychological transformation.* Toronto, Canada: Inner City Books.

Woodman, M. (2005). The eye that cannot see. *Spring, 72,* 31-42.

Woodman, M., & Sieff, D. F. (2015). 'Spiralling through the apocalypse: Facing the Death Mother to claim our lives'. In D. F. Sieff (Ed.), *Understanding and healing emotional trauma: Conversations with pioneering clinicians and researchers* (64-87). London, England: Routledge.

Yellin, J., & Epstein, O. B. (Eds.) (2013). *Terror within and without: Attachment and disintegration: Clinical work on the edge.* London, England: Karnac.

Yellin, J., & White, K. (2012). *Shattered states: Disorganised attachment and its repair.* London, England: Karnac Books

Young M. L. (2008a) Death comes. *Qualitative Inquiry, 14*(6), 990-998. doi: 10.1177/1077800408321467

Young, M. L. (2008b). A handbook on bears. *Qualitative Inquiry, 14*(6), 999-1009. doi: 10.1177/1077800408321975

Young, R. M. (2001). *Oedipus complex: Ideas in psychoanalysis.* Cambridge, England: Icon Books.

Zelas, K. (2017). *The trials of Minnie Dean: A verse biography.* Wellington, NZ: Makaroa Press.

Zweig, C., & Abrams, J. (Eds.). (1991). *Meeting the shadow: The hidden power of the dark side of human nature.* Los Angeles. CA: Tarcher Press.

Appendix

Minnie Dean – A Brief Chronology of Events

1863 Arrives in Southland, with one daughter and pregnant.
Lives with her aunt, Granny Kelly.
Works as a teacher and/or governess.

1872 Marries Charles Dean.
Financial difficulties increase.

1880 Adopts 8-year-old Margaret Cameron after Margaret's mother dies.

1882 Minnie's daughter Ellen and her children drown in the well: apparently a suicide-filicide.

1884 The Deans are declared bankrupt.

1885-7 Move to Winton. Financial difficulties.
Becomes a childcare worker.

1889 First infant (May Irene Dean) dies. Adopted in May, dies October.
Takes on more children.

The original house burns down and Charles Dean builds the small wooden cottage called The Larches. They all squeeze into it.

1893   Second infant dies (Bertha Currie).
Takes on more children.
Police begin surveillance of Minnie's business.

1890   Around this time Minnie adopts 10-year-old Esther Wallis to help with babies.

1895   Infant Life Protection Act passed.
Two infants disappear – not missed until 1895 (Cyril Scoular, John Clark).
Neglects a baby in Christchurch.
Third child disappears (Willie Phelan).
A mother visits looking for her child (Mary McKernan).
Fourth infant disappears (Sydney McKernan).
Collects Dorothy Edith Carter and Eva Hornsby on her last train trip.
Police search reveals both children found buried in Minnie's garden.
One other child skeleton found in garden.
Court trial for child-murder.
Death by hanging.

Minnie Dean took in 27 children (that we know of). Eleven survived, seven died. This leaves nine unaccounted for. Of the original 27 children, 18 were traced by Minnie's biographer Lynley Hood (1994).

CPSIA information can be obtained
at www.ICGtesting.com
Printed in the USA
BVHW080904151121
621685BV00004B/96